Twist

the Familiar

Additional copies may be ordered from the publisher for educational,
business, promotional or premium use.
For information, contact ALIVE Book Publishing at:
alivebookpublishing.com

Book design by Alex P. Johnson

ISBN 13
978-1-63132-228-0
Library of Congress Control Number: 2024904608

Library of Congress Cataloging-in-Publication Data
is available upon request.

First Edition

Published in the United States of America by ALIVE Book Publishing
an imprint of Advanced Publishing LLC
3200 A Danville Blvd., Suite 204, Alamo, California 94507
alivebookpublishing.com

PRINTED IN THE UNITED STATES OF AMERICA

10 9 8 7 6 5 4 3 2 1

Twist
the Familiar

Your Playbook for Success,
One Story at a Time

Gary Hernbroth

ABOOKS
Alive Book Publishing

To my mom and dad, Robert and Gail Hernbroth, who gave me boundless love, great foundations, and taught my brothers and me right from wrong and the value of family. And to my "miracle" sons Gregory and Michael, both sources of endless pride, joy, and laughter for me.

And, most certainly, to my loving wife and beautiful soulmate, Marie. I'm still so very thrilled that she picked me. God only knows what I'd be without you.

In Loving Memory

Gail Hernbroth
(1936 - 2018)

Robert Hernbroth
(1933 – 2025)

You know, we just don't recognize the most significant moments of our lives while they're happening. Back then I thought, well, there'll be other days. I didn't realize that that was the only day.

~ Burt Lancaster as Moonlight Graham
in Universal Pictures' *Field of Dreams*

Contents

Foreword

When Gary asked me to write the Foreword for this book, I must admit, I was intimidated, having never worked in the corporate world. My work experience was as a teacher and football coach at De La Salle High School for 40 years. I have been retired for four years.

When his book arrived and I held it in my hands, my immediate reaction was, "Holy cow!" It has 61 chapters and is 437 pages long. For a day or so, the book sat on my dining room table like a huge gorilla. Every time I walked past it, a little voice would say, "Read me." After passing that dining room table numerous times, I finally got my courage up and started reading. Three hours later, I put it down. Reading it transformed me. What I discovered in that initial read was what a fantastic writer Gary is. He takes the difficult and makes it easy to understand in small doses. What a gift.

The beauty of this book is that as you read it, common sense hits you over the head like a hammer. Gary's anecdotes are spot-on, which made me think, "Why didn't I think of that?" This book is not just about the corporate world; it's about how you conduct your life every day. It's about interpersonal relationships and bringing your best self to the table no matter where you are, who you're with, or whatever situation you are in. Instead of thinking about why you can't get something done, he teaches you how to brainstorm and figure out ways you *can* get it done. I love the way that Gary breaks up the chapters into small lessons of "Let's get to the point and move on." This makes his book an easy and enjoyable read.

I love this book. It is for everybody and anybody, a book of *action*. It is more than a business book, as Gary's straight-forward, common-sense approach applies to everyday living situations. Throughout *Twist the Familiar*, Gary deftly illustrates some business practices that I recognized as reflections of what my wife and I try to accomplish in our family. For example, we collaborate on everything, and work together on creating a loving, creative environment for our family. We guide our children and help them realize their potential; we encourage them so that someday they will create honest, moral, and loving families themselves. We show them how to "give back" and "pay it forward."

I would like to thank Gary for sharing his world and putting his thoughts to paper. Gary's wisdom in *Twist the Familiar* will enable all who read it to be better, more creative, and loving people. And that takes some strength and conditioning, which Gary and I believe is the key to success. That idea lines up with one of my favorite concepts from Helen Keller, who believed that character isn't developed in ease and quiet, but that it takes some trials and setbacks before the soul can be strengthened, ambition can be inspired, and success can be achieved.

With Gary's easy-to-understand writing style, he shows us that where preparation meets opportunity, greatness can be achieved.

—**Bob Ladouceur**, *Member, National High School Hall of Fame & Bay Area Sports Hall of Fame; coached De La Salle High School to eleven national football championships, twenty unbeaten seasons and a record 151-game winning streak; six-time National High School Coach of the Year*

Introduction

Thank you for engaging me as your "strength and conditioning coach." When I first heard my client, Randle Harwood of the City of Fort Worth, introduce me that way to his department prior to one of our training workshops, I was bursting with pride. I let him know it, too. "Well," he replied, "that's exactly what you do for us." The label caught on from there with other clients, too. Thus, I set out writing this book with two goals in mind; to be your personal strength and conditioning coach and to also help you build your own personal playbook for whatever it is you want to achieve.

I've also written this book to do what a book should enable you to do: stop your merry-go-round long enough to do some reflection. Visit your inner temple. As scholar Dr. Ruth J. Simmons said, "Stop and reflect...it's hard to read (a book) without reflecting." She offers that it's a form of meditation, "and that's a good thing. The busyness does not make our lives more meaningful. It is the interior life that makes the greatest difference to us in the end."

This book can serve as a true journey – yours! Of course, we're in this together, and we'll have lots of help along the way, too. There are plenty of stories here of regular folks doing irregular things, and doing things in uncommon, unique ways, creating success along the way. I'm betting that everything within these pages is also within your reach, if you want to make it so.

My goal is to give you the internal confidence, coupled with valuable tools, to help you:

Think differently
Act differently
Expand your creativity
Make different things happen
Improve and expand your skill sets
Do common things in bold, uncommon ways
Put yourself and others in positions to be more successful

This curated collection of stories is as eclectic as you might find anywhere in a book of this genre. In these pages, our journey will take us to divergent places such as Pebble Beach, Pearl Harbor, Valley Forge, a U.S. Army base, a college classroom, classic baseball stadiums, a Civil War battlefield, and inside luxury hotels, to name a few. As you will see, such a wide variety of seemingly dissimilar locations will make perfect sense and offer you dynamic settings in the pursuit of twisting the familiar. They are meant to inspire, enlighten, challenge, and motivate you. They are intended to spark emotions into actions, and to help you see possibilities you may not have considered before, both personally and professionally.

We will be looking at things through new lenses. Whether it's overcoming great odds, recommitting to fundamentals, creating something new by trial and error, learning from flubs and goof-ups, or capturing "aha" moments, it's all here to help create sparks for you. And it's all authentic, too. These aren't superhero comic book tales of make-believe. Everything here is within your reach in some way or another. These stories happened to regular people like you and me.

Consider this book's coaching moments to be your jet fuel. Whether you are a front-line team member, mid-level manager, salesperson, leadership executive, or business owner, I'm confident you will find value here. These stories were brought together to appeal to a wide range of people, whether you are a business veteran or a budding college graduate just starting out on your journey.

Setting the tone for our journey together

People have asked me, "How long have you been writing your book?" My answer is, "My whole life." That's because it takes many years of experiences to make a book like this legit. This effort has been several years in the making because I am a serial writer. I am constantly journaling about interesting people and unique situations I encounter in my travels as a speaker and business coach.

Just like you, my journey is one of many soaring triumphs and a few tortured moments, too. I guess that makes us human! Many people have helped shape my life and various careers along the way, whether they knew it or not. Some were outstanding, many were average, and others were comically, disappointingly, and downright awful. I learned from them all, one way or another.

I purposefully delayed writing most of this book until the Covid-19 pandemic had largely passed. I made the decision to wait for business and life in general to start coming back to life again, to calm down from the catastrophe. In some ways we're still feeling our way around this, and even more perspective will come with time.

Some social media bloggers have opined that "Covid-19 changed everything." I wholeheartedly disagree. That's too broad a brush with which to paint. The pandemic certainly changed many things in our world—there is no debate there. But not *everything*. While it would be dismissive not to embrace technologies and innovative ways of doing things brought about by the pandemic, we are finding in our post-pandemic world that things some people considered to be old-school or obsolete, are truly timeless. One of my core beliefs is that the pursuit of quality and excellence within us and others should never be considered trendy.

Pre or post-pandemic methodologies? I'll argue that it's not a zero-sum game here—we can have both, can't we?

We sure can. The successful post-pandemic "rebounders" are embracing those tried-and-true principles that were successful in pre-Covid times. Core business values, all of which are discussed in this book, such as customer care, communication skills, creativity, teamwork, smart leadership, sales professionalism, initiative, honesty, accountability and trust—they never go out of style. They are as necessary today as ever before, and maybe even more so.

I was recently asked in one of my keynotes, *"Gary, how do you see our best path forward?"* This was my response, and it serves as a byline to this book:

"The most successful people and organizations will be the ones who learned lessons from the crisis and can now apply those valuable experiences and move forward armed with new knowledge, a tougher resilience, and a renewed spirit."

The time is now. Why wait? After all, as Eleanor Roosevelt once said: "Today is the oldest you've ever been, and the youngest you'll ever be again."

How to put this book to work for you

Take advantage of the "Building Your Playbook" questions provided after the chapters. You can apply them to yourself and also include your team members and colleagues, too. They are designed to help you relate to the story on your own terms, whether you are solopreneur, small business owner, executive, manager, or front-line team member. Hopefully, they'll make you think and help you act.

Please keep this in mind as you discover the unique tools within these chapters: not everything works for everyone, in every situation, in exactly the same way. Use these stories and examples as inspiration and suggestions as to how you can make them your own. Ideas and tools vary depending on how and when they are utilized, which can vary person-by-person. Think, "different strokes for different folks."

Also keep in mind that this isn't a novel. You don't need to read the stories in any particular order. You can jump around to the sections you want to read when you want to read them. Just enjoy cruising and choosing the areas you want to peruse, and come back to the other sections later.

And most of all, have fun with it!

What's behind the idea of "Twist the Familiar?"

When I was vetting my title of this book, many people were intrigued by the phrase "twist the familiar" and how I came up with the idea. Here is the quick back story:

It's a phrase I coined from one of those "epiphanies" that just pop into our heads sometimes. I just made it up on the spot while presenting a training workshop for the sales team at Colonial Williamsburg several years ago. We were work-ing on coming up with unique ways to do things differently, such as methods of presenting proposals. I was urging them to think about doing something more creative and crazy-good so that they stood out from their competitors in a memorable way.

I didn't want to say something tired and trite like, "think outside the box" or "let's find a new paradigm." Blech! I wanted to offer something more original. I was a bit tongue-tied, searching for just the right words to use, when I started moving my arms in the air like I was twisting an invisible lightbulb into a socket. Then I said, "Let's find ways that we can twist the familiar." The term caught on with the group and it was off to the races.

If I could write a description of Twist(ing) the Familiar" for a dictionary, it would entail the idea of thinking and act-ing differently in order to make a difference or get a differ-ent result; a way to stand out in a healthy, productive (non-violent) way. I would also include taking creative ap-proaches, making a positive impact for you and others in memorable ways to solve business or personal challenges by doing something unique.

Here is a perfect example to help illustrate the concept. If you recall the TV show "MacGyver," he solved dilemmas and got people out of dangerous jams by designing and building things out of disparate materials he found lying around. He used his knowledge of science and his gift of creativity to do things such as building a lifeboat using only PVC pipe, duct tape, and milk cartons. That is truly the essence of the idea behind twisting the familiar.

Interestingly, the name and personal brand of "Mac-Gyver" is now in our vernacular as a verb, such as going to the hardware store and saying to the clerk, "I'm trying to MacGyver this, so what parts will I need to buy?"

Of course, some of the ideas and coaching suggestions in this book will take longer to accomplish than others. Some are easier to do than others. But they are all within reach. Don't get discouraged. Be diligent, persistent, and patient. Incremental change may be small but it is change nonetheless. Celebrate your small victories, they add up to the bigger ones.

Now, let's go and MacGyver this!

Chapter 1

Two Isn't One, But It Sure Beats Three!

*"Even imperfection itself may have its ideal
or perfect state."* —Thomas de Quincey

This very thing about achieving success without perfection happened to me while playing my favorite sport of golf, a game that doles out more lessons about humility and imperfection than one would ever want. Indeed, Hall of Fame golfer Raymond Floyd once famously said, "They call it golf because all the other four-letter words were taken."

On a steely overcast day several years ago during a memorable round at Cypress Point Club in Pebble Beach, I was standing on the tee of what is routinely referred to as the most famous par-3 in the world—the 16th hole. And I had just launched a lifetime drive.

I certainly wasn't the first golfer to stand jelly-kneed while teeing off at "The Sistine Chapel of Golf" as Cypress Point Club is often referred to. This particular meeting of land and sea at the 16th is the most beautifully treacherous inlet of swirling surf and fairway you'd ever want to see. Long celebrated as "one of the most visually stunning golf holes in the world" by *Golf Magazine,* it is an artist's and photographer's dream.

The greatest golfers and many of the world's most famous celebrities through the ages have stood on that tee and faced the same watery challenge as our foursome was facing. And no matter your fame, financial standing, or playing status, nothing is guaranteed in golf. You can't "buy" a good shot here. An eight-time winner on the professional tour once recorded a 16 on this par-3 hole.

Playing here, it's easy to get swept away by it all. Amid your thoughts of the setting and the moment you are blessed to be living in, you somehow have to clear your head, grab the right club out of your bag, and find a way to successfully hit your doggone golf ball. If you love a challenge, this is the moment.

Golfers have essentially two choices from the tee box here: Launching a shot toward the green that has to carry some 233 yards—it looks and plays much longer, especially in the wind—while avoiding the Pacific Ocean surf and craggy rocks for a shot on the green that you'll remember forever. But if your ball falls short of the plateau, penalty strokes await you like the sea otters lurking in the waves below, waiting for a tasty lunch of fresh sea urchin. The alternative route is to hit a shorter shot over the cove to a bailout on the narrow spit of grassy fairway off to the left. But forget any birdies and maybe even pars over there.

Risk-reward time. And I sure didn't come here to lay up.

I squinted to see my little white golf ball fly off the face of my driver. I'd given it all I had in my swing. I recall nervously watching it sail over the chasm of swirling blue-gray sea foam, headed on a straight path—fairly rare for me—toward the green nestled on the rocky plateau. My heart started pounding in my chest. Was I the only one who could hear it? My ball was somehow not doing its normal slice off to the left. It was cutting through the wind in a beautiful arc, streaking toward the promontory. Those 233 yards of carry felt like a mile.

As my little white ball continued lifting over the surf, I

actually lost sight of it briefly in the gray sky until it hit the front edge of the green. It gently bounced a couple of times and started rolling, rolling, rolling in a straight line through the middle of the wide green toward the yellow pin flag. That's when my caddy, Bob, who was watching my shot with the practiced eyes of thirty-plus years as a looper at the club, quietly said over my shoulder, "You're number eight."

My heart jumped in my chest because I knew immediately what Bob was referring to. At the time there were only seven golfers who had ever achieved a hole-in-one on this hole, including the famous entertainer Bing Crosby, a member of Cypress Point Club during his lifetime.

"You're number eight," Bob repeated confidently. From that distance, I couldn't see my ball on the green. Adrenaline was surging through my entire body. Could it actually be true—had I just aced this landmark hole?

As we walked up the left-side patch of fairway towards the green, my heart was in my throat. I felt like a kid making my way down the stairs on Christmas morning—I didn't know exactly what was waiting for me but I knew it was going to be good.

About thirty yards from the yellow flag snapping in the breeze I could see that my ball had come to rest a few inches from the hole. A millisecond of disappointment immediately gave way to the voice in my brain: "Now, Gary, you'd better make that putt for a two." We measured it at twenty inches.

My caddy broke into a smile and deadpanned, "Nice shot." My brother Terry, displaying brotherly competitiveness and absolutely no mercy, blurted out, "Hey, we're hitting in turn. You have to wait until we all get up there and putt in order." He and my other brother Ron, along with our

Uncle Don were off the green with their shots. So I'd have to agonize over that putt for a few very l-o-n-g minutes.

After their putts, my brother snapped a picture to prove for posterity where my tee shot had landed. It was finally my turn. My putt now looked three times its distance. I wanted to sink that ball more than any other golf stroke in my life. My caddie didn't give me a read on the putt lest he clutter my mind for the moment. I was on my own.

Trying to settle my nerves, I exhaled and pulled my putter back, stroking it straight through. The ball looked to be in slow motion and seemed to take forever to roll straight into the cup. It was the longest twenty-inch putt I ever made. Hearing the ball rattle in the bottom of the cup was both relief and joy at the same time. I retrieved the ball—it's a treasured keepsake—and looked back at the tee, still processing that I had covered that distance in two strokes.

Although I had narrowly missed achieving those 12,500-to-1 odds of perfection in getting a hole-in-one that day, my birdie-2 was nevertheless a pretty special achievement for me, one that I still treasure. It proves that you can still crush it without perfection. And let's be realistic—when you're a casual golfer like me, just avoiding a silly number on this iconic hole is considered a very worthy achievement in itself.

Sure, two isn't one, but it sure beats everything else.

Building Your Playbook:

- *In relation to your work or passion, how do you define perfection vs. being successful? What does it look like?*
- *Have you ever achieved absolute perfection in something? In what way?*
- *How were you able to accomplish it?*
- *Is perfection absolutely necessary for what you want to accomplish? (When perfection isn't achieved, can you still get the win or have success with the next best thing?)*
- *Choose a specific target or goal of yours. Next, determine which factors could affect your end result. What you will need to do or have in order to get the win, the best-case scenario for your goal? Does it have to be a perfect result in order to be successful?*

Chapter 2

Being Successful Doesn't Mean Being Perfect

"And now that you don't have to be perfect,
you can be good." — John Steinbeck

During the recording of one of the greatest albums of all time, the greatest group of all time had trouble finding perfection. According to *Music Spotlight's* "The Beatles," while the group was laying down tracks for their masterpiece "Abbey Road" album, "tempers rose perilously close to the surface as [Paul] McCartney made his fellow Beatles record the basic track for the song 'Maxwell's Silver Hammer' over and over, searching for an elusive perfect take. "If no less than the Beatles found perfection elusive, then what does that mean for the rest of us?

When you establish your goals, do you laser in on perfection as the ultimate center of the bullseye? What happens if you miss it by just a little . . . or by a lot? Are you still going to be able to operate, to produce excellent work, to survive? And can you still get the win and flourish if the bullseye is not achieved?

In other words, can we be successful even if we're not perfect? After all, we're humans.

The answer is a resounding "Yes!"

But still, shouldn't we aim for the bulls-eye of excellence? The idea is that if we *aim small* at a smaller target—such as the bullseye—within an overall goal area, we are more likely to *miss small* if the bullseye is not hit, meaning that we have better odds of hitting at least the surrounding area.

Conversely, if we only *aim big* at just the general overall goal area and we miss that, we're going to *miss big*, meaning the entire area itself.

One of the most-quoted coaches of all time, the legendary Vince Lombardi, whose Green Bay Packers won the first two Super Bowls, had a similar take on the concept: "Perfection is not attainable, but if we chase perfection we can catch excellence."

Since perfection is often difficult, then why not just dial it back and "settle" for a lesser goal to achieve. Wouldn't that be easier and less stressful? Let's delve into that for a moment.

Perfection comes in a variety of applications

There are unquestionably some occupations that require perfection more than others. Think of air traffic controllers, surgeons, and pharma scientists, to name just a few. There is no "settling" there or bad things could happen. Achieving perfection is a wonderful feeling because it means you can't do any better—it's the top of the top.

It's also very rare. Consider golf. According to the National Hole-in-One Registry, the odds of the average golfer making a hole-in-one are 12,500 to one. And there are a lot of exceptional golfers who never get an ace.

Perfection in many things is a great target to shoot for, so why not go for it? Customers pay for your products to work *perfectly*, don't they? They don't want things that only work most of the time.

I've asked many clients, *"What does perfection look like in your organization?"* They overwhelmingly struggle answering that query; they usually don't have a clue on how to answer that.

Bob Ladouceur, a man you were introduced to via his foreward in this book, is someone I admire for his approach to life, preparation, accountability and work ethic. His accomplishments as a high school football coach are the stuff of national records, books, and even a Hollywood movie.

During his tenure as head football coach of De La Salle High School in Concord, California, his teams earned a national record of 151 consecutive wins. That's twelve years without a loss! He was named the National High School Coach of the Year by USA Today three times. The NFL honored Coach Lad with its first Don Shula High School Coach of the Year award. In his book titled "Chasing Perfection," he explains how he would address the idea of perfection to his players:

"I don't expect a perfect performance. But what I do expect—and what you should expect of yourself and one another—is a perfect effort from snap to whistle."

Fundamentals make excellence achievable

One of Ladouceur's foundational beliefs is that you have to have strong techniques and fundamentals, and that everything emanates from there. That's where his idea of "perfect effort" comes in—putting in the hard work to do things the right way, consistently, at a higher level than your competition.

Another highly successful coach, Nick Saban, also weighs in on the pursuit of perfection and the reality of actual performance. He has led several teams to the college football national championship:

"If you know you will not be perfect, then those mistakes can roll off your shoulders as you move on to the next play.

But if perfection is your ideal, those mistakes will cripple you with frustration. So be realistic, understand that you and others will make mistakes, and use those as building blocks for the future."

That makes good sense for business, too. You or your team may not always achieve perfection, but if your fundamentals and techniques are iron-strong, you'll have a good shot at winning. You'll be putting yourself and others around you in the best position for success.

No one said this would be easy, but give it a try anyway

There is a remarkable scene in the film *A League of Their Own* with Tom Hanks as the manager of a World War II era ladies professional baseball team and his star player, Geena Davis. She nervously tries to think of a reason to justify to Hanks why she is quitting the team on the eve of the World Series: "It just got too hard," she said. Incredulous, Hanks leans forward and admonishes her: "It's supposed to be hard. If it wasn't hard, everyone would do it. It's the hard that makes it great."

Davis' character in the film wasn't perfect, but she was the league's best ballplayer and an admired natural leader among her teammates. Her character illustrates how perfection is not necessarily a prerequisite for success—but full effort is. She demanded a lot from herself, her teammates, AND her coach.

For many of us, the road to excellence and achievement is wrought with potholes. For example, the most successful multi-million-dollar salespeople aren't perfect. No salesperson alive gets every sale they attempt. If they claim otherwise, I like to say they're either lyin' or they ain't been tryin.'

Perfection for an Olympic gymnast or skater is 10.0, but you can still win a gold medal without that score. You can win a Super Bowl with an imperfect season, too. The only "perfect" team (undefeated and untied) in the history of the National Football League to date is the 1972 Miami Dolphins, amassing a 17-0 record while winning the Super Bowl. No team has gone undefeated since then, and yet every year a new Super Bowl champion is crowned with an imperfect record and is considered a "great team."

So being perfect and winning is not a zero-sum game.

Be careful of settling

But be careful—that's not necessarily a license to take our foot off the gas pedal. When we do that we can get blindsided, maybe by our competition, maybe somewhere else. Why not instill a culture in your company or team of giving what coaches such as Ladouceur refer to as "perfect effort" every time? Aim small, miss small.

Do you and your team have the commitment to excellence and the fundamentals and techniques to get you there? Settling won't get you to where you want to be; it won't often get the job done. And once you start dialing back and settling, it can be a slippery slope into mediocrity before you realize it.

Unfortunately, many people actually shoot for much less than excellence or perfection, For them, being "good enough" or mediocre is just fine with them. They don't relish the hard work or the price to pay that it takes to get to a higher level of performance.

So they dial it back. Have you ever worked alongside others who prefer to do that? Their work never seems to dazzle. It's sad to see that they could probably attain so much more, yet they prefer to throttle down. And when they do, that's when the dominoes start to fall for the entire production line. Their less-than-stellar efforts put the rest of the team or business unit in peril of putting out shoddy or late work, and of letting down the rest of the organization and its customers. You can see how that will put a drag on the larger mission of the organization.

French philosopher Voltaire coined the phrase *"good is the enemy of great."* Settling for *good* because it's easier and not as risky can be the lazy way to mediocrity and being average. If you run your own business, you likely know that being average can tarnish your brand and cost you customers. Can you imagine selling "average" hamburgers in a town with much better hamburger restaurants? You wouldn't be in business very long. Middle-of-the-pack folks don't usually try to twist the familiar, either.

Aim for the bullseye

Let's examine a simple yet profound method to build a plan for your approach that helps put your goals in clear focus, enabling you and your team or organization to put its best efforts into the right areas.

The premise is to determine three possible outcomes: Best, most likely/realistic, and worst. What is the *very best* we can achieve? What are we *realistically or most likely* to achieve? What is the *least* we can accept? Think of a dart board for this example:

Best-case scenario: Perfection (Bullseye)

Realistic scenario: Exceptional, very good (the inner couple of rings around the bullseye)

Worst-case scenario: The bare minimum we can accept (getting at least one dart to score on any number in the outer ring).

Even the GOATS miss perfection—yet they still crush it

Take heart. History is full of the Greatest of All Time (GOATs) who weren't perfect. And things turned out just fine for them. But it wasn't by luck or wishing upon a star. They applied their talents and put in the hard work, the fundamentals, and the endless hours of practice. They put themselves in a position to be successful.

They overcame imperfection and landed in excellence.

Great examples of this are the players considered to be the game's elite in the Major League Baseball Hall of Fame. Not only were they imperfect in their craft, they actually failed more than they succeeded during their storied careers. How can that be?

Here is how the late, great Ted Williams, who is generally regarded as the purest hitter in the game's history, told it: "Baseball is the only field of endeavor where a man can succeed three times out of ten and be considered a good performer."

To Williams' point, the average HOF enshrinee failed to get a hit approximately seven times out of ten trips to the plate during their playing days. In your line of work, would you even be around if you failed 70 percent of the time, let alone be considered *great* or hall of fame material?

So it turns out that writer John Steinbeck was on to something about this perfection thing, after all?

Yes, he sure was. This topic of not being perfect came up during a webinar where I was one of the panelists. I was asked by a member of the audience, "Is failure a bad thing?"

I answered that "it depends." I went on to explain that if you let failures and setbacks overtake you and debilitate you—and you never learn from them—then, yes, failure is a bad thing. But if it forces you to change something, do something differently, come back up off the canvas and learn from it so as to do better next time, then you're actually using failure as a catapult and not a millstone.

Speaker Rick Rigsby, a former journalist and college professor, puts it like this: "Shoot for the stars to be the best you can be. Good enough isn't good enough if it can be better. And better isn't good enough if it can be the best."

Kirk Cousins, former Big 10 champion quarterback out of Michigan State and a Pro Bowl NFL quarterback, puts it this way about setting your bar for performance: "Pursue perfection and hopefully you wind up at excellence." There's aim small, miss small again.

Don't be frozen in place and afraid to try because you fear not achieving perfection. Let the idea motivate you, not scare you. Set the highest of standards for you and your organization or team and don't just settle for average. Do your thing as best you can and apply your very best efforts. That way, you'll be better suited to create success, even if it isn't necessarily perfection.

And that brings us back to the Beatles. The best-selling music act in history was the gold standard for other groups to be measured by, yet nevertheless the Fab Four felt that they recorded some clunker songs. John Lennon once proclaimed: "'Eight Days a Week' was never a good song. We struggled to record it and struggled to make it into a song.

We both [he and Paul McCartney] worked on it, but it was lousy anyway."

Music fans didn't agree with Lennon. They bought over a million copies of the record. "Eight Days a Week" is considered one of the Beatles' biggest hits, becoming certified gold and making it to number one on the USA Billboard charts in 1965.

You can do this. Accomplishments—great or small—start with the decision someone makes to say, "I'll try!"

Building Your Playbook:

- *Are you aiming to achieve perfection in your business or in life?*
- *What happens when perfection isn't achieved?*
- *Do you manage your team or business with the goal of hitting perfection in certain things?*
- *From the above, what are the results?*
- *Evaluate how you and your team members view success—how high is the bar?*

Chapter 3

Adversity as a Gift—Use it wisely

"Champions are not the ones who always win races. Champions are the ones who get out there and try. And try harder the next time. And even harder the next time . . . They compete to best themselves as much if not more than they compete to best others." —Simon Sinek

L et's face it. Some days you just don't have it. Whether it's at work, playing sports, during a sales pitch, or in your own kitchen trying to whip up a new recipe—you tried and it just wasn't there. It happens. You didn't capture the sale, you didn't get the job, your design wasn't approved, or your prize bull didn't take home the blue ribbon after all.

Sometimes you just can't make a winning hand out of the cards you are dealt.

Have you ever done any kind of writing? If so, you've been there. We've all stared at a blank page or screen because the words and ideas weren't coming. It's happened to me, waiting for that lightbulb moment that causes a gusher of ideas to flow.

So here is the great news! It happens to all of us at one time or another.

You can overcome the blahs or setbacks in a number of ways. You can reframe them, laugh in the face of them and shake them off, or put the mental and physical work into overcoming them, depending on their severity or importance to you. It may not be easy, but it will be worth it.

Twist the familiar and try a different angle or think more creatively. Maybe "it" comes to you in a spark of inspiration. Maybe you should go back to the drawing board and start all over. Change your mechanics or fundamentals. Practice often. Improve your outlook. Get others to help you.

It's all about going through the process of setbacks and coming out the other side with some type of success. Most great stories of achievement have that kind of story arc somewhere in their past.

Let's grab some inspiration here from people you may recognize, those who didn't give up when faced with early obstacles:

Abraham Lincoln lost eight elections before he was successfully elected as President of the United States.

In 1954, an unknown Elvis Presley performed a couple of songs as a tryout at the Hi-Hat Club in Memphis, Tennessee. Unimpressed, the club's band leader told Elvis to "stick with driving a truck because you're never going to make it as a singer."

Author J.K. Rowling received turndowns from twelve publishing houses for her first "Harry Potter" book, and fellow writer Theodor Seuss Geisel ("Dr. Seuss") was turned down twenty-eight times for his first manuscript.

Golfing legend Arnold Palmer shared an episode in his book, *A Life Well Played*. Early in his rookie year, Palmer overheard a famous golf teacher say this after seeing him hit a few balls on the practice tee: "Better tell him to get a job. With that swing of his he'll never make it out here on tour."

Setbacks taught these folks important lessons on their roads to greatness. Setbacks and defeats happen to us more times than we want to admit. They're not fun, but they're usually not fatal, either. It sounds strange, but it may work out better for you sometimes *if you don't win*. How so? Setbacks can teach you valuable lessons, as we will see here.

Think of setbacks as a way to cultivate winning

Unquestionably, success can be found in making some sort of progress from where you were previously. Inch by inch, customer by customer, dollar by dollar, whatever your measurement is. Inventors know this. Thomas Edison's teachers said he was "too stupid to learn anything." And he was fired from his first two jobs for being "non-productive." As an inventor, Edison made one thousand unsuccessful attempts at inventing the light bulb (more about the rest of his inventions later). When a reporter asked, "How did it feel to fail one thousand times?" Edison replied, "I didn't fail one thousand times. The light bulb was an invention with one thousand steps."

The Napoleon Hill Foundation wrote this about Edison: "There are few obstacles in life that will not succumb to consistent, sustained, intelligent, positive action." Wow, what a powerful idea! Let's ask ourselves: why can't we make that our credo to live and work by, too?

Maybe it would help to think of obstacles and adversity as much-needed wake-up calls for all of us. Winston Churchill, who doggedly guided Great Britain to victory as Prime Minister through World War II, gave the world this wonderful mantra on this topic: "Success is not final, failure is not fatal: it is the courage to continue that counts."

This sentiment to get back up off the mat after being knocked down is reinforced in one of my all-time favorite motivational movie scenes. In the MGM film *Rocky Balboa*, Sylvester Stallone delivers a powerful life lesson to his adult son about taking responsibility for handling the adversity in his life:

"The world ain't all sunshine and rainbows . . . It ain't about how hard you hit, it's how hard you can get hit and keep moving forward. How much you can take and keep moving forward. That's how winning is done."

Successful people have learned how to deal with not always winning, and not always getting what they want. And that can be a tough pill to swallow. Losing isn't fun. It sucks. But nobody wins *every* time. Strangely enough, winners know this lesson very well because they've been there. It sounds counter-intuitive, but *winners have their losses to thank for their successes, whether they realize it or not.*

How can that be? Because winners learn important lessons from their losses and put those "L's" to work for them in their next efforts.

Work as best as you can towards success, including getting help where and when you need it. Remember, it's the final result that matters most. Sure, going it alone may have its advantages, but results count the most. Don't be a lone hero and fail because you didn't enlist some helping hands to lighten the load.

Alliance Partners can be powerful together

Those helping hands I'm referring to are people or teams I call alliance partners. This idea has been very successful for a large number of my training client organizations. They embrace it enthusiastically when I illustrate how it makes them and their teams—and ultimately the entire organization—stronger and better.

Alliance partners can be people or internal teams

aligning with each other within an organization such as sales and customer service, or externally with two or more separate companies creating the alliance together. Let's face it—we all need help from others at some point or other, and there are those who need us and what we bring to the table. It's a true partnership of *give 'n get*.

The winning math for Alliance Partner results: 1 + 1 = 3

The premise behind this very powerful equation is this: two teams or businesses working together to combine their efforts and resources to create results greater than either entity could achieve on its own.

An example would be a cake bakery and a florist. Since both serve the weddings market, by combining their products in a package offering or combining their sales efforts, they could work together finding more wedding business as an alliance than either one of them could find on their own: thus, $1 + 1 = 3$.

Alliance partners bolster each other up, make plans together, offer resources and ideas, hold each other accountable, help each other in the work to be done, share strategies and tactics, and also share the fruits of their partnership, too!

Building your playbook:

- *Do you have setbacks/adversity episodes that you have learned from?*
- *What lessons and subsequent changes did those episodes create in your life?*
- *Think of who could be your alliance partners: How would you align your efforts with each other? What kind of support or added benefits would you each bring to the other? What kind of results would you plan to achieve together?*
- *Draw up a plan in your life or business to put 1 + 1 = 3 to work for you.*

Chapter 4

To Win, Winners Must Learn How to Lose

"If you play the game long enough you're not going to be successful all the time. You'll get on a little roll, but somebody will bring you down to school. You have to keep grinding ahead. You can't let failure determine your future success." —Kirk Gibson

As a youth sports coach, I knew my teams weren't going to win every game, far from it. But my steadfast role was clear to me: Strive to put players in positions where they have the greatest opportunity to be successful—for the team and then for themselves. We coached the "team first" notion, not for individual glories.

And we coaches tried to teach our players to learn from their less than stellar moments in games—ugly strikeouts, errors, and botched plays. Sure, it's sports and those things happen. But nobody wanted them to become habitual, including the kids. And in some games those wacky moments came in bunches and they cost us.

We used those instances in our practices as coaching moments to re-address their fundamentals. The kids had pride and didn't like to lose, especially to "lose ugly." While mistakes are certainly OK, the goal was to try and not make the same mistakes twice. When we were successful at improving their fundamentals, lo and behold we won more games. And the kids took joy in their improvement as players. The games became more fun for them. They had experienced the lows, didn't like them, and naturally realized that the highs were worth the extra effort.

My parents taught me early in my childhood that life isn't fair, and that life doesn't owe anybody anything. To that point, I found this little slice of inspiration on a sign in a souvenir shop in Monterey, California. It speaks well to this lesson:

"Prepare the child for the path, not the path for the child."

And it isn't only for children, by any means—it applies to adults, too. Prepare, prepare, prepare. And be ready to have things go differently sometimes. *Shift happens.*

When proper training in the fundamentals and techniques kicks in with children and adults alike, they have the motivation to perform and succeed because they are armed with the proper tools. They are set up for success. It's less about *rah-rah* and more about having confidence in their roles, and the internal motivation to do well. When people are confident, they want to make something happen. It's rewarding and fun when that occurs. It's a recipe for success for any business owner, manager, or supervisor to put into practice in their businesses.

We also know that even with careful planning, shift happens. The best-laid plans can go up in smoke in an instant. It's best to prepare for some bumps along the road—big bumps, little bumps, and even some deep sinkholes, too. What are your contingency plans, your "Plan B's?" That's not a loser's outlook, it's an experienced outlook. Successful people and organizations ask themselves beforehand, "What am I (or *are we*, if referring to a team) prepared to do when shift happens?" Do we go around it, work through it, or break down because of it?

Own your setbacks and put them to work for you

As Winston Churchill attested, losing isn't fatal, but it also isn't much fun, either. Losing doesn't have to be fatal to your business or your plans *if* you learn from it and do something about it to prepare for the next opportunity. If you are in business, think about why or how you lost a customer. What contributed to that? Is there something that can be avoided or "fixed" for next time? Did you present an idea or proposal at work only to see it get turned down? Same thought process for your interview that didn't land the job. Assess what happened.

It's a tough lesson to learn, but setbacks can be the very shot in the arm you need for embracing change of some kind. Failures help you figure out what it will take to do better next time. Use a loss to your advantage. It's like giving yourself or your team a healthy dose of *tough love*.

My all-time favorite golfer, the late Arnold Palmer, spoke about humility in a very similar way, as excerpted from the book *Arnie* by Tom Callahan: "The good thing about bad losses is they bring you back to earth. And in my experience, they arrive at just the right time, when you need them the most. The moment you become a little too full of yourself, they come along and turn you into a real person again."

Keep this in mind about assessing losses or setbacks: maybe you did nothing "wrong" per se; it's just that others might have prepared better, executed better, or made better use of the circumstances. Learn from it by being accountable. Then put the work in to improve and kick your game up a few notches next time.

Don't operate in a vacuum—review your performances

Sports teams and athletes use game film/video to review their performances to analyze the hits and misses, the blown opportunities, the flubs. As Kirk Gibson referred to in the quote at the top of this chapter, at some point everyone gets taken to "school" in some way. Smart people go to work fixing, tinkering, and re-committing for their next contest or game. For the rest of us, it could be before our next sales pitch or company initiative. Re-assess, re-train, re-deploy. It's got to be part of your business or success strategy, too. Nothing runs forever, like perfect clockwork, all the time. Life gets in the way.

What is your "game film?" It could be Yelp/social media reviews or other means of customer or employee feedback. Do you ever analyze "what happened" in your business— taking stock of your lost opportunities or setbacks?

Speaking of watching our performances, I had the opportunity to meet thoroughbred jockey Martin Garcia several years ago. He had recently won the 135th running of the Preakness Stakes at Pimlico Race Course in Baltimore, Maryland, a prestigious Triple Crown Race. He won aboard the horse *Lookin At Lucky*. I asked him if he enjoyed watching the video of his victory once in a while. "I've never seen it," he said to me with a grin. "I never watch my wins. I only watch my losses so that I can see what I need to do to improve."

Garcia's answer took me back a bit. I didn't anticipate that response. But I think it's brilliant. How many of us take the time and care to really study our setbacks? How many salespeople fret over why they lost the sale to a competitor? It's the critical time for learning, to do some introspection to see what might have been done differently to win. Maybe you did all the right things but the customer just liked the alternative better. It happens. But the savvy professional still asks those tough-love questions anyway, looking for difference-makers for the next time.

If you never fall down, you'll never learn how to get back up

A young rookie golfer was in the lead heading to the last several holes of a recent PGA Tour event. He had never won a professional golf tournament, and with each successive hole he was visibly feeling the pressure of what a life-changer his first career win would be. Victory was so close he could taste it, yet there was still work to do.

With just a few holes left in the final round, he hit a terrible shot into a sand bunker. He then made a poor recovery shot and missed the putt. Suddenly, tragically, he began to press and as the saying goes, *his wheels started coming off.* His confidence was waning like the diminishing daylight.

The TV camera showed a close-up of his face and he looked totally overwhelmed by the moment. TV broadcaster and Hall of Fame golfer Nick Faldo offered an insightful veteran's perspective from the broadcast booth: "He's finding out that you've got to learn how to lose before you can know how to win."

Ask a winner or a successful person, and if they are honest they will tell you they've lost sometimes, maybe lots of times. That doesn't mean they liked it. But I'll bet that their setbacks helped them see what it would take to win. It certainly works for me: I may not like it, but I'm going to learn from it and use it to my advantage next time.

Put your adversity in perspective and turn it into positive energy. Own it and make it your mission. The late Pat Summitt, who was the all-time winningest women's college basketball coach and achieved eight national championships at Tennessee, said this about the topic: "There is an old saying, 'a champion is someone who is willing to be uncomfortable'. . . and losing forces you to re-examine."

Motivation for re-examination and self-reflection in the pursuit of success can come in a variety of ways. An example of a type of reverse motivation that made an impression on me is from the film *Moneyball*, starring Brad Pitt as Billy Beane, the general manager of the Oakland A's at the time. The scene shows Pitt explaining his mantra to some of the players as they were trying to turn things around from a losing streak: "I hate losing. I hate losing even more than I want to win. And there is a difference."

Building Your Playbook

- *Think about the times you've lost at something—a game, a sale, a promotion, a relationship. Did you think about why or how you lost, and then use it as a lesson to put to good use for the next time?*
- *Take an introspective look at the factors at hand when you didn't get the win: List them and how they might have impacted the result.*
- *Next, take each factor and write down what you could have done differently, or what you will do differently should those circumstances arise next time. This is key to preparation for your next challenge.*
- *If you lead a team, go through a similar exercise in analyzing your losses/setbacks with them. Come up with steps to stop something, change something, add something, etc., so as to not repeat the same mistakes or missed opportunities. Remember: maybe nothing was done "wrong" per se, but the question might be: where do we need the jet fuel to gain the win next time?*

Chapter 5

Sometimes it's Better to be Lucky than Good

"The race is not always to the swift." — Ecclesiastes 9:11

We've been focusing on pursuing perfection and achieving excellence. How about an instance when being mediocre actually meant winning? Is that even possible?

In a strange twist, flying under the radar despite his best efforts to excel actually paid off for my dad when he was serving his country in the Unites States Army.

He was drafted into the Army in 1956 and sent to Fort Leonard Wood in Missouri for basic training. To set the tone for the story, a bit of background about that Army base in the 1950s is essential.

"It was out in the middle of nowhere, surrounded by woods and rocks," my dad recalls. The luxurious accommodations for the Army personnel stationed there were barracks that my dad referred to as "tar-paper shacks." The frigid winter winds would whistle through the wooden slats in the thin walls. He and his fellow GIs called the army base "a sh**hole."

The Korean War had recently ended in 1953, thus a number of veterans were still among the soldiers at Fort Leonard Wood. Their memories of the climate in Korea were still fresh, so they nicknamed the base "Little Korea" because of its wild weather swings, "from 20 below in the winter to over 100 degrees in the summer," according to my dad.

After eight weeks of basic training that converted my dad

from a youthful schoolteacher just a year out of college to an infantry soldier, he was assigned as a clerk-typist at the post. Along with eighty other newly minted soldiers, he was destined to start his military adventure riding a desk.

My dad and the other GIs quickly learned that when it came to the art of being clerk-typists in the military, the skill of typing was actually a necessary thing. For many of the infantrymen, typing proficiency was not in their wheelhouse. For their training, they were armed with Remington model typewriters. This explains why my dad humorously refers to himself as a proud member of *The Remington Raiders*, a tongue-in-cheek nickname from across all branches of the service back in the day. There was a lot of typing needed back then. It's been said that if an army moves on its stomach then paper is a close second, and you'd get no argument from my dad.

The rumor mill starts churning

During the course of those typing classes, rumors, a time-honored military tradition to be sure, started swirling around that the best typists were going to be able to transfer to a different army base, leaving the miseries of "Little Korea" in Missouri far behind. Ah! That was the Golden Ticket if you could get it. My dad and his fellow GIs now had a huge incentive to kick up their typing games.

My dad had a good buddy in his company who had a job with IBM in his civilian life. That experience enabled him to make his Remington typewriter sing at sixty-plus words per minute. On the other hand, my dad was what they called a "hunt-and-peck" typist, all thumbs. His thick fingers came down with authority on the keys, one at a time, resembling a rooster pecking at grain in the barnyard. He whisked along at a paltry pace despite his best efforts.

My dad pushed himself. But he had football fingers, not a typist's fingers. My dad's football-playing days spent blocking on the offensive line in high school and college did not help his hands lithely dance upon the typewriter keys. No matter what he did, he topped out at a number he still clearly remembers: twenty-seven words per minute.

As the course cruised along, the better typists carried themselves quite confidently, while the others kept struggling to increase their typing speeds. My dad recalls that while the Army never officially promised anybody anything about transfers based on typing scores, the officers cunningly said to the soldiers: "It would be in your best interest to do your best." Wink, wink.

It's not just a job, it's a typing adventure

It didn't look to my dad like he would be leaving Fort Leonard Wood any time soon. My mom was pregnant with me back in Michigan, and was hoping to join him should he get another posting somewhere else — anywhere else. But at twenty-seven words per minute, he considered himself out of the running and apparently doomed to more frigid winters and stifling summers stuck at Leonard Wood.

To add to the pressure and the incentive to type faster, twenty-five words per minute was the minimum to stay in the clerk-typist pool. Any mark lower than that, and you were moved to the engineering corps on the base. Nobody on the base wanted anything to do with that duty if they could help it.

"We would see those guys in the engineer corps out in

that awful weather, doing all sorts of building and construction work," he recalls. "I'd look out my window during a winter blizzard and see those poor guys climbing up an ice-covered telephone pole in the blowing snow, 10 degrees above zero. Their uniforms were all covered with cold snow as they were working on the wiring way up there at the top. I even saw some guys lose their footing and fall off the pole. No way did we want that duty."

Thus, with motivation like that, my dad gamely powered through the final typing exams. When they were completed, the officer in charge of the "Raiders" posted the final scores on the bulletin board for everyone to see, with their words-per-minute tally listed next to their names. There was a red cutline drawn on the scoresheet showing twenty soldiers above the line, supposedly being rewarded with a transfer to another base. There were sixty GI's who were below the red line, including my dad, who could see that their Army destiny was going to be tied to Fort Leonard Wood and all of its seasonal charms.

Sure enough, my dad's IBM buddy was near the top of the list at sixty-plus wpm, and he was absolutely beaming over his score. My dad's twenty-seven wpm was far below the red cutline.

"Not so fast, guys!"

But the U.S. Army was about to throw them all a big curve ball.

The top brass at Fort Leonard Wood were no fools. As my dad tells it, "They weren't dummies. Do you think they were going to ship all of their best typists off to help other bases and keep the guys who couldn't really type? They wanted the best clerk-typists in their own offices. That cutline on the list was exactly the opposite of what we all thought it was."

Unfounded rumors are ubiquitous in the Armed Services, and this ruse was on those soldiers who assumed that their superior typing talents would earn them a ticket out of town. My dad chuckles when he recalls how it all worked out:

"They kept the top twenty guys in that class at Leonard Wood and shipped the rest of us off to other places for our assignments. I got Fort Sam Houston in San Antonio, which was considered a utopia compared to Leonard Wood. In fact, when they announced where we would be going, my sergeant said, 'Hernbroth, you are headed to San Antonio. That's the country club of the Army.'"

My dad's mediocre typing skills meant that he got to serve out his two years of duty at a much better post, San Antonio, where he had opportunities to improve his skills, earn a promotion to corporal, and be offered a spot in Officer Candidate School. My mom joined him in San Antonio a few months later and I came along in the spring.

At least in this case, being mediocre really paid off. I suppose sometimes that it's better to be lucky than good.

Building Your Playbook

- *Has this happened to you, where you got a pleasant surprise after thinking you failed?*
- *What about misguided groupthink in your organization—has it caused problems?*
- *What has motivated you to try harder to achieve a goal?*
- *What motivators are most important to your team members to achieve their goals?*

Chapter 6

Dialing in Focus When it Counts Most

"It is those who concentrate on but one thing at a time
who advance in this world."—Og Mandino

Something dangerous in my wife's heart acted up
within weeks of her fortieth birthday. No thanks to an
atrial septal defect—a hole in her heart from birth—
she needed a heart ablation.

When the doctor performed the procedure, he came out
to the waiting area and informed me that although the ablation was technically a success, she was not out of the
woods yet. She would now require open-heart surgery.

I was in shock. The thought of a forty-year-old needing
open heart surgery seemed incredulous. The fact that it was
my wife was scary as hell.

The weeks leading up to her surgery were extremely
nervous times for our families. I was a jumble of nerves that
pre-dawn morning as I drove her and my mom to the hospital. It was one of those times in life when prayers and
one's faith in God was front and center.

I also thought about my wife's heart surgeon. I knew of
his stellar reputation from the physicians and other hospital
staffers who recommended him. They said he was one of
the best in the area. They trusted him, he was a real pro, that
kind of thing. Still, my nerves needed calming.

When it came time for my monumentally brave and at
least outwardly calm wife to be rolled down the hall on her
gurney and into surgery, I kissed her and watched the

nurses wheel her away. The doors closed and I tried to fight the jitters, but the "what ifs" were winning the battle for my thoughts. Marie had taught me about cleansing breaths during her deliveries of our sons, so I tried a few of those and turned for the elevator to go to the waiting room. As she reminded me, she was in God's hands.

As the elevator door opened, I walked in and looked up to see others already in there. It was my wife's heart surgeon and his team.

I must have looked awfully pale and nervous to him because he looked at me with a sympathetic face and broke the uneasy silence in the elevator by quietly saying, "Don't worry, son. I've done three hundred of these operations."

I processed that for a quick moment. Then I looked him square in the eyes. I could feel the back of my own eyes swelling with fluid: "Yes, doc, that is good to know. But the most important one you'll ever do is the one you're about to do now."

No one said a word. The surgeon just nodded.

Time in the waiting room was heavy. I remember trying to read a book but I kept reading the same paragraph over and over again. My mom and I played some cards as a distraction. At some point hours later, a staffer showed me the way to the ICU recovery area where my wife was sleeping.

I pulled up a chair, hearing those "beep-beep-beeps" from the imposing machine Marie was hooked up to. Her skin color was quite peaked but her nurse assured me that was normal after such major surgery. The nurse must have sensed I looked extremely concerned as I stood over the gurney and took it all in.

"She's doing great" she said, quickly glancing at the monitor to make sure before walking away to see another patient. I was left to wait nervously for Marie's surgeon to appear and give me his post-op report.

After what seemed like an excruciating amount of time (although it was probably less than ten minutes), the doctor walked into the ICU and made his way straight to me. I stood up and could hear my own heart pounding inside my chest.

"She did great," he said with a confident smile, shaking my hand. "She's going to be fine." I let out a long breath. My prayers had been answered.

The next thing he said absolutely rocked me.

"And I want to thank *you*."

Huh? *Wasn't I supposed to say that to him?* My emotions were so jumbled, he beat me to it. I said something like, "You do?"

"Yes," he replied. He looked straight into my eyes. "That comment you made to me in the elevator this morning, it really dialed me in. It made me think about something very important—that no matter how many of these procedures I've done, it only matters to the patients and their families how *this one* goes, that *this* operation comes out all right. Thank you for reminding me of that."

Blessedly, my wife's open-heart surgery was 100 percent successful. And the surgeon's comment about helping him dial in his focus has never left me.

Focus—it's everything, really

It's so easy to lose focus sometimes, isn't it? We get distracted, we get cocky, we get sloppy. We let our auto-pilot kick in. However successful or "hot-stuff" we think we are, we need a proverbial splash of cold water to the face every so often, a convincing "aha" wake-up call when all of a sudden things look clearer to us. When we shut out all the other noise and concentrate on what we are doing, we perform better.

Being mentally laser-focused enables us to better apply our talents to our immediate task. Golf legend Bobby Jones said as much when describing what it took to play top-level golf: "Competitive golf is played mainly on a five-and-a-half-inch course—the space between your ears."

That cerebral component certainly holds true for more than just golf, especially in organizations where top performance counts and quality means something.

Whether you are a heart surgeon with over three hundred successful open-heart procedures or a teacher, salesperson or restauranteur—re-focusing makes us better.

Building Your Playbook:

- *What helps you re-focus?*
- *What factors contribute to you or your team losing focus?*
- *What can be done to eliminate or diminish those distractions?*
- *How do you "dial it in" before doing your job or performing your role?*
- *If you manage a team, how do you help the team members re-focus?*

Chapter 7

Rolling Rocks and Ticking Clocks

"The definition of insanity is doing the same thing over and over again and expecting different results." —Narcotics Anonymous, 1981

Call it an epiphany. While shopping one day, I came upon a random pairing of pieces on a store shelf, sitting right next to each other: A desktop resin sculpture of a man trying to roll a big round rock uphill and a wall clock propped up on a stand.

The juxtaposition hit me like a thunderbolt. Most likely, a store clerk just placed those items next to each other without any thought as to what they might represent together. But the idea lit me up.

Why the thunderbolt? One of the illustrations I frequently draw on flipchart paper in my workshops is of a person struggling to push a big rock uphill, trying to accomplish their goals all by themselves. This resin sculpture I saw sitting on the shelf was of the tragic Greek figure of Sisyphus. Per Greek mythology, Sisyphus was punished by the gods for his deceitfulness and compelled to roll an immense boulder up a hill, only to watch it roll back down. This action was to repeat itself for eternity. Legend says that the gods thought there was no more dreadful a punishment than futile and hopeless labor.

Everyone has "rocks"
—it's all in how you decide to roll them

The Sisyphus piece positioned next to the clock got me thinking: How much *time* and *energy* do we waste trying to push our "rocks" (missions, projects, goals, challenges or duties) uphill by ourselves?

Everyone has rocks to haul somewhere. They come in all shapes, sizes, colors, and weight. Often, help is available around us to share the load, but for some reason(s) we don't always summon those resources. We don't notice them. We want to go it alone. We don't look out from behind the big rock in front of us to notice that help is near.

And all the while the clock is ticking, eating up precious time that we can't get back. Indeed, the parallel to our own lives is crystal clear.

Let's plan better. Let's take more control of our destinies. Let's work to cut down the distractions. Let's shelve our egos and be brave enough to ask for help to roll our rocks. Helping hands can make for lighter work. Share the load and you'll save time, valuable energy, and reduce your stress level. You will likely reach your goal sooner, too.

Does the idea of pushing rocks uphill alone sound daunting? Has it ever happened to you? Have you ever seen this happen with others, struggling by themselves to figure something out, to make a deadline or to handle an order? It's painful to watch. And it's even more painful to experience.

Good news! In today's world—unlike Greek mythology—this frustrating redundancy can often be avoided.

Why not get help?

I don't know of any badge of honor that exists for doing things the hardest way, do you? I've always thought that doing things the *best way* is what counted the most.

We learn very valuable lessons from our travails of trying to roll rocks uphill alone. Steve Peterson, a veteran finance executive of several business start-ups, tells a sad tale of trying to go it alone while working for a software start-up early in his career: "We spent a lot of time pushing our rocks uphill, and we failed because we didn't hire the experts to deliver the solutions our customers needed. I over-extended myself by trying to develop skills that I didn't have any formal training in. I tried to wear too many hats—sales, marketing, business development, and implementation. It was nuts."

Peterson isn't alone. "If you don't bring the proper resources to bear, you'll end up losing," states Richard Rue, president of The Volare Group, an executive recruiter for Fortune 1000 companies in Silicon Valley. "I was a B2B software salesperson at the time, and I went into my presentation to customers without enough technical resources, including people who could have done a great presentation along with me. We needed a team, and we didn't have a team. It was a mediocre effort and we did not get the business. I was naïve about my chances of going it alone."

Peterson and Rue learned tough and long-lasting lessons about rolling rocks uphill by themselves. Who hasn't felt the time-suck and the whirlpool of impending disaster, even in little tasks, when their rock's weight overwhelms even their strongest solo efforts? It can be debilitating.

Tough experience is a great teacher

"You learn from experience," adds Peterson. "Another tech start-up I was involved with was a clear case of rocks and clocks. Our big rock was the acquisition of new customers, which we were doing at a rate faster than we could support them. And the big clock was ticking for us because if we didn't provide the timely network service and support, we would lose customers . . . Instead of trying to roll that rock uphill by ourselves by just throwing more hardware at it, we brought in experts to help us roll the rock in the right direction and make us smarter, better able to respond to our customers' problems and opportunities. We wanted to get to the point where the rock was actually rolling *downhill*."

Now there is a goal to work towards!

When you are a one-person show such as a solopreneur, you have to get out in front of your rock pile or you could be swallowed up, as tour operator David Rubens experienced: "I can't reinvent the wheel when putting together my clients' events. I'm only one person, and I know it. It was a lesson I had to learn the hard way. I was setting myself up to fail, going in a million directions. Nowadays, I know enough to bring in the experts necessary to help me provide my customers with a successful event."

Even managers with established teams around them need to recognize that it takes helping hands to roll the bigger rocks up to the top of Success Hill in a timely and effective manner. Isn't that the essence of the word "manager," as in knowing how to manage the process?

Former hospitality executive Phil Anderson shared a tale

on this topic from his days as general manager of a luxury resort in upstate New York: "When I got there, the food and beverage operation was not turning a profit. My big rock was being tasked with turning it around and making it profitable, in addition to my other duties. With my hotel background I had overall knowledge of food and beverage, but I did not cook omelets, trim steaks or bake pastries."

"I hired those niche professionals," he continued, "and shared the goals, defined what our success should look like, and then—most importantly—I got out of their way. We turned it around in that first year, but it took many hands all working together to do it. Each person played an important role in getting that rock up the hill. It was definitely a team accomplishment."

What's a leader to do?

If you lead teams or organizations, it is paramount that you keep your eyes and ears open for signs that the heavy rocks are accumulating. It could be that people are struggling to get their tasks completed, missing their deadlines, unable to handle multiple priorities, inconsistently producing quality output, or even stop working altogether. Left untended, the pile will grow and you know what it's like to try and move a big pile of boulders.

There can be tremendous and dangerous fallout from too many rocks and not enough help, or over-sized rocks that could be better handled if they were just chiseled into smaller pieces. Burnout, disgruntled team members, frustration, distrust, communication breakdowns, lack of morale and camaraderie, slippage in quality, lack of caring, quitting (and don't forget about quiet quitting!) and insubordination are some of the fallouts in the rock yard.

And keep in mind that there is a clock ticking somewhere representing a deadline for accomplishing the goal. It can be very stressful.

An ounce of prevention is worth a pound of cure

The recommendation here is to get your arms around the situation as quickly as you can. Try to anticipate the next rock rolling your way, and get out in front of it if at all possible. Keep in mind that *prevention* is *future-focused* and *crisis management* is dealing with the *now*. Prevention is easier— and better. Leaders with clear, prescient thoughts of what may be coming down the pike, rather than waiting for the next rock to come to rest at their feet, are better suited to make the necessary plans—and twist the familiar—to get people ready.

Manage the process or the process will manage you

To help set you up for success in a project management mode for a rock-rolling mission you may be facing, I've developed the following set of questions focusing on *who, what, where, when, how, and why.*

Building Your Playbook:

- *What is going on? (situational assessment)*
- *Why is it happening? (the root causes)*
- *What needs to be changed? (identification)*
- *Where do we start? (priorities)*
- *How will the changes be brought about? (processes)*
- *What resources are needed? (alliance partners; people, products, procedures)*
- *Who will do what? (assignments/responsibilities)*
- *When will we begin/what is the date by which we need to have this accomplished?*

Chapter 8

Herding Kittens

"Responsibility equals accountability equals ownership. And a sense of ownership is the most powerful weapon a team or organization can have." — Pat Summitt

"Gary, I just don't think I can do this anymore. It's like herding kittens, it's a full-time job."

This was said to me by someone who was resigning as a committee chairperson for a volunteer organization. It wasn't anywhere near the first time I had heard that from someone nor was it the last. Herding kittens never pays enough.

Everyone should serve on a volunteer committee at least once in their life. It can be one of the most rewarding feelings you'll ever have, knowing that you had a hand in managing or producing an event that impacted lives in some way, such as charities, etc.

Conversely, the experience can also be headache-inducing, like herding kittens when all the kittens want to do is play and run around in different directions.

The following section offers tools for managing committees and boards, whether they are within your organization where people are paid to be there or volunteer organizations and committees staffed with people who have "day jobs."

I've had the honor and pleasure to serve on many different types of boards and committees in various industries, with purposes ranging from charities/fund-raising, special events, golf tournaments, education, and hospitality. Observing the dynamics that play out in those experiences, it's a veritable palate of different colors of "the good, the bad, and the ugly." The make-up of these committees are largely free-agent volunteers, aka wild cards, brought together for a common good or purpose.

Often, they have very little in common in terms of business acumen, handling details, follow-up, and experience working together in small groups. Diversity of backgrounds is one thing, but a group that has trouble pulling together is quite another.

If you've served on volunteer committees or boards, you know exactly what I'm talking about.

Most of the committees I have been involved with were extremely successful, thanks to a winning recipe of outstanding leadership, clear understanding of our goals, shared responsibilities, and sterling accountability for follow-up. Essentially, we put all of our rocks into their proper boxes and we did it on time.

In those instances, the people who showed up to our meetings (that's hurdle number one!) were generally engaged and also dedicated enough to pitch in and help with the heavy lifting. Not surprisingly, we flourished and our events or missions were successful.

Other committees or boards more closely resembled the kittens. It was tough getting some people to show up. Not enough people pitched in and the accountability for follow-up was poor. At times we needed paranormal experts because we were being ghosted by some of the group. In those cases, the ultimate results could have been so much better.

The road to success via Highway 2-6-2

For an educational conference of the Society of Government Meeting Professionals, I was asked to speak on the dynamics of board volunteerism and getting more people involved with their association. The board president, Kit Gonzales, asked me to tie in their theme, *On the Road to Success*. I drew up a "Highway 2-6-2" road sign to illustrate my message on what can typically happen with committees. Here is the premise based on my experiences:

Assuming a typical committee of ten people, I've found it to work like this many times: two people do most of the real work, six come in and out of the process as they can (or want to), and the other two folks never manage to show up or pitch in for whatever reasons. They are the committee ghosts. Thus, 2-6-2.

Sound familiar?

The real equation to success here is 1+1=3. Remember, this equation illustrates two parties adding their efforts together to create something greater than either party can produce on their own.

That's what happens when two or more people pitch in to help roll the rock.

The keys to running a successful committee are not boilerplate because of the differences in personalities, mission, available budget and resources, time constraints, etc. However, here are six elements that will impact just about any committee and its ability to be successful:

1) The efficacy of the leader
2) The personalities/abilities involved
3) The resources available to the members

4) Attendance and level of engagement

5) Accountability for follow-up in the work assigned

6) Time management and deadlines

Committee leaders: You don't often get blank checks on time into infinity and beyond. There is usually a deadline of some kind that is looming, such as an event date, membership election, budget year, etc. Prioritize your "rocks" by size and importance and divide your rocks up among members. Pay attention to the ticking clocks and how your time is being spent—or frittered away.

Avoid having Sisyphus on your committee

Nobody wants to mimic Sisyphus, or welcome him to their committee. Get some help with your wagons of rocks. It comes down to this: either it's you working alone with 100% of the weight-bearing load, or, for example, finding four others to pitch in, and now the load is spread among five people – or 20% each. In that way, each person brings something to the table. More hands make for lighter work.

With respect to my comment in the previous paragraph about extra hands, just be sure not to dilute, delay, or destruct the overall goal or mission simply because you're adding more unqualified or un-trained hands handling the rock. There is such a thing as too many cooks in the kitchen.

The best people to run committees are true leaders who can coalesce strangers and big-ego type-A personalities (as those types of people usually find their way onto boards and the like). There's nothing wrong with that, but they can't just be there for the political optics or as a resume-builder.

As a longtime association management executive with

many years of experience dealing with boards and committees told me: "Remind them right off the bat that they are there to *work!*"

These guidelines will help you and the other worker bees manage the process:

• Don't wait too long to decide that you need help. There is nothing wrong with forming alliance partnerships to help. Anticipation is better than reaction.

• Bring people on board who have the expertise, time, and inclination to help move the process forward with you. Train and coach them where needed.

• Explain the rules of engagement up-front, plus your desired quality outcomes, communication protocols, and time deadlines. In other words: Who does what with whom, and how, by when?

• Divide the work up in ways that make sense, utilizing the talents and expertise at hand, and properly deploying your team.

• Periodically check on things—do not trust autopilot! Hold people accountable for their share of the load (not in a heavy-handed way), and make sure there is one person who is unquestionably the team leader for the project. The buck stops . . . *where?*

Of course, all of this has to be done diplomatically, and you'll certainly get better results with a friendly approach. But it can be frustrating. When you are driving down Highway 2-6-2, keep your eyes on the prize of why you are all on the journey together and what your ultimate destination really is.

Building Your Playbook:

- *What does your load of rocks look like—what are the components or the end number for your goal(s) to be accomplished?*
- *When do you have to accomplish your goal?*
- *What resources will you need such as people, supplies, technology, etc.?*
- *What potential roadblocks do you anticipate, and what is your plan for dealing with them?*
- *Apply this exercise to your team and across your different departments.*

Chapter 9

Three Pillars of Success

"You cannot force someone to comprehend a message that they are not ready to receive. Still, you must never underestimate the power of planting a seed." —Anonymous

D id you ever have a moment of perfect clarity when something just comes to you, random thoughts triggered by some little thing that makes perfect sense and seems to explain so much? To me, it's like a brilliant box of light just opens up in my head.

Just such a thought hit me while I was sitting in a golf cart during an enjoyable round of golf with some buddies on a warm winter day. My cart partner and I were sizing up how we should attack the hole from the fairway. We were locked in a friendly little match for a few bucks against our buddies. The elevated green was 150 yards to the front of us, surrounded by several menacing sand bunkers.

As my partner sized up his next shot, I reminded him that we needed to avoid those sand traps. I tried to gently focus him in on his next shot. "Play it smart. Try to keep the ball left and away from the traps."

He nodded his head and assented, "Yeah, I know." He quickly grabbed a club, assumed his stance, and then took a really ugly swing, gouging the turf and sending a divot of sod high into the air. The divot got more air than the golf ball itself. His ball spun right into — you guessed it — the largest trap nestled in front of the green.

"Damn!" he snorted. "I shouldn't have used that club. I didn't think the trap was that wide." He stomped his feet on the ground as if trying to put out smoldering cigarette butts in the grass. "And for some reason," he continued, "I keep hitting the ground first before the ball." He was upset to say the least. As much as I felt for him as my match partner, I began sizing up our next shot in hopes we could still win the hole. Crying over spilled milk has no place in golf.

He walked around the cart to let off steam. I knew better than to say anything, so I kept quiet and let Mt. Vesuvius expel its lava. "I heard you," he said to me, plopping down hard into the cart next to me, arms crossed, and fumes coming out of his nostrils. "I just didn't think about it. I didn't understand how big those traps really were. And I swung like crap." I kept quiet. No sense beating a dead horse.

His tirade flicked on a lightbulb in my brain. I quickly grabbed the scoring pencil and scribbled three words on our scorecard, three pillars of success, so that I wouldn't forget them after the round:

Listening, comprehension, and execution: L-C-E

If you're thinking that a whole different meaning of the word "execution" might have crossed my mind at that very moment after such an ugly shot by my partner, well, I plead the fifth. Essentially, the three words came to me when I considered the sequence of events in his golf shot: My partner had *heard* me about the traps — he admitted that. But he didn't *comprehend* the distance and size of the traps. And then, to top it off, he made a lousy swing — he didn't properly *execute* his shot.

There it was, popping into my brain in the span of just a few seconds — a useful coaching tool that I could develop and use in my coaching: *listening, comprehension, and execution.*

To me, they go together like peanut butter, jelly, and bread. Since that day on the golf course, I've come to call them my *Three Pillars of Success*.

While there is a lot more to success such as talent, effort, timing, opportunity and such, we really can't accomplish much without the components of listening, comprehension, and execution at the root of the issue. It's like pouring the cement foundation when building a sturdy house. Got to have it.

Testing the equation

Three steps, three pillars; L-C-E. Simple thoughts, yet maybe not so simple to consistently achieve. Let's test the theory: just try taking one of the three out of the mix, and what do you have? It will most likely be a wobbly result. These three elements need each other in order to perform at full tilt. The process ultimately fails if you take just one of the three out of the mix:

If you're not listening and paying attention, you won't know what the mission, job or task is, and you'll miss the mark;

If you don't comprehend the concept or instructions, then you may apply the wrong tactic and that can lead to the execution being incorrect, misguided and off-target;

If you do not or cannot properly execute, the entire task or mission craters or underperforms.

Here is an example of how just one missing component of the three pillars can render the entire process a fail:

During one of our epic golfing days at Cypress Point Club with my dad, his caddie was explaining to him how to hit a certain putt, pointing out the best angle and speed and showing him the spot to aim for on the green. While my dad always tried to strike a good golf shot, he was fully aware of his limitations on the links and never let his game bother him or take away from the experience of the day. My dad thanked him for his read and assumed his putting stance. Standing over a putt, he resembled an ice fisherman holding an auger ready to drill a hole in a frozen lake.

My dad banged his putt and it meandered across the green and over the soft undulations, landing about ten feet from the spot where the caddie had coached him to go. To be fair, the greens on Cypress Point can be very tricky. With no malice of any kind, my dad just walked over to his ball to hit the next putt. He looked at his caddy and lightened up the moment. "Bud, it's not your fault. It was a good plan on your part. My mind was willing but my body was weak."

This little episode sums up the concept nicely. My dad *heard* the caddie and he clearly *comprehended* where the putt should be aimed, based on the spot the caddy physically showed to him. But the third component of L-C-E was lacking—my dad's *execution*. Try as he did, he just hit his putt to the wrong side of the green. So it was two out of three and certainly good intentions all around, but not the desired result. The same thing happens in businesses everywhere, every day. I'll argue that in this case, the old saying "Two out of three ain't bad" is all wet. Sorry, Meat Loaf.

Include L-C-E into your training-coaching regimen to help build a strong foundation for just about everything you're working on or trying to impart to others.

Sometimes, our best inspirations can be the unintentional consequences of a flub. Thank goodness my friend hit that lousy golf shot.

Building Your Playbook:

- *Think about how you communicate verbally to get your ideas across, or how you process communication from others. Have you ever had the breakdown happen somewhere along the process? What happened?*
- *With the example you've just thought of, re-construct how it happened and insert L-C-E to see how it broke down, and what could have been done differently using the model.*
- *List three pieces of information that you need to communicate to others, and apply the L-C-E model to them. Make that your game plan for rolling those pieces of information out. Let's see what happens!*
- *If you manage or lead a team, try the formula and practice it with them; make it the mantra for improving communication.*

Chapter 10

If We're Not Getting Better, We're Getting Worse

"Why diminish your soul being run-of-the-mill at something? Mediocrity is a hairball coughed up on the carpet of creation." —Tom Robbins

Sometimes, you never know what you'll get when you ask a simple question.

This is the story of one of my training programs deep from the inside to illustrate how a group of individuals were lifted up out of mediocrity and became a team. Picture your organization facing some of these same challenges and how you might handle them.

A former client of mine, general manager Phil Anderson, was plotting the points with me in advance of my training campaign for his upscale historic hotel in downtown Atlanta. As part of my due diligence, I suggested that we should take a temperature reading of his management/leadership team to see what they felt were the top issues facing the hotel. I do this regularly with my clients as I tailor their programs to focus on the biggest elephants in the room.

Subsequently, Anderson and I composed a survey for his managers. In his words, "mediocrity was running rampant" when he arrived several months earlier as the new GM. He was beginning the process of weeding that characteristic out of the hotel's culture, and my upcoming training program was to be the catalyst.

We started by asking his executive committee members

to submit what they thought the hotel needed to do first in moving the hotel forward. Keep in mind that these are the top managers in the hotel. Three of the responses have been sources of laughter for us through the years:

- "Enhance the stains" (from the director of housekeeping)
- "Sustain the turnover" (from the director of food and beverage)
- "Complicate the uncomplicated" (from the director of rooms)

You can't make this stuff up. I had my work cut out for me.

Taking the mediocrity pledge

In addition to the survey, Anderson spent a copious amount of time observing the team members in every department of the hotel while performing their roles. Anderson sent this brilliantly funny, tongue-in-cheek—or so he thought—memo to me, asking me if I liked the idea:

From: Anderson
Sent: Tuesday, June 19, 2007 4:21 PM
To: Gary Hernbroth
Subject: Mediocrity Pledge

What do you think of me offering the group the opportunity to sign a Mediocrity Pledge?

I _____ pledge to sustain the level of mediocrity in my department. I am a mediocre manager and can not move my department from mediocre to good let alone good to great. I pledge to be mediocre and look for the easy way and the path of least resistance. Training, coaching and corrective action are beyond my core skill set. Proactive planning and organization are outside of my capabilities. I will remain reactive and go from fire to fire always appearing busy yet accomplishing nothing. I am mediocre and will live and breath mediocrity.

Accepted by_____ on _____

Declined by_____ on _____

If nothing else, it can be used in your book. I am heading to my room to shake my head in frustratiuon...........

I told him: "Go for it!" It might act as the icebreaker for people to realize that mediocrity was indeed "a thing" at the hotel. He had a healthy sense of humor in getting this important point across.

Anderson issued his Mediocrity Pledge a few days before my arrival. When I got to the hotel for the initial training, he called me and deadpanned: "Gary, I've been getting the Mediocrity Pledge back from the managers." He paused. "And I don't know if I should laugh or cry. Several of them actually signed the pledge and agreed to it!"

"Whaaaat?" was my first reaction. If it wasn't so tragic it would have been hilarious. Did the people who agreed to it actually read it? Did they comprehend it? Did they agree to it just to be funny? Anderson and I headed to his hotel's bar to figure this thing out. Somehow, the bar made the most sense to us at the time. We needed a proper setting in which to digest this exercise and plot the points for this journey.

Mediocrity or bust!

We used this revealing exercise as a launching pad to determine which areas we would address first and foremost in my training program. There was no quick fix here.

In my role as the hotel's "strength and conditioning coach," Phil tasked me with getting the idea across to his managers and supervisors that improvement and performing up to their potential was paramount. They weren't really a cohesive team, just a group of individuals working under the same roof. Prior to his arrival, the hotel was under-performing, and he was there to get it turned around. He was an affable, approachable leader with a great sense of humor, but he was nobody's patsy.

Anderson gave one of the more straightforward speeches I've ever heard when introducing me and my training program to his group. Standing in front of his twenty-five or so department heads, managers, and supervisors, he explained a bit of the background of the hotel's recent lackluster performance, and also gave the broad strokes about the upcoming training initiative. Then he bravely said, "And some of you probably won't make the cut." You could hear a pin drop in that ballroom.

Anderson's message was clear; mediocrity was not an option any longer. The hotel's owners—real estate investors—expected better performance from them, top to bottom. He said that having worked with me before at his previous hotels, my approach of *work hard-play hard* got results, and that they would learn a lot if they paid attention and threw themselves into the program.

He didn't sugarcoat anything but he also didn't yell or wave his arms. He just spoke in calm, dulcet tones as a confident leader would. Essentially, he laid out the rules of engagement such as being on time, doing the training assignments, and being personally accountable for results and improvement. He was straightforward and honest with them.

It was refreshing to hear an organizational leader speak with such frankness. For his closing, he wisely lightened it up with a relatable, funny story from his previous resort that involved golfing with me and being caught by a fast-moving rainstorm, soaking us through to the skin.

The anatomy of bringing a group of individuals together as a team

Following Anderson, I walked to the front of the ballroom and took off my shoes and socks. That sure got their attention.

A few weeks in advance I had explained my idea to Anderson, and he put Chris Kennington, his director of engineering and one of the best follow-through aficionados I've ever encountered in my hotel training experiences, in touch with me. Over the phone, I had asked Kennington to build a wooden box about three feet square, and put about four inches of sand in the box. He built it perfectly and my sandbox was waiting for me at the front of the room, covered with a tablecloth.

I removed the covering and stepped into the sandbox, facing the group. There were some chuckles and some gasps. People were buzzing to each other, exactly as I had hoped—keep them guessing!

I did this strange opening to bring home two of my starting points. First, with this program we were going to twist the familiar, do different things that weren't the norm. Second, the sandbox represented my concept of "shifting sand leadership."

I rocked back and forth on my heels to illustrate that I was on unsure footing, and that the sand shifts quite easily, much like the lives of managers and people in leadership positions. Things are always changing under our feet and around us. I pointed out that no matter how safe and solid we feel at a given moment, things can change quickly. When we are managing people, products, processes, and customers, we must pay attention to the shifting sands. The symbolism was a big hit with the group, and I later found out that it was from that moment that they knew the program was going to be anything but boring.

Don't ever stop learning—it won't end well

In one of my initial discussions with the group, I explained one of my favorite truisms: "We are either getting better or we are getting worse."

There is no in-between. All living organisms operate in this manner—think of houseplants—as time doesn't allow us to stand still. So the choice is simple. It's better to try and get better because the alternative isn't so great. Once you stop learning you stop growing, and once you stop growing, you begin the process of dying in some way.

The hotel managers largely embraced this, pitched in to the program, and we had a lot of fun along the way. Though a couple of people didn't choose to heed the call to overcome mediocrity and thus moved on to greener pastures, everyone else welcomed the fresh air of new ideas and threw themselves into the exercises and discussions with each other.

Creating a powerful alliance, brick by brick

Without really realizing it, the hotel's leadership group was beginning to raise its own expectations of performance, and to hold each other more accountable for topnotch efforts and results at a higher level. Across the entire hotel, it no longer was a "miracle" that things got done in excellent fashion and on time.

Inexorably, brick by brick, a real team was taking shape. The duck quacking was going away and the soaring of eagles was on the rise.

To be sure, it wasn't all calm water sailing. We worked through some time-honored thorny issues and land mines, including clunky ways of getting things done. We stream-lined processes by cutting out unnecessary steps. We knocked down silos—those impervious structures between people and teams that breed territorialism, keep things in, and keeps other things out. We adopted sensible communication protocols that saved time and raised responses to a new art form. We designed new twists to the familiar that enhanced their guests' experiences.

Through it all, trust was steadily built among the team and their staffs. Much of the sniveling between departments was receding. I designed contests and team challenges that enabled the managers to let off some steam. People proved to be quite competitive, too. For example, the group was divided into teams of five and tasked to theme, plan, and create one of our group breaks, and then the entire group voted on the best one. I recall the winners creatively wrote and performed their own theme song to go along with their July 4th-themed break. They were dancing and high-fiving when they won the group's vote. We also played "pumpkin bocce ball" and mini-golf in the ballroom and foyer areas during different break times. *Work hard-play hard*, as I had promised.

It's all about the baked potatoes

Engineering whiz Kennington displayed one of the best examples of twisting the familiar and thinking like an owner. As a department head he rotated every few week-ends with the other executive managers to be the hotel's "manager on duty" or MOD, as they are called. The role involved staying in the hotel over the weekend and being responsible as the de facto general manager in Anderson's absence.

One evening, Kennington went down to the hotel's dining room for dinner and ordered a steak. He noticed that the steak was served with mashed potatoes. As he tells it, "Nobody wants mashed potatoes with their steak. I like my steak with a baked potato. No wonder we weren't selling a lot of steak. So, I went out the next morning and bought a ten-pound bag of potatoes for about five dollars. I gave them to the chef and asked him to serve baked potatoes with the steaks instead of mashed potatoes. I also suggested we add a five-dollar upcharge for them. We started selling a lot of steaks."

A few weekends later, it was Kennington's turn to be MOD again. Same thing, the restaurant had reverted back to mashed potatoes. This time the intrepid engineering director went out and bought several ten-pound bags of potatoes and hand-delivered them to the kitchen again. Even with the five-dollar upcharge, they sold out of steaks.

"At a meeting, Phil Anderson asked the food and beverage director, 'Our food and beverage sales on these two weekends were higher than the other weekends. Do you know why?' He was told about the steaks served with baked potatoes and the five-dollar upcharge. Guess what? We kept baked potatoes on the menu with the steaks. I guess it all started because I just like baked potatoes with my steaks, and we found out that other people did, too."

Accountability matters

One of the biggest features of my design was to have the people who were joined as alliance partners work on their plans for whatever it was that they were going to tackle together. It wasn't make-believe; they were slaying real dragons in the hotel. They made a short stand-up presentation in front of the entire group, committing to getting their goal(s) done, or at least put into tangible motion, by the next training installation a few months down the road.

The next time I returned to the hotel, we started off with each pair of alliance partners again presenting to the group on the status of their previous plans. We discussed their progress, their hurdles, and ways to complete their goals. Teammates offered help and ideas. This exercise on responsibility, teamwork, and accountability significantly raised the completion rate of the projects. It also served as a catalyst for those managers who just didn't get it in gear as well as some of the other people. It is a terrifically successful aspect of the training and it pays big dividends on many levels, including its positive effect on customer care.

And it all starts with writing goals down.

What gets measured gets done

From the get-go, I knew that I had to build a strong foundation among the group, taking nothing for granted. I also knew that we had to have people engaged from the same starting point, like a horse race. That helps make for better consistency across the different teams and departments. Thus, I began by coaching the managers on how to build their SMART Plans: *Specific, Measurable, Achievable, Relevant, and Time-sensitive.*

Having the managers write their plans down and present them to each other was a crucial step for them to begin accepting ownership and accountability, and to overcome mediocrity. The managers were encouraged to put a lot of thought into their SMART plans and to consult with each other if needed, because these goals would become their playbook and guiding light moving forward. Of course, goals and needs change over time in one way or another. If so, you just make another SMART plan. I suggested that they "slice the elephants into small pieces" to make them more manageable.

Why is writing goals down so important? Is it cliché to say that people who write goals down actually accomplish more? Studies abound on the topic, and *Forbes* cites a report that says: "You are 42% more likely to achieve your goals if you write them down … People who don't write their goals down tend to fail easier than the ones who have plans…" It also helps you remember them better.

Talking is one thing, writing things down and doing them is quite another. The dictum "what gets measured gets done" is one of my favorites, and has proven itself over and over again in my work with all types of organizations. In his first few months at the hotel, Anderson got so tired of hearing people say at meetings, "we've been talking about that" without seeming to ever take action beyond that, that he outlawed the phrase in the hotel. I made a humorous sign with that phrase resembling a no smoking sign for him to hang in his office. Though the sign was a light-hearted way of making a point, people got the message.

Bye-bye, mediocrity!

In the final analysis we saw people really grow professionally and blossom as true managers and teammates.

The management team ultimately got more things accomplished in fewer steps and with more enthusiasm and effectiveness than before. Not only did the results show in increased guest satisfaction, increased business, and diminished turnover, but the hotel was a much more fun place to work, too. The team enjoyed pulling together rather than pushing apart. They held themselves to higher standards, they took their commitments to each other seriously, and they grew as individuals and as a team.

The Mediocrity Pledge, once a catalyst, was now a thing of the past.

Building Your Playbook:

- *What have you used as a catalyst for change?*
- *How did it turn out?*
- *When is the last time you did management or team assessments?*
- *What did they reveal to you or the organization?*
- *What is the call to action for investing in upskilling/ training/coaching in your organization?*
- *List the elements you think should be included in such a plan, the end goal(s) to be accomplished, and a time for being completed*

Chapter 11

Everyone Gets Their Butt Kicked Sooner or Later

"Confidence is a beautiful thing. When you have it you never think you'll lose it. And when you lose it you never think you'll get it back." —Paul Azinger

My friend and business colleague Gary Brown related to me an indelible lesson about humility that his dad once gave him: "Today you're a peacock but tomorrow you could be a feather duster." Entertainment icon Dolly Parton adds a similar warning: "A peacock that rests on his feathers is just another turkey."

It's good to have a healthy dose of humility, no matter how self-important you think you are. I've never met a person in business or otherwise who lived their life totally unscathed from getting their butt kicked at least once, including me. I also don't know of any winners who have ever avoided a setback or loss. No one is perfect, no one wins 'em all.

Hotel industry sales executive Wade Bryant had his "feather duster" moment of truth thrown at him when moving to a new job. There is a lot to be learned from his story. When we talked about it, he minced no words as he dove right in:

"I thought I was hot sh*t. Then I got my a** kicked."

Bryant arrived in Nashville from California, where he had accepted the position of director of sales and marketing for a brand hotel. He had been on the job for two or three months: "I remember that day very clearly," he explained.

"I was in my office cleaning out some of my predecessor's filing cabinets when my general manager walked in. Up until that time, we'd had a decent relationship, but he wasn't a very engaged person.

He shut the door and sat down.

'Wade, the bleeding has to stop,' he said bluntly. 'We hired you because you sold us a bill of goods and it's not happening. This isn't going to work. You need to get it fixed. You need to stop the bleeding.' Then he just got up and left. It was a one-way conversation.

"As a background, we had been going through a poor profit/loss performance which I had largely inherited. My GM must have gotten his own rear end handed to him by our management company so he walked into his highly paid director of sales' office to ask me what I was going to do about it. Only he wasn't asking.

"That was a tough day, one I've never forgotten. That moment accelerated everything for me. I knew that I had to get my sh*t together.

"I honestly didn't know how to read a lot of the corporate reports we had to deal with. We hadn't used them in my former property in Monterey. Nobody had ever asked my former general manager and me for these types of in-depth reports. For years, the two of us had just gotten along by preparing the reports we needed. It was a looser, independent resort hotel. There was no corporate oversight, just the general manager and me, handling all the reports we thought were necessary.

"It was a clear case of *I didn't know what it is that I didn't know.* I didn't have to.

"Here I was at this brand hotel with a tightly controlled corporate management company. I had to make sense of things like variances and also analyze and interpret data. I was now involved in things like gross operating profit and profit/loss. These were things that my previous GM in Monterey always handled because that was the way he managed.

"As funny as it seems now, all of a sudden I found myself Googling things like net operating income, gross operating profit, EBITDA (Earnings Before Interest, Taxes, Depreciation and Amortization), profit margins, you name it.

"I didn't want my friends in the industry to know that I didn't know this stuff. And I surely didn't want my team to know, either. They all assumed that I already knew these things. I was really feeling behind the eight ball and I didn't have a big network that I could call upon and ask for help, either.

"I started to doubt myself. Did I sell them a 'bill of goods' after all? Heck, in my previous hotel, I was used to being the superstar, the guy who got things done. Now, I was making a lot more money and I didn't know half of what they were throwing at me. I felt that my sales and leadership skills were intact, but this was a whole new world of accountability for me in reporting and questions that were being thrown at me. And I was trying to play catch-up, fast."

Aha moments should spring us into action

For Bryant, it was a career aha moment. So how did he pull himself out of this potentially damaging career tailspin?

"I went into complete self-education mode and also complete cover-up mode, too. I was just waiting for the next set of questions to drop. I was hoping to learn quickly so I could have the answers.

"My self-doubt made it hard to perform my duties at

times. It took about three months to get it figured out. I didn't let my team know that I was scared sh*tless in those days, either. It was certainly one of the most scary, humbling, and critical periods of my professional life.

"What got me through was the confidence of knowing that I wasn't a dumb guy. I still had my strengths but not all the answers I needed to have. No one in my previous positions ever told me these things were important or showed me how, or asked me to figure it out. So, how do you know what it is you need to know?

"The harsh words from my Nashville GM actually helped me begin to ask more questions, to become more knowledgeable, and to become more accountable.

"The key for me was asking questions, trial and error, and using resources like Google to find out what it is I didn't know and what I needed to know.

"My advice to pass along here is this: The single most important thing before you take a new job is to go ask the people who are doing that job already. Ask about the problems, the learning curve, etc. Go in with your eyes wide open. Have a network of people you can call on for help and engage with those mentors.

"I can also see now that people in the same job or workplace for ten-to-fifteen years don't necessarily know what new questions to ask. That's a challenge too.

That day I got my a** kicked was singly the most pivotal moment of my career."

Powerful setbacks make for powerful lessons learned

Bryant learned a valuable set of lessons that could happen to any of us. People can get very full of themselves, preening like, well—a peacock. He went from peacock to feather duster in a short one-sided conversation. It was his career wake-up call.

Life is about choices. Bryant made his choice to stay and learn, and to plant his flag. He picked himself up off the canvas after his boss gut-punched him. After a bout of anxiety, he self-assessed and went back to the drawing board, schooling himself in what he needed to learn.

Are you comfortable being uncomfortable?

Here is a question I've often asked audiences when doing leadership training: "Are you comfortable being uncomfortable?" The self-awareness aspect of that question is important because that's the reality for people in leadership, sales, or even parenting roles—things can be a bit uncomfortable in some way or another because we are dealing with the "X" factor—people.

In this case, Bryant was extremely uncomfortable not knowing the things he needed to know. But he was comfortable in his own self-confidence to know where to look for the answers and save his job.

It's not that way with everybody. Sometimes egos are raging and it's tough to work with those types of people. I've found that some folks with overactive egos are "all hat and no cattle," as the phrase goes. They talk a good game but their effort and results are missing in action. It reminds me of an apropos quote by author/orator/educator Booker T. Washington:

"Ego is the anesthesia that deadens the pain of stupidity."

We can do amazing things when our backs are against

the wall. With some people, they shine the brightest at times like that. Some athletes play better from behind rather than in the lead; they come alive when the game is in the balance.

In this case, Wade's career may have been hanging in the balance that day. Instead of folding, he got up off the floor and set about twisting the familiar of what he knew in search of what he needed to know. That's what winners do.

Building Your Playbook:

- *Have you ever had a wake-up call like this?*
- *If so, what happened? What did you do about it?*
- *What changes came about as a result?*
- *If you manage others, who might need the benefit of such a wake-up call from you?*

Chapter 12

Your Solo Adventure May Only be a U-turn Away

"It is in your moments of decision that your destiny is shaped. It's the quality of our decisions that determines the quality of our lives." —Tony Robbins

Making a U-turn while driving a car is not really all that difficult for most drivers; get the green light, check for oncoming traffic, turn the wheel, and you're on your way in the opposite direction.

However, making a U-turn to change both the entire direction of your career and your life at the same time? Now *that's* a bit more daunting. It's the genesis of our story and may just be the jet fuel you need to twist the familiar, too.

A former high school classmate of mine did both. He took a U-turn in his car that turned out to be a change in direction in more ways than one. His chronicle illustrates how we can choose to pivot from one life to another, and in this case, taking a leap of faith from a W-2 job into flying solo as an entrepreneur.

I've known Ron Schlaupitz since our days at Cousino High School in Warren, Michigan, where we were teammates on the varsity football team. Maybe the competitive spirit we developed in school through sports helped us develop our drives to excel in starting our own businesses many years later.

After college, Ron worked his way up the ranks in the financial management business, all the while raising a family with the big dream of one day starting his own CPA firm.

"While I was a CFO for a tooling manufacturer in the Detroit area," he recalls, "the state of Michigan was in the throes of a very tough economy. The loss of jobs and closures of automotive plants were affecting a lot of industries in the Mitten State, including ours."

Ron was feeling the drag of his situation, as if the walls were closing in on him. Often, the seeds of discontent can spawn the entrepreneurial heart into action.

"The economy was struggling, and the company was down in sales," he laments. "I was very frustrated because the tooling industry was in shambles. I knew the company I worked for was heading in the wrong direction."

The time to take the leap was now!

Ron was sent by his company to meet with their "work-out banker," whose job it is to assess the risk of the bank's loans made to a company and negotiate the debt; never a pleasant task. After that grueling appointment, he got into his car to drive back to his office, emotionally worn out from the ordeal.

Driving down the street, Ron had his epiphany moment: "I suddenly thought, screw it, I'm not going to do this anymore!" he recalls. "I was close to the office and I did an immediate U-turn on the next corner. I drove home, changed into my jeans, went straight to the FedEx Office and printed my own business cards as a business financial consultant. I wrote out my resignation letter the next day."

Wham, just like that! Certainly, there was no lack of courage on his part. It didn't take long, however, for reality to settle in.

Ron's fledgling solo enterprise started modestly, as many

do. "I initially started working out of the house," he recalled, "and through that summer after leaving the tooling company, for the first four months, I had no income."

Like other smart solopreneurs, he was smart enough to seek advice from outside sources. If you want to succeed with your own business, take some tips from the savvy pros, especially if you are starting on a shoestring. You don't have to adopt all of the tips you get (some can be pretty lame), but having experienced people whom you trust point out some of the land mines and thick tangles a newbie owner can encounter can save you time, money, and grief.

"I had lunch with a business associate who recommended that I practice as a CPA rather than a financial consultant," he recalls. "Making the switch, it took a few more months to get clients, but then I got three in one week! I was taking people out to lunch and networking with attorneys and bankers, grassroots stuff."

Humble beginnings can be stressful

Solopreneurs must be true to who and what they are. Kevin O'Leary, known as *Mr. Wonderful* on the popular TV show *Shark Tank*, once corrected a solopreneur who was pitching his product on the show: "First of all, you aren't a company, you are a product." It's an excellent reality check for people who run their own solo entity. Don't get ahead of your skis.

Job One

And dialing yourself in means finding customers who will pay you for your services or product. Period. Everything else, at least initially, is just "stuff." Building your sales pipeline with viable prospects as soon as possible is a smart number one priority to focus on.

Self-employment is a veritable roller coaster. And as is the case with spouses and families of solopreneurs, the stress level at home can be palpable. They get nervous when the income is not steady and paychecks aren't coming in every two weeks. Ron explained his start-up strategies to his wife Linda, putting an emphasis on his leads and his works-in-progress. People who don't own their own businesses can sometimes get really impatient about those things.

"I showed her my appointment calendar and the fact that I had nine different appointments that week. I explained how I had to prepare for each one, do the appointment and also the follow-up, and all of that takes time. I didn't always bill people when they asked for a bit of help, either. I was just trying to develop relationships."

What? Not charge people for your expertise? How can that be? It's often all you have to sell! Actually, not charging everyone who calls to ask you for business advice, as Ron pointed out, can be a savvy investment. I know this from firsthand experience. It is a very friendly thing to do and certainly helps build relationships.

It also works to solidify you as a *subject matter expert* and *trusted advisor*. And word can spread rather quickly. That's exactly the sweet spot where you want to be with people. As I often say to my audiences: "Today's apple seed is tomorrow's apple tree." Giving people a sample of your expertise is like making a bank deposit in brand-building. It may pay big dividends down the road.

The brand, the brand, the brand!

That sweet spot is indeed an important part of your brand. Build, nurture, evolve, and protect your brand *fiercely*! I cover branding more in depth in another section of this book, but it bears mentioning it here, too. *It's that important.*

Putting forth solid salesmanship, goodwill, and fellowship are brand virtues, especially when you're trying to grow your fledgling business.

And then there is your competition, and it may not always be who or what you think it is. For independent business owners and indeed salespeople everywhere, there is another competitor that is often overlooked: *Status quo.*

That is described as doing nothing, changing nothing, staying on cruise control. It can be maddening to overcome this stance with a prospect. Getting potential customers to move off the good ship "Status Quo" is sometimes a harder task than selling against your tangible competition. Your proposal may very well lose to a litany of responses such as "We're not going to do anything right now It seems like a lot of extra work, It sounds expensive, We can't get everyone together, We've never done that before, We're not sure we need it," yadda yadda yadda.

What to do? Craft your messaging and laser focus your approach to solidify the benefits in your prospect's mind of why your product or service beats the heck out of what they are currently doing. Point out the potential dangers of "doing nothing" vs. the benefit of what your product or service can bring them.

Luck is what happens when preparation meets opportunity

"The great thing about being an entrepreneur is at any time you can take your destiny into your own hands, lead your own life & create a business. That's freedom." —Lori Greiner (also of "Shark Tank").

And sometimes, that freedom is hard to define. I've worked with people who started their own small businesses and they explain their success this way: "Aw, I just got lucky."

Well, maybe. And then maybe they made their own luck with hard work. In addition to his Job One as a CPA, Ron also had to wear the small business owner's hats of prospector, marketer, salesperson, advertising, public relations, customer service, purchasing, printing manager, mailroom/postage clerk, IT engineer, troubleshooter, insurance buyer, and bookkeeper—all things that go into running one's own business.

And you only have twenty-four hours in a day, so your time and priority management must be rock solid. Start thinking and operating like an *owner*. You have to be brutal on how you spend your time. You can't get so caught up in the minutiae that you lose the big picture and what Job One is. It's no way to run a successful business. Don't miss the entire forest by staring at only the tree in front of you.

"Life begins at the end of your comfort zone."
—Neale Donald Walsch

Aside from very rare cases, starting one's own business is most definitely out of any comfort zone. It's risky and it's not for everyone. The anonymous quote: "Everything you want is on the other side of fear" compliments the quote above. And with hard work, diligence, and some breaks, that fear of "will I be successful?" can definitely morph into the extremely satisfying feeling of knowing that you've worked hard to build your own enterprise up from nothing.

Still, there can be scary times outside of a comfort zone. I asked Ron if he ever had that "uh-oh" moment starting out.

"Oh-h-h yeah," he responded. "I looked at my client base after that first year of going out on my own, and it certainly was not the quality that I had hoped for. I only made $20,000 for an entire year of hard work."

It took a few years, but Ron's grassroots efforts doggedly worked out for him, and he eventually built a solid book of business. He put himself in a position to take on a partner, expanding his client base and building his reputation in southeast Michigan. From the humble beginnings of his home-office, he fulfilled his dream of owning a company and growing his firm to twenty-five employees and almost $4 million in annual revenue in just eight years.

This success story was no overnight sensation. It was one of steady, pragmatic, and tenacious pursuit of business and dedicated customer service. One of Ron's core beliefs is that as much as you must continue to look for new customers, you should always take great care of the customers you have.

> **"I am who I am today because of the choices
> I made yesterday." — Eleanor Roosevelt**

I asked Ron to share his top tenets of business in this book, to help other established entrepreneurs or those who are either just starting out on their own business or considering taking such a leap of faith:

• **Face your fears:** "My greatest fear was starting something on my own when I had a family to provide for. But I put that fear aside that day of my U-turn and just said, 'Screw it!'"

• **Think big ... or big enough:** "What you want to do with your business has to become big enough to make it worth all the effort and risk."

• **Commit to it:** "If you have a good foundation of skills and a good idea of what you want to do, you just have to go out and do it. Once you've committed to do it, every day you have to think: 'What do I need to do to go forward?' Then go do it!"

• **Take it step by step:** "Don't take on more than you can accomplish at once. Finish what you start. Take small steps if you need to. Your opportunities will expand as you accomplish each step forward in your plan."

• **Remember, it's *your* business:** "You have to address those issues that invariably come up in your business, and you have to address them every day. However, the big difference is that you are working on those issues that ultimately help your own business instead of someone else's."

• **The essence of self-employment:** "It is an epiphany when you decide to do this. You must be creative. You must be thoughtful. You must make smart decisions every day. Set your goals, be realistic, and focus on the top two or three things that will make the most difference and accomplish them. If you can't focus on those, then nothing will get done. Seek the counsel of others. You don't have to think up all the ideas and have all the answers by yourself, as if in a vacuum."

The Entrepreneur's Toolkit

Being a small business entrepreneur myself for over two decades, and also coaching and collaborating with other self-employed business operators, I have found certain things tend to rise to the top. Here are my twelve recommendations in what I refer to as *The Entrepreneur's Toolkit*:

- *You have to first thoroughly learn your craft or specialty inside and out, up and down. This separates the amateurs from the professionals.*
- *You have to get knocked down a few times, and then learn how to get back up. Learn from your setbacks and mistakes. Never stop learning.*
- *Business ownership is not for the timid or weak. You must decide if you are in it for the long haul. Have a tough skin.*
- *Choose your business name ("dba"), logo, "look," and your brand carefully—you're going to be stuck with it for a while. It's an extension of you, so what does it communicate? Make it memorable, not garish. Bring in others for input, but the ultimate decision is yours.*
- *Build, evolve, and fiercely protect your personal brand. It can mean the difference between success and failure.*
- *Running one's own business takes a village, and help can come in all manner of sizes, shapes, colors, and opportunities; find your mentors.*
- *How healthy is your financial war chest? You'll have months where you'll need a wheelbarrow to carry your money to the bank, and months where the only thing in your wheelbarrow is dirt and weeds. You will need a good amount of "seed money" to start. Any investors? You've got to have the stamina, faith, and customers to survive the rollercoaster ride.*

- *Never, ever take even one customer for granted. Treat them like gold. You probably aren't the only game in town so they don't have to do business with you—they choose to do business with you.*
- *Master your social media skills. You're going to need the internet.*
- *Invest in a good web design and make sure you can self-edit. It will save you tons of money.*
- *Be prepared for a ton of spam and junk mail from thousands of people (not all legit) selling services and products to small business owners. They can eat up your time. Guard your time preciously.*
- *You will certainly need some breaks along the way. If you have strong fundamentals, techniques, and a commitment to excellence, you'll find that you make your own breaks.*

Life is full of U-turn opportunities of all kinds. Like Ron Schlaupitz, you may decide to turn the wheel in a blink of an eye and change the course of your life. Or, you may do a slow burn, building up to your moment when you embark on your own journey to becoming an entrepreneur. Whichever you decide, make the most of your opportunity and enjoy the ride.

Building Your Playbook:

- *Use the two checklists above to apply them to your own situation. Make notes for each bullet point on where you are with each one, where you need to be, what you will need to do to get there, and when you want (or need) to get there, such as a deadline or target completion date.*
- *Are you considering running your own business? Why? What do you want to accomplish?*
- *What excites you about that idea?*
- *What scares you about that idea?*
- *What is your product or service?*
- *Try writing an initial statement of purpose for your new business.*
- *How about ideas for the name of your business?*
- *List your top three attributes (strengths) that best describe you.*
- *How will those attributes help you build your business?*

Chapter 13

The School of Hard Knocks is Now in Session

"If you think education is expensive, try ignorance."
—Robert Orben

My dad spent his professional career in education at different levels—teaching, counseling, and administration. Along the way, he picked up many tips and tools that were not taught in any textbooks. The lessons here are things he learned in the "School of Hard Knocks." That makes a lot of sense if you consider my dad grew up in the rugged 1930s and 1940s in Oak Park, Illinois, a suburb of Chicago. Through adversity, you develop life tools such as integrity, accountability, trust, decision-making and the benefits of hard work.

His career in education included positions in high schools, colleges, regional occupation programs, and a time in the corporate sector. In addition to teaching, he was a high school football coach, assistant principal, college counselor, and assistant superintendent of schools in Davison, MI. In the mid-70s, he and the superintendent, along with school board members and faculty, frequently had run-ins with a teenage school board member, a young demagogue by the name of Michael Moore—yes, *that* Michael Moore. My dad also pioneered the first vocational education program in the state of Michigan where high school students built residential homes.

As an educator, my dad had a keen sense of observation and an intuitive sense about people and situations. He liked to share stories in the classroom with his students to help make the dry book material come alive, and thus make it more interesting and compelling to grasp. My dad told it like it is, and his students ate it up.

He finally retired in 2019, having taught advanced college courses until he was eighty-six years young—that's sixty-one years in front of classrooms. Though he earned two master's degrees, he's always put more stock into real-world learning rather than book learning.

Here are two of his most popular lessons:

Section One: "Twenty tactical approaches to problem-solving solutions for managers and supervisors in the workplace"

1. Stand up when you hear: "Got a minute?" If you allow them to sit down in your office, it's going to be twenty minutes or more.

2. Don't let things fester, such as employee conflicts including office romances, tardiness, and personal matters. If not handled, further action will most likely be necessary down the road. It will infect your team, too.

3. Don't just come into my office, "vomit" a problem on my desk, and then leave. If you bring me a problem, offer an idea or possible solution to the issue.

4. No end-runs on my team. Have enough respect for me to try and talk it out with me first.

5. Have a "Plan B" for all situations. You never know when you will need it.

6. Ethics: Would I want my family, pastor or best friend to know of my decision today? Would I want it printed in today's newspaper or shared online, and read by my mom

or grandmother?

7. Don't have too many rules and regulations. Keep it simple and more impactful.

8. Learn to take the blame when deserved and give credit to others when earned.

9. It is your time, efforts, and energy that you give to the organization. Make all those efforts count fully to the best of your ability.

10. Form a quick huddle in the morning that covers information needed for the day: Who goes where, who does what, what can you share, how can we help each other? It's communication 101.

11. When you give someone responsibility, you must also give them the authority to act on that responsibility.

12. When you wrap up your day, reflect on what you accomplished, how you spent your time, and what you will do first thing tomorrow.

13. Be comfortable in your own skin. Don't try to be someone you aren't.

14. Look for the good in others, and then tell them about it.

15. Learn from this simple approach to leadership by Jack Welch: "Always seek the truth and build the trust."

16. Write handwritten notes to those who deserve one. They are valued more than you know, and are reread more than once.

17. When you apologize, make it sincere and mean it.

18. What is keeping you from being the best you can be?

19. Trying to satisfy everyone is "The Impossible Dream."

20. The first day that you cut a shady deal with one of your team members is the last day that you are truly effective as a leader. You're then on a slippery slope.

Section Two: "Have to vs. Get to"

My dad shared this profoundly powerful exercise with me while I was driving him home from dinner one evening. It's an inspirational way to help us keep things in perspective. I found it to be extremely impactful, and I hope you will, too. It certainly twists our familiar in terms of seeing common things through a different lens.

He offered this example of "have to vs. get to" when you say, "I have to go to work today." Instead, give thought to those unemployed people who would love the opportunity just to say, "I get to go to work today."

Here is another one: "I have to pick up my child from school today" sounds like a chore, while "I get to pick up my child from school today" sounds like a blessing.

Or how about this one: "I always have to keep my house clean" vs. "I get to keep my house clean." How about those who don't have a house to live in or call their own?

With this method of comparing the way we look at things in our world, so many of those things take on a whole new perspective. This little exercise really dials me in and refocuses me on what is important and what matters most.

Have to vs. Get to: As my dad puts it, "One is an obligation; the other is a privilege."

We lost my mom the summer before this conversation. Becoming choked up talking about this lesson on our drive home, my dad spoke in a low voice: "I *have* to take my wife out for her birthday vs. I *get* to take my wife out for her birthday." I watched a tear well up in his eye as he gazed out the window, when he softly added, "I would love to be able to say that again."

Building Your Playbook:

- *What are the top three to five lessons you've learned or you've admired along the way during your own personal journey?*
- *What would be your top three lessons from this list to initiate on your team or for yourself?*
- *Draw up your own Have to vs. Get to exercise; reflect on what you have; it might help you appreciate things in a different light.*

Chapter 14

Lessons on Creating Excellence from Pebble Beach

"The quality of a person's life is in direct proportion to their commitment to excellence, regardless of their chosen field of endeavor." —Vince Lombardi

Does excellence come from an organization and thus have its effect on the people working there, or does the excellence emanate from the people working there, and thus elevate the organization? Can't both things be true?

When I think of a business where both statements coexist, I think of Pebble Beach. It's a place my family and I have been blessed to visit many times, living in northern California just a little less than two hours away. I recall that the first kindness I ever received at Pebble Beach was in 1980 from the director of golf at the time, Steve McLennan, the humble and friendly director of golf , the "quiet leader" type. After Steve moved on, RJ Harper assumed the reins. I got to know RJ too, a special gentleman, and always very kind to me and my family. After a round of golf there with family, he would ask me, "Did your dad enjoy it?" He would say how much he relished the idea that my dad could play golf with his sons and spend those special days together.

Both Steve and RJ had enormous responsibilities leading the golf departments at such a world-class iconic place, host to numerous U.S. Opens, annual Pro-Am tournaments, and countless hundreds of other events, not to mention legions of golfers coming from all over the world to live out their dreams on those links.

While both men were unquestionably committed to excellence befitting a place like Pebble Beach, I have absolutely no doubt that they would have been equally impressive running a dusty old driving range in a backwater town like the Kevin Costner character in the movie *Tin Cup*. If you have a commitment to quality inside of you, it is transferable wherever you go.

I had several occasions to see RJ interact with his staff and people who weren't celebrities or golfing royalty, just "folks," and I was very impressed that he treated them just as kindly and courteously as if they were celebrities like Tiger Woods or Clint Eastwood. He enjoyed doing nice things for people.

Sadly, RJ is gone, but he touched a lot of lives during his time at Pebble Beach. He is still revered there. How does somebody earn that kind of respect and admiration? How did he twist the familiar in terms of leadership and setting the example?

If you're going to live, leave a legacy. Make a mark on the world that can't be erased. —Maya Angelou

What goes into our personal legacy? To be sure, it's no single thing. It's in how we act and treat others, and how we don't compromise our principles or bend the rules for some. It's also in how we comport ourselves and act in pressure-cooker situations. It can be how we treat others with kindness and care, and how we own up to things vs. make excuses or blame others.

It can also be in our sense of fairness and how we

approach challenges and make decisions. It's also in how we earn and give respect and trust, and our ability to relate to different kinds of people. It often includes our ability to give and take and to display flexibility, which is not to be confused with being wishy-washy.

We may never know to what degree we've made impressions on other people—how they view us or how we've affected them. I told my own two sons when they were growing up: "You never know who is noticing you and seeing what you do, so do things right and do the right things."

Many of us accumulate memorable life lessons during our journey. I came upon such a post from one of those lives RJ Harper touched, James L. Bosworth, Jr., who wrote of the life lessons he learned from RJ while working for him at Pebble Beach. No matter your chosen field of endeavor, these lessons are impactful. Some are simple, many are profound. All told, they have universal value and really nothing to do with golf.

The following section was originally published in 2017 as "Life Lessons from the Prince of Pebble Beach" by James L. Bosworth, Jr., CEO at The Spyglass Collective, and is edited for content/space and presented here with permission:

"He had a special way of challenging, encouraging, and kicking you in the a**—all at the same time … most of the time doing it with a twinkle in his eye and a broad smile on his face. He believed in earning your opportunities through a combination of hard work and attitude. He would always say 'the cream rises to the top.' His merit-based promotion system produced some of the finest individuals in and around the world of golf, and it taught me the importance of never taking a shortcut or the easy way out."

Here are a few of RJ's life lessons:

"Be early, even if you are opening up the pro shop at 4:30 a.m.

Show everyone respect and kindness.

Smile—the world loves a friendly smile.

Introduce yourself with pride. I was a little shy and intimidated. RJ had me take an entire day to introduce myself to every tourist and guest on the front steps of the Pro Shop to get used to meeting and greeting new people. His explanation was that most people would be intimidated to be at the mecca of golf, but it was my job to humanize and enhance their experience, to create a friend, and a lifelong memory for those lucky enough to be there. What a gift— thank you RJ.

Work hard and don't be afraid to learn. I remember even as our director of golf he took a calligraphy course. I was shocked to see him attending what is mostly a class for assistants, but he thought it would be fun and helpful if he got a little bit better at it—and he was great at it!

Be enthusiastic about both big and small wins.

Dress well and make sure you know how to iron.

When you screw up, admit it and take responsibility.

Never take your good fortune for granted. Always use your gifts to enhance the lives of others.

Sing even if you're bad! It's one of the joys of life.

Celebrate the achievements of others.

Take a moral stand—it's good for you.

Be a present parent. RJ was a great dad and a role model to many of us single dads. I never had a call or a meeting with RJ where family was not at the center.

Help those who can't help you. Life is about what you

give, not what you get.

Compete hard and win! If you fall short, give credit to others and take the responsibility for the loss.

Take your hat off when you walk into a building. People respect your 'hat head' more than your perfect hair."

Harper's duties at Pebble Beach called for him to often work closely with the owners, including Arnold Palmer. They became good friends.

During Palmer's nationally televised funeral service near his home in Latrobe, Pennsylvania in 2016, CBS sportscaster Jim Nantz took to the lectern for his tribute to Arnie. In his remarks, he included a mention of his friend RJ, who was back at home unable to attend due to the progression of his illness. Later in the ceremony, golfing great Jack Nicklaus spoke tearfully about the loss of Arnie, his very close friend and longtime competitor. He included this quote in his closing remarks:

"Don't cry because it's over. Smile because it happened."

As I reflect back on that telecast, I believe Nicklaus' words would also have applied to RJ Harper and his legacy at Pebble Beach. I sincerely hope he would be OK with my reference here. It's a moving quote that I think can apply to all of us at one time or another in our lives.

Consider for a moment the people whose lives you have touched. What do you think your own personal legacy of excellence would be?

Building Your Playbook:

- *How would you describe "commitment to excellence" in your own words? What does it mean to you?*
- *What do you do personally to pursue that?*
- *How about your team—do they subscribe to having a commitment to excellence?*
- *What personal lessons, like that of Harper's above, would you have on your own list from your own experiences?*
- *What can you do to instill such a commitment in others?*

Chapter 15

Tooting Your Own Horn is Not Always Easy

"There is only one thing in the world worse than being talked about, and that is not being talked about." —Oscar Wilde

**Success is not just *who you know*.
It's more often about *who knows you*.**

Have you ever been asked to "toot your own horn," so to speak, to tell others about your talents, abilities, and qualities? Certainly, if you've ever interviewed for a job, validated yourself to a customer, or crafted a resume or online profile, you have. Did you find it easy to talk about yourself that way? For many people, it can be a real struggle.

But love it or loathe it, there's no denying that it's a necessary thing in our world today, especially in business. This book will give you the keys and confidence to help you tell your story and put your personal brand attributes and traits to work for you.

Expressing your own attributes to others can be a bit off-putting, right? Whether you're the one sending those messages or the person receiving them, if it's overdone, it can be downright uncomfortable and cringeworthy. While some people see it as a welcome opportunity to talk about their brand or do a bit of self-promotion, others are very uncomfortable with talking or writing about themselves. To them it seems like bragging or being an egomaniac.

But that sentiment can be a big detriment to one's career.

You can't successfully interview for a job, justify yourself to a customer, or build your social media profiles without talking about yourself, your accomplishments, and your attributes. Just don't be a jerk about it.

Let's face it, we're not all wired the same way when it comes to self-promotion. Muse.com offers this: "Whether it makes you feel too self-promotional or you simply don't like being the center of attention, talking about yourself isn't a skill that comes naturally to everyone . . . But there's no getting around it: You have to learn to talk about yourself."

The good news is that you already do it

When someone is uncomfortable tooting their own horn, I coach them to look at it this way: "You already do it, but maybe you don't realize it!" Whether it's expressing your credentials on your resume, talking about yourself in a job interview, or crafting your social media personal profile, you've already had to put yourself out there by telling the world about your attributes and strengths in the quest to make a case for *Brand You*.

Sometimes I'll hear a person say, "Gee, I don't like bragging about myself." I respect that. But to label it bragging is really a bit harsh. Sure, if you apply your wonderfulness in a bullying, standoffish way, then it is bragging. Who likes a braggart? It won't get you very far in business or life. So I'll repeat: don't be a jerk about it. There is a big difference between being self-confident and being a jerk. I'm reminded of Will "The Thrill" Clark, a former Major League Baseball player and six-time All-Star. Playing for the San Francisco Giants, Clark was asked by a reporter if he was bragging when he said his Giants were going to beat the opposing team in the upcoming playoffs. He famously replied: "Well, it ain't bragging if you can back it up."

Brusque as they may be for some, Clark's words have always made sense to me. It's all in the delivery.

Be proud of your attributes—it's your personal brand

Everyone has stories, everyone has attributes. You should always be prepared to have yours ready to use when needed. Stories contribute and help flesh out your personal brand. They give your background vibrant colors and may explain certain things about you—all part of your brand. For example, what background stories about yourself would you use to answer these queries?

"Can you tell me what your strongest attributes are, the ones that would qualify you to be the manager of our department?"

"Which experiences in your background would tell us that you have faced challenges, that you are ready for the next level?"

"I'm considering entrusting my company's business to you. What strengths do you bring to the table that would show me that I'm making the right decision?"

Boom! Those are deer-in-the-headlights questions, aren't they? What do you say? You can't hem and haw. You'd better have believable answers and convincing talking points along with enough self-confidence in order to articulate them. Are your self-talking points game-ready?

Does your online story need an "attribute makeover"?

Have you reviewed your own online profiles lately? Are

you looking to build, update, tweak or start over with a better way to tell your story? Maybe you should. It's good to revisit your profiles often. It's a poor reflection on your own brand to have an outdated profile, and I've seen a ton of them. It's a sloppy look.

Let's start with the thing people will see first – your photo. Oh my . . . please invest in a professional headshot with great lighting and appropriate attire for what you do. No poorly-lit fuzzy photos, with someone's arm around your shoulder that you cropped out of a spring break photo ten years ago. A bad profile photo, or no photo at all, is a red flag. You've been fairly warned.

The next most critical piece is your one-liner branding description below your name, since that will show in searches and messages. Craft a definitive and catchy statement that describes what you do, who you are. Between your photo and your description, it's sometimes all that some people will take the time to look at before they decide to move on. It sucks, but it's true. People spend an average of seven-to-fifteen scant seconds checking each other out online, so what you present initially had better be great. If so intrigued, they'll next venture onto your *About* section. It's like opening a book. After an intriguing introduction on the cover, people will be more inclined to open the pages and see what you are all about. Here is where a lot of folks get it wrong.

It's about YOU, not your company's website excerpts

Too many people think that their *About* section is the place to copy and paste the talking points about their company, often lifting the salesy text, word-for-word, right off their company's website. No, no, no! Don't do it. It's a sure cure for insomnia. This space is yours, not your company's! A brief mention of your company and what it does is fine.

Keep in mind that people visit your profile to read about *you*. If they want to read about your company's factoids, they'll go to its website. Craft a compelling thumbnail sketch of yourself, making it interesting for visitors who have stopped for a look at your "billboard" while traveling at warp speed on the e-highway.

Questions that help us talk about ourselves

My overriding advice is to be *genuine* and *authentic*. Avoid like the plague those bland phrases that many others tend to employ. LinkedIn makes available a list of overused trite phrases and words. Check your profile against those and see how many of them you've included and then get rid of them. Find other ways of saying what you want to say. Yes, twist the familiar in how you write!

For example, "proven track record" is on that trite list and is my most disfavored phrase. Yuck! It's a term that doesn't mean anything tangible, yet legions of people use it. They don't know what else to say so they copy what others use. Yawn. Can you actually prove your track record from years ago? Is anyone going to ask you to do so?

I developed the following list of questions to help you identify or come to grips with your best traits and draw out some interesting anecdotes that people will find compelling about you. Use as many of these as you like, in any order:

What inspires me?
Why am I in this business?

What do I enjoy most about what I do?

What kind of person am I to work with?

What do I find most gratifying?

What am I most proud of?

What was the biggest challenge I've had to overcome or the biggest problem I had to solve?

What are my top three attributes? This is a good place to use what others have said about you, i.e., customers, peers or colleagues.

What three adjectives best describe me?

What do I bring to the table? This is why someone would benefit from engaging with you, hiring you, or working with you.

S-A-R: (see below)

People love stories. I coach the "SAR" method to help people get the most mileage out of their stories. It is a simple formula that works as a snapshot to illustrate one episode or assignment in your career to highlight as a short story that paints an overall picture of how you roll. It is a powerful opportunity for you to put your best foot forward via a mini story. You are limited by the number of characters, so be pithy.

S — Situation: Start with a brief background of the situation, job or assignment you inherited or were tasked with accomplishing. What were the conditions when you entered the picture?

A — Action: What action(s) did you take to solve the problem, cure the illness, fix the issue, book the sale? What resources did you bring to bear? What systems did you design or implement?

R—Results: What resulted from your action(s), and what came about as a result of your solution(s)? How did this help or fix your clients' dilemma or pain point?

Creating "A Call to Action"

As you craft your *About* section's closing, keep in mind that you want to end strong so that people will be intrigued enough to keep going through the other sections of your profile and ultimately connect with you. Build a powerful, compelling "Call to Action" because visitors to your profile are likely to ask themselves:

"Can this person help me solve my problem or take my pain away?"

"Is this someone I would like to connect with?"

"Can this person bring value to my life in some way?"

Mention any solid differentiators that you offer or represent, something they can't get from the thousands of other people that do what you do. Twist the familiar and separate yourself from the pack. Maybe you serve a particular niche or have a unique attribute. Don't keep it a secret—now is the time to use it!

Are you ready to start writing? Great! Just remember to keep it real. Nobody walks on water even though some folks' online profiles come close to insinuating that they do. Instead, craft your honest story. It's what most people want to see—authenticity. And relax—you don't have to write your entire story alone. It's very effective to ask your customers and colleagues to help you tell your story via written recommendations on your profile that will support and validate your claims.

With all of this, you will gain more confidence in talking and writing about yourself. I'll bet that you will also see an increase in your connection invitations from others. Your network will grow. Write a strong, bold case on your own behalf and you will compel people to engage with you.

And that will ensure that the notes you play while tooting your own horn will sound oh-so-sweet.

Building Your Playbook:

- *Examine your answers to the questions in this section in order to construct your "About" section. You have a lot of characters to use but it is limited, so learn how to edit your more verbose sections.*

- *Write, edit, write again, edit again—you'll become a better writer. Plus, your tastes change over time in how you want to say things. Watch your punctuation and grammar. Have a second pair of eyes check your work.*

- *Some things need more explanation than others, but keep your stories short.*

- *Read your section when finished and ask yourself: Would I want to read this? Would I find this person interesting or engaging? If not, edit again.*

- *Update your profile frequently. You will change over time, and so should your profile. Why would anyone be satisfied having an outdated billboard?*

- *If you lead a team, check out your team's individual profiles. Do they represent well? Are they saying anything that goes against the company mantra that might prove embarrassing? Does their profile create a compelling case that will attract customers? Are they sloppy with typos, poor phrasing, punctuation errors, or poor grammar?*

Chapter 16

Embrace Your Brand and Make it Work for You

"Your brand is what people say about you
when you are not in the room." —Jeff Bezos

"I could have been better . . . And then, when I walked down the street, people would have looked and they would have said, 'There goes Roy Hobbs, the best there ever was . . .'" (From the 1984 TriStar Pictures baseball film *The Natural*, starring Robert Redford as Hobbs.)

Sitting on his hospital bed recovering from surgery, professional baseball player Roy Hobbs reflected on how different his baseball career could have been. He fully comprehended his legacy—his *brand*—as a star ballplayer. But as outstanding a player as he was, Hobbs still felt regret over things in his past that prevented him from being the best ever.

The best there ever was. I'm guessing that's a personal brand legacy that any one of us would like to own, no matter what we do for a living.

So what's stopping you?

What is *your* legacy? Have you given it much thought? Your personal brand works to help determine your legacy and how you are viewed by others. It is the world's window into your soul. And it's 100 percent yours and yours alone. You own it.

That's pretty cool when you think about it.

Everyone has a personal brand whether they want one

or not. Some people push back on the concept because they don't see themselves as a brand per se. They may fight the idea because they incorrectly label it as "profiling," which has a negative connotation in our society. That's a harsh way to look at one's attributes. Regardless of whether we want to believe it or want to agree with it or not, people see us in specific ways. The fact is that we all have a personal brand so we'd better make the most of it. Much of what we accomplish in life (or don't accomplish) ties back to the essence of our brand characteristics.

Why is my personal brand so important?

Your brand can enable you to soar, and it can also hold you back.

Branding is how others perceive you—the world's window into how you roll. It affects how others treat you, respond to you, believe you, trust you, follow you, spend time with you, respect you, engage with you, buy from you, listen to you, admire you, hire you, promote you—*or not*.

It's essentially a work in progress, since we've all had a certain set of characteristics evolving with us since birth and through our formative years. In our professional lives, our personal branding carries a lot of weight in our careers and with our peers and customers. Indeed, personal branding is a lifelong journey, and it can change in several ways along that road.

What can I do to elevate my own brand?

Consider this: Your smile is your **logo**, your personality is your **business card**, and how you leave others feeling after an experience with you becomes your **trademark**.

Let's explore how you can build, enhance, or reinvent your personal brand. A good starting point to self-assessment is this question: *What do I bring to the table?* Start by defining your *value* to others. Your brand works to help "sell" your value and your ideas to others, to solidify your believability as an authentic person.

It's easy to see how outside salespeople must project a believable, trustworthy and knowledgeable personal brand to customers, but how about others who don't sell for a living? Well, everybody sells something at one point or another. We frequently sell our ideas and opinions to family members, friends, neighbors, work buddies, etc. Organizational/team leaders are in sales, too. They have to constantly sell their vision, ideas, and goals to their teams in order to get forward movement.

Branding isn't just for big companies

The concept of personal branding is easier to comprehend when we think about some of the iconic companies present in our lives every day, many of whom we grew up with: Gerber, Hershey, Coke, Pepsi, Walmart, Microsoft, Apple, Titleist, Amazon, Ford, Tesla, etc. Those brands conjure up some type of emotional response in us, triggering an inclination to buy or not to buy, to believe in them or not, depending on how we perceive the brand and the problem or need it solves, or the value it brings to our lives.

Think about your trip to the grocery store: Why do you throw certain products into your basket and leave other similar products by different manufacturers on the shelves? There must be some equation going on inside your head that says, "I'm buying X because I like it better than Y." For whatever reason(s), such as your previous experience with the product, price, taste, convenience, effectiveness, or appeal, you make your decision on buying one brand vs. another.

Your personal brand works in much the same way via its effect on other people.

You and other people make the same type of branding decisions about each other every day. Personal brand characteristics draw us toward some people and away from others. Why do we say *yes* to some people and *no* to others? We trust and believe some people more—or less; we want to spend time with some people more than others; we choose our partners and friends based on certain factors, and personal branding is ever present in the equation.

How do we grow our personal brand? Be the lobster!

Why a lobster? Lobsters grow by molting. This process entails them struggling out of their old shells, while simultaneously absorbing water that expands their body size. In order to grow, a lobster needs to shed its hard shell and replace it with a newer, larger shell. We can learn from lobsters by constantly "molting" and growing our personal brand via our actions, thoughts, words, etc. You can't stay rutted in your old shell, you won't grow. And thus, your brand won't really evolve, either, limiting your upside potential for success.

And if you're looking for an easier path as in "fake it 'till you make it", that's a crock. Today, most people and organizations value genuine, authentic people with brands that reflect those same qualities. Being a fake is a short-term play that can end badly.

Seven key branding characteristics for you to build on

In working with people at all levels in all types of organizations, I've identified seven key characteristics/attributes that define a large part of an individual's personal brand. How do you stack up here?

Uniqueness: What sets you apart from the crowd? What makes you different from others?

Image: What imagery do you create? It's both subjective and objective. How do you appear to others? It may sound trite in talking about looks, but think about it. It's often part of the gig. It's not always about looks, of course; it can also be something intangible. People can make judgements and branding decisions in milliseconds based on how someone looks, their wardrobe, or how they carry themselves. Do you walk proudly or sulk? How is your hygiene? For example, halitosis is a bad branding characteristic! Body language, facial signals, and voice inflection are huge telltale signs to many people. Do you have a friendly smile or are you always frowning?

Signature Traits: What do you bring to the table? What traits are you best known for? Are you accurate in your work? Are you a good writer? Do you have an ear for music? Are you good at making decisions under pressure? Do you come up with creative ideas?

Reputation: It's about what others think of you. You have to earn your reputation in others' eyes. Are you reliable or always running late? Are you always playing the contrarian? Do you pay your own way or always borrow from others? Do you cheat or do you respect rules? Can you keep a secret? Are you considered a "go-to" authority on things?

Principles: What do you stand for: Trust? Honesty?

Doing whatever it takes? How do others perceive your ethics, your sense of right from wrong? What guiding principles drive your decision-making?

Attitude: Are you known as a negative person most of the time? Are you candy-corn super-sweet much of the time? Are you typically over the top with even the simplest things? Are you known as an optimist or a pessimist? Are you cheerful and approachable, or snarly and gruff?

Skill Set/Talents/Abilities: This is where it gets real. At some point, you have to have the actual necessary skill set and the talents to pull off whatever it is you are trying to do. You can have the best attitude and intentions in the world, but if you can't do the job correctly because you don't have the skills, well, you know how that will turn out. If you need to add skills or learn new talents to improve your brand, don't wait for Christmas. Get help, start upskilling.

Protect your brand—fiercely!

I can't stress this strongly enough. As many high-profile celebrities, politicians, and athletes know only too well, a personal brand can be quickly and irreparably shredded in the blink of an eye. It takes years to build a brand—just ask someone who has built their own business—but it can be smashed into pieces in one idiotic moment.

Do whatever you can to protect your brand, including recovery and damage control if something goes sideways, even if it wasn't your fault. You can try to build your brand back up. Thankfully, many people have short memories and some people are more forgiving than others. But it takes time and effort. Golfer Tiger Woods is a well-known example of that. His personal brand went up, then way down, and then back up again. But it's not always easy, nor is it guaranteed.

And for crying out loud, *be authentic!* This is far and away the number one piece of advice on personal branding that I can offer to you. Without authenticity, the rest of your branding components can't really be on solid ground.

Teams have brands, too

Teams of people have a brand of some sort, too (whether they know it or not), be it a Little League team or a team of nurses in a hospital ICU. Heck, even the a.m. shift and the p.m. shift within the same department can have very different brand characteristics. I experienced that with a convention center client of mine, it was literally night and day. The trouble is, with almost every team to whom I've asked the question over the years, they have had absolutely no clue what their team brand is, or what they stand for. It is alarming.

Would it surprise you to know that in 95 percent of the cases, not only do the team leaders or department managers not know what their team's brand is, but most of the members on the teams have never even *heard of* the concept of team brands!

To help rectify that, an exercise I'll employ with my clients is to test the various business units/teams/departments within an organization on what they each bring to the table. We examine how they integrate, what they do, and how they do it. I help them come to grips with their individual team brands, strengths, and characteristics. It's an exercise you would find valuable in your own organization. This is the critical point: Do the various team brands tie back to and support the overall organizational brand or mission? Does it all fit together as a strong, productive fabric? Branding-wise, with companies and their team members in the various business units, the whole should be greater than the sum of its parts. In other words, it's the 1 + 1 = 3 formula again.

My experience is that most teams have an "identity crisis" in that they don't know what their identity is. If you lead a team, my strong recommendation is to invest time on working together to identify your team brand: what you do, what you stand for, how you roll. It also helps build a better sense of camaraderie. It will be time well spent.

To summarize, if you build, nourish, and protect your brand properly and carefully, who knows? Just like Roy Hobbs, maybe someday someone might say as you walk by them: "There goes the best there ever was."

Building Your Playbook:

- *How would you fill out your seven key brand attributes in terms of your own characteristics?*
- *What do others think of your brand? Has anyone ever said anything to you about any of your characteristics? Was it a viable observation? How did that make you feel?*
- *Test your own branding perceptions of others in your life: How do their characteristics pull you towards them or pull you away? Does it affect how you believe them, trust them, interact with them, buy from them?*
- *Which branding attribute of yours do you most want to improve?*
- *Which branding attribute do you lack but want to acquire? Go get it!*
- *What is your team brand at work? How do they live their brand, and does it properly reflect the organization and its overall brand?*

Chapter 17

A Twist on The Concept of "Off-Season"

"There is no continuum for success. Just because you won last year, it doesn't mean you don't have to go earn it next time… Success is momentary." —Nick Saban

Many things in our world have annual cycles or seasons, such as sports leagues, holiday shopping, the school year, farm crops, you name it. There is usually a slow (or slower) season and a busy (or busier) season, with two very different activity levels in play.

Your organization or industry likely has its cycles, too.

Although it's not always either/or, most businesses have those high-season times when it's crazy-busy, frantic to the point of pulling your hair out, just to keep up. Then there are the not-so-busy times when it's more like "Wake me up when a customer comes in the door." The latter economic condition is commonly referred to in business as "the off-season."

You've likely heard this: "Come and visit during the off-season. Our rates are much lower because no one is here." Or this one: "Wait to buy those in the off-season, as we run a lot of specials because we're really dead at that time of year." What a sales approach—the idea of being dead. That really makes me want to buy.

So it's your off-season? Keep your team awake

Learning about my clients' business cycles while developing a customized training program for them, they inevitably tell me about their off-season when business is slower, such as a summer resort in the winter or a Christmas products company in July. There is usually an entirely different mindset around companies when business slows down or goes with a skeletal staff to handle the trickle of business. They begin to "coast," and here is my case why that can hurt a business in both the short term and the long term.

It's my experience that for many businesses during the so-called off-season or off-times, their service level slips as staffers gear down. In baseball parlance, *they lose their fastball*. Ho hum. The team's performance slumps as cruise control takes over. Chill, baby, chill.

That's exactly why I try to forego eating in restaurants on really slow nights. Almost without fail, we get much better service on busy nights. Go figure.

Here's my take on that: When it's busy—and this was certainly true for me during my waiter days back in college—people seem more focused, more in motion, more fired up to deliver. Maybe it's because the adrenalin kicks into gear when customers seem to be coming out of the woodwork. More transactions are happening, money is flowing, and it's just more active. People have less time to daydream and ponder because they are in motion. They seem more alive as their bodies give off bundles of kinetic energy. Motion creates energy. Energy creates results. Busy times fend off the NoDoz pills.

On the other hand, slower nights (or slower seasons)

seem to cause our attention spans to wane and our energy levels to sag. We make more mistakes. Our focus isn't as sharp. Wake me up when it's over. It's often *Yawn City*, except for your customers, who are there to do business with you and are still expected to pay for the goods and services they are buying. They deserve your A-Game. Did we forget about them? Check your own guest/customer satisfaction scores. I'll bet that they lag behind during your slower times or off-season. How do you correct that?

Stop calling it the "off-season"

Get rid of the term "off-season!" Erase it from your brain. Lose that mindset. Just don't refer to it as that anymore. It's got the word "off" in it, and that can't be a good thing for your team. It's the subliminal idea that something is a bit "off," such as your need for attention to details, service quality, customer care, or product delivery.

Rather, refer to it as your "pre-season," as in *preparation season*. It's a mindset, to be sure. As sports teams do, use your slower times in a much more productive fashion, getting your team prepared for the busier times to take stock of what needs to be done, such as:

Work out the kinks in your operations and deliverables

Get people fired up and recommitted to Job One — why are they here?

Retrain and upskill staffers to refresh, refocus, reinvigorate, redeploy

Think anew, twist the familiar; what else can we do? What do we need?

Streamline processes that have become clunky

Tweak things to make them better. You don't have to reinvent all the wheels

Add some things such as more products, more variety, more choices, etc.

Eliminate other things: Wonky procedures, unnecessary components, products or services that don't sell

Refresh both "soft" goods such as attitudes, and "hard" goods such as furniture, paint, renovations, etc.

Practice! Practice! Practice! Get the new way of doing things down to a science; Get people game-ready!

How twisting the familiar turned around a seasonal resort

Let's look at a short case study. Although it is a hospitality example, you can easily apply these same concepts to your own business or industry.

I suggested this concept to a lake resort client located in a seasonal area, with the bulk of their business being in the summer months. They told me their customer service marks always suffered in the off-season. I wasn't surprised. They had more issues in the slower months than the busy months. Though the resort didn't close its doors in the off-months and they still entertained paying guests, business significantly slowed down. They had bunches of seasonal layoffs and their "mojo" slumped.

I suggested to the resort general manager that we begin with removing the term *off-season* from their vernacular. His reaction was predictable: "What?" He was initially taken back by this strange suggestion of how we should twist the familiar on an age-old term in the industry. I was breaking new ground with him, explaining my 30,000-foot strategy: everything starts with the mindset of a *preparation season* (or *preseason*) vs. clinging to the term *off-season*.

This sea change wasn't accomplished overnight. I designed a total immersion, a necessary approach for real success to happen. Both the management team and the frontline team were exposed to the idea of a *preseason* and the benefits behind it. We kicked preparation into high gear, starting with a review of the recently concluded high season. Once people got the gist of what we were trying to do, they embraced it because they could see that their lives at work were about to get better when business cranked up again.

One of the initial components of my program included my "Four Pillar Questions" method (we'll delve into it in greater detail in another chapter). When starting to craft a project or campaign it's a good idea to take a pause first, and look backward in order to plan forward—to learn from mistakes and successes and analyze where we are going. The Four Pillar Questions are:

Where are we?
How did we get here?
Where are we going?
How will we get there?

Change can be painful, but stagnation is fatal

Sports teams and athletes watch game films and videos to see their past performances and scout their opposition, all for the purpose of getting better and improving their performance. The successful ones break down their past games, looking for nuances, missed opportunities, and ways they could have done something better. The film or video is a cruel teacher because it doesn't lie.

Like Saban and other successful winning coaches, they use their team's game films to plan their approach to the next game. They build on their past efforts and design their next game plan with the goal of working to eliminate their mistakes. It's called improvement. You can apply the same idea to your organization.

For a business, including this particular resort client, their "game film" could be a variety of tools such as customer reviews, social media feedback, visual observations, tangible results, profit and loss, etc. Use these resources to prepare your game plan moving forward, just like a coach. You don't want to repeat the same mistakes or redundancies from last season.

During the resort's preseason, I helped them challenge their status quo. Everything was on the table for examination. We analyzed, planned, trained/re-trained, practiced, executed, and evaluated. We got people and teams ready for their prime time busy season. Ultimately, that resort's team was better prepared and more fired up for their high season than ever before, and their results showed it. Their customer satisfaction scores soared and earned them a bonus from the owners. It also resulted in more leads for future business.

Reflecting on this assignment, my first challenge was getting them to change their mentality. Indeed, the term *off-season* was now R.I.P. at that resort. Good riddance.

Since this approach of preparing in the preseason works for teams and athletes, I'm confident it can succeed for your business units, too. But it takes some work.

"Great teams know that championships
are won in the off-season" — ESPN

For example, every summer, football teams all over the country gather again in the throes of preseason preparation, doing the "grunt work" of getting ready for the upcoming season. They are conditioning, learning, relearning, getting back into game-ready shape, and syncing up with each other so they can perform as a team. New coaches are getting to know their players and vice versa. They are changing up what didn't work so well last season and instilling new plays with new players in new positions.

Does some of this sound familiar when thinking of your own organization? The whole idea is to put your slower times and low seasons to work by investing in the fundamentals and techniques—some call them the X's and O's—to improve and compete at a higher level than before.

Is the idea of "no continuum for success" a valid one?

Is Coach Saban's idea a correct one? Does success have to be earned all over again, even though you've won in the past? I concur 100 percent with that notion. There is nothing in winning something once that brings a guarantee of winning it the very next time. There are no handouts, you have to earn it all over again. And we know that shift happens. We can improve the odds—that's exactly what we're doing in this chapter—but there are no guarantees.

Have you heard those long-running commercials for investment companies? Their disclaimer says: "Past performance is no guarantee of future results." The investors have to earn your trust every day, with every transaction. It's the "What have you done for me lately?" business. If you've ever wagered on a horse race and made your picks based on the horse's past performances, you know all too well that the next race is a different race altogether, and anything can happen.

The best leaders and coaches know there are no magic beans here. If you want to win again, your preparation must include going back to your standards and hitting the fundamentals and techniques all over again. No one is going to hand you a victory in business just because you kicked butt last year, last month, or even last week.

You build championship efforts one brick at a time

Get your various teams and business units involved in their own piece of the puzzle. Refer to the list here as a blueprint. It can be a good starting point for team-by-team preseason analytics. Then bring everyone together and see how the "bricks" stack up.

When people at every level of an organization get involved in this initiative, more people get behind it and become engaged. When they have a hand in the project, they tend to support it more. Otherwise, this entire initiative might just seem like extra work to the supervisors and frontline staff and in a slow business period, that will be a grind and a hard sell.

What about your competition in the *off-season*? This is a great time to get a leg up on them, too. Commit to doing the little things better than they do. Let them coast on autopilot during their off-season or slow periods if they so choose. Without some "preseason" work, they are inevitably going to repeat their same mistakes from the previous high season, armed with the same old procedures and baggage, too. Like the saying goes: "If you always do what you've always done, you'll always get what you always got."

Meanwhile, your organization is getting better by putting

the work in, and preparing throughout its preseason to come out with engines revving. The sweat equity you expend in reviewing, planning, adjusting, and practicing will pay off.

As a capstone for our topic, this quote from former Michigan State and NFL quarterback Kirk Cousins does the job quite nicely. After capturing the Big Ten football title as the underdog team several years ago, Cousins explained his take on the hard work and the preparation that goes into the preseason to bring about winning during the actual season:

"Championships are built on a thousand invisible mornings, when no one is watching."

Building Your Playbook:

- *What steps do you or your organization take during the slow periods or low season to put in the preparation for future efforts when it gets busy again?*
- *Which areas would you address first in your preseason work?*
- *Draw up an initial plan outlining the most important issues: What would you change? Refer to the list in this section as your guide.*
- *What barriers or resistance do you think would get in the way of this initiative?*
- *What can you do to overcome these and move forward?*

Chapter 18

Leadership by Example—the Best Kind!

"You are shaped by how you play, not by what you say."
—Anonymous

This story is about attention to detail, leadership by example, and creating a culture where people want to give their top performance. Although it is a story based in hospitality, you can easily apply these same ideals and put them into practice in your own business. When you do, you'll be twisting the familiar far above your competition.

The luxury hotel that recruited me out of The School of Hospitality Business at Michigan State was the iconic Westin St. Francis, a famous San Francisco landmark. It was one of the few major buildings that survived the destructive 1906 earthquake without major structural damage, while much of the city was in flames and rubble.

Throughout its storied history, it has been the hotel choice of many U.S. presidents, royalty from many nations, and legions of A-list celebrities. Its list of glitterati who have stayed there reads like a who's who.

It also has a robust record of hosting many movie sets and important events. In 1945, when world dignitaries gathered in San Francisco to sign the Charter of the United Nations, many of the events took place at the St. Francis.

As such, I was extremely proud to land a management development position right out of college at such a respected and historic grand hotel. A small army of people worked hard to sustain that first-class image and deliver the goods every day. The "St. Frantic," as we lovingly called it internally on crazy-busy days, wasn't just about marketing schmaltz.

Leaders set the tone

We learn quite a bit in our lives by what we see and observe. Part of our success at the St. Francis was due to the tone and tenor set by our general manager, Robert B. Wilhelm, or "RBW" as he was called internally. He was classically trained in old-school hospitality and was impeccably dressed most often in Brooks Brothers suits, looking every bit the part of the classic hotelier-in-charge. He garnered respect from the staff and to be fair, a little bit of intimidation with some folks too, as he set high bars and expected people to give their "A" games.

RBW ran a fairly tight ship but he was not without dry humor. I recall my very first shift as night manager of the 1,200-room hotel when I was twenty-three years old. I had just a year of management training there and I was about to be the person in charge of the entire hotel from 11:00 p.m. to 7:00 a.m. (known in the industry as "the graveyard shift"), when lots of things could and often did happen. We had bars, lounges, and a chic dance club on the top floor of our tower that closed at 4:00 a.m. With over a thousand occupied rooms, front doors with full-on street access to Union Square, and an opulent lobby that invited looky-loos and random people all day and night, what could possibly ever happen during the night?

I got to the hotel an hour before I was expected to be there; I was leaving nothing to chance. I armed myself with my trusty walkie-talkie and walked over to our desk. RBW walked through the lobby in my direction. He gave me a smile, handed me a large heavy ring of thirty or so keys on it, and succinctly said, "OK Gary, she's all yours. Don't let the place burn down. If it does, then call me." That was it, his entire instructions to me. Then he simply walked out to his car.

The lesson of trust our general manager placed in me that night has stayed with me all these years. It gave me tremendous confidence, and I wanted to perform commensurate with his trust. It's a lesson that greatly impacted my career.

"The quality of a leader is reflected in the standards they set for themselves." —Ray Kroc

No matter the business, leaders set the tone. And if that leader is you (or you are an aspiring leader), then be self-aware that people are always watching you and how you set the tone. All of your personal brand characteristics, such as how you dress and carry yourself, the words you use, your temperament, your care for others, your decision-making—it's all out there for people to see. And what they see rubs off on them, including how they treat each other and *your customers*.

RBW's style and messaging made us fully aware that we had a truly "grande dame" of a hotel to represent and keep in tip-top shape. It was really impressive to see the pride in peoples' work there, polishing and cleaning things, and going to great lengths to serve our guests. It was a never-ending job to make that substantial hotel sparkle. Our general manager instilled in us the chops to treat our hotel like our own home. We weren't perfect by any means, but we ran a fairly tight luxury ship.

We were indoctrinated with a culture of class and a sense of belonging to something bigger than ourselves. Much of that emanated from RBW and his executive team. They didn't just walk around and point fingers, they coached and counseled. As a result, the staff treated our guests and each other with respect. We addressed guests by "sir" and "ma'am." We never forgot who paid the bills.

Twisting the familiar meant washing our money!

A reflection of our overall commitment to quality was the fact that we even washed our coins at the St. Francis. Yes, you read that correctly. We were world-famous for that. And nobody else even tried to copy us; they wouldn't have dared. It was an institution with us. As silly as this may sound now, to many people across the globe, this was one of our hotel's leading trademarks.

A very kindly gentleman, Arnold Batliner, had the decades-old job of washing all the coins we used in the hotel. He was a prideful soul who absolutely loved his job and the impact it made for our guests and visitors. Washing coins was his Job One—and two and three. That's all he did, and he did it marvelously.

Batliner had been featured in the media several times, so we would get people from all over the world approaching our huge front desk, asking us to make change. They would inquire, "Is this the hotel that washes its money?" When they were handed the lustrous coins they marveled at them as if they had been handed precious newly minted gemstones.

Batliner was a bit of a solitary soul, working alone in his little room above the front desk, but he enjoyed pleasing people. On several occasions I was asked by a tourist if they could have their picture taken with the man who washed our coins. I would go upstairs to Batliner's little room and ask him if he would mind coming down to the lobby for a photo. He never turned anyone down. In his presence, people acted fairly giddy while lining up their photo with him, almost as if they were meeting one of the Beatles.

What's so important about the coin-washing? It was part of our brand and our pride. The fact that we washed our coins was part of the overall "class act" atmosphere that rubbed off on the rest of us. From a purely fiscal viewpoint, would it have meant less work and less expense for the hotel's management to discontinue the program? Of course. Would it have been easier to manage a much simpler cash-handling process like all of the other hotels in San Francisco did? Without a doubt.

But one would argue that not everything can be solely about the profit-and-loss statement. Not everything that is done *easier* is done *better*. Our hotel would have lost a lot of its luster, both figuratively and literally, had RBW discontinued the program. Instead, we owned an edge over every other hotel.

What can you do in your own business akin to the coin-washing specialty? Is there something unique you can do to twist the familiar over your competitors?

"We pick everything up off the floor here"

So with all of that, you can imagine our hotel's culture when it came to pieces of paper or litter of any kind. It was THE no-no. One of the first things I was told during my orientation as a management trainee was: "Here at the St. Francis, we pick up any trash we see on the floors or carpeting.

ANY little paper, no matter how small—it's a big deal around here. Don't let RBW ever see you walking past a piece of paper on the floor without picking it up."

OK, got it, fairly warned. That short tutorial was something I've never forgotten.

"But the president might be waiting . . ."

That admonition was about to manifest itself into a firsthand lesson for me, and is one that can be transferable to your business too.

I was the assistant manager on duty one very busy afternoon. We were expecting President Jimmy Carter and all of his Secret Service detail, plus a phalanx of local police and an entourage of officials and media to be converging upon our hotel at any moment. The president was coming to deliver a luncheon address to a convention group in our grand ballroom. I was ready to go with my little lapel pin with an "A" on it, signifying that I had been vetted with a high-level security clearance by the U.S. Secret Service. They gave those pins to management and service staff that would be assisting the president.

The Secret Service always sent us the visiting dignitaries' schedules in advance, and then they never followed them for reasons you can imagine. RBW was pacing back and forth, a bit nervous, and I think a bit put off at the change in schedule. In the hotel business, your main goal is that a visit by a VIP such as the president happens without incident—a nice clean arrival and getaway, no problems. Once the dignitary departed, then everyone could breathe again.

While I waited in the front office making last-minute checks, RBW continued his pacing out in the lobby like an expectant father. Suddenly, my walkie-talkie sprang to life. Our security chief alerted me that "the eagle has landed." I sprang into action, immediately moving to get RBW to the arrival area on the other end of the hotel. He saw me coming, nodded, and turned on his heels to make for our ballroom. He was walking very quickly, like a man hurrying to make the plane as they close the doors, but still maintaining decorum.

I was a few feet behind him, trying to keep up.

As we passed the bank of lobby elevators, RBW suddenly, deftly, as if practiced hundreds of times before, bent over *while in stride*, and picked up a wad of crumpled paper that had missed the trash urn next to the elevator. Plunk! Into the urn it went. He never even missed a beat. Down the hall he flew to his moment of photographic destiny with Jimmy Carter.

That little act in a millisecond of time made a huge impact on me. I figured that if our busy general manager could pick up a piece of paper while hurrying on his way to meet the President of the United States, then the rest of us could pick up litter, too. He could have played the big shot or pulled rank, or pointed at the paper and told me to pick it up because he was in a hurry to meet President Carter, but he didn't do that.

What an impressive way to hammer home a point and prove that no one was above our hotel's rules, including the top executive. My general manager's message was impressively received by me, whether he intended to send it or not: "Do as I do, not just as I say."

Even our celebrities cleaned up their messes

I've often wondered what RBW would have thought had

he known that one of our frequent celebrity guests made an accidental mess on the floor and owned it just like we employees did, too.

The late actress Cindy Williams ("Shirley Feeney" of the popular 1976-1983 hit TV comedy series *Laverne & Shirley*), was a guest of ours every few months or so. She got a kick out of me asking her what was going to happen on the upcoming episodes, and of course she always demurred: "I can't tell you that, Gary. In fact, sometimes we don't even know ourselves until we get the scripts." She was such a genuine, down-to-earth person, very likeable and sincere. Our staff loved her.

One evening, Williams came scampering down to the front desk, looking all stressed out. "Gary, Gary," she called out from across the lobby as she approached the front desk at a fast walk. With a look of embarrassment she leaned forward, and in a quiet voice said, "I did something really silly and I feel awful about it. I need your help." I couldn't wait to hear this.

She explained to me that she had brought her own candle to her guestroom, lit it, and had accidentally knocked it over, and that there was now a big blob of hardened candle wax on the carpeting.

Smiling sheepishly and looking like a girl in middle school who accidentally spilled her milk at lunchtime, she said, "Please, I want to clean this up. I think if you get me some ice I can get it out."

We didn't expect our guests to clean up accidental messes. "Cindy, don't worry about it," I assured her. "I'll call housekeeping to get it out."

"Oh no," she countered. "I made the mess and I want to clean it up. No one else should have to clean up my mess. I feel terrible about this. If I can't get it out I certainly want to pay for this."

I was smiling at her conviction to want to do this, all the while trying to convince her that our industrious house-keeping staff had some miracle solutions and concoctions for which to remove stains and such.

One of our bellmen got a bucket of ice for her and escorted her up to her room where she and a housekeeper worked on that wax. She called me thirty minutes later, very excited and happy, proud at getting the spilled wax off the carpeting. She was certainly one of the nicest people — celebrity or otherwise — that I encountered during my time at the St. Francis.

I suppose you know that you are running an effective operation when even your customers want to clean up their own messes!

Building Your Playbook:

- *In what areas of your own business or organization can you apply and/or design the concept of luxury and pride in the business, and of going above and beyond for your staff and customers?*
- *How would you implement, manage, and sustain such changes in expectations and behaviors?*
- *Sometimes the expense of something (like coin-washing) scares us into falling back to status quo, of cutting corners. Put pencil to paper on how much your ideas in this area would actually cost. Is there an R.O.I.?*
- *What are your organization's "house rules," such as the example of picking up paper? Are they understood? Are people held accountable for them?*

Chapter 19

How Many Does it Take to Unscrew a Light Bulb?

"Two things are infinite: the universe and human stupidity; and I'm not sure about the universe." —Albert Einstein

D o you know the answer to the riddle of how many people it takes to unscrew a light bulb? This story may answer that question once and for all. It also exposes many things that can be easily translated to any business when it comes to problem-solving and the crazy idea that more is always better. It's not.

While doing my normal pre-training setup in a meeting room at a suburban big-name franchise hotel, I was going through my typical pre-check list and prepping the room with various supplies. I like to get to my training sites plenty early to get a leg up on Murphy's Law, just in case.

Good thing, too.

Working with the audio-visual tech, I did a check of the projection onto the screen and was horrified to see that "Murphy" was indeed present in the room with us. The hotel banquet team had set up the projection screen directly underneath a fisheye light bulb in the ceiling. It was perfectly situated so that the light was shining fully on the screen and giving off a glare that rendered my slides absolutely impossible to see. That wasn't going to work at all.

I mentioned this to the AV tech. He shrugged his shoulders and his reply was underwhelming. "Well, they pretty much set up all of the groups in this room this way."

Oh no, not *that* lame response. Were there really that

many professional people out there who just "settled" for a lousy setup when holding a meeting in this room? Apparently so, but I don't like to settle when something can be made better. *Twist the*.... Yup, you got it!

When I hear someone say, "Everybody else does it that way," or "Nobody ever brought that up before," I shake my head and wonder why. And then I get into my *MacGyver* mode. Instead of simply settling, I look for ways to make things right (or better) if at all humanely possible.

A gathering of eagles, this was not!

The AV tech called the hotel's banquet captain who arrived and summarily flicked the light switch in the back of the room—up, down, up, down. Lights went off, lights came on, rinse and repeat. It became readily apparent that the lighting was only wired to do two things—turn on and turn off. The hotel's meeting rooms were apparently not wired for state-of-the-art dimmer switches.

Only with "lights off" could the slide deck be seen on the screen. Not wanting to deliver my training workshop in the dark, I asked the banquet captain if they had another way they could tweak the room setup, even at this late notice. Given my hotel background, it was ingrained in me to look for solutions in all nooks and crannies.

He looked around the room, then up at the light. He got his walkie-talkie and called the engineering department. By now, most of my training group was beginning to arrive. It was the hotel's sales and services team so they were "chill" and perfectly happy to hit their own coffee break, find a seat, and slam down Danish rolls while waiting for this escapade to play out.

Several minutes later, the engineer showed up and he brought a second accomplice. Apparently this situation was worthy of a two-alarm engineering response. So picture this: The AV tech, the banquet captain, two engineers, and the conference services manager were standing in front of the screen under the light with hands on hips, staring at the light bulb like it was the Christmas Star.

One light bulb had tied up five hotel staffers for twenty minutes. I kept a straight face and tried to give them some space to do their jobs. I broke the impasse by politely asking them if we could just unscrew the light bulb from its socket, thus no light would be shining its glare down onto the slides.

The group of five standing under the light bulb looked at each other and nodded. The engineers left the room without a word and returned five minutes later, carrying a long-handled tool resembling a harpoon. It extended to about eight feet and was designed to replace light bulbs in hard-to-reach places. Both men held the tool as they aimed it up to the ceiling light socket and gingerly removed the outlaw light bulb, just as if they were pulling out an elephant's wisdom tooth.

Out of the corner of my eye, I caught the hotel's general manager standing in the back of the room just grinning at me and shaking his head. He later told me that he learned a lot about his team just watching the drama unfold.

I've often wondered if they ever unscrewed that light-bulb again for another group or just put it back in its socket and let it be the next customer's problem.

For me, the answer to the riddle at the top of this story will forever be "five."

Building Your Playbook:

- *In what ways are you or your organization complicating the uncomplicated?*
- *Take a hard look at how you would answer this question: "How easy are we—really—to do business with?" Do you have any customer feedback to help you answer this question?*
- *What can you do to get your people up to speed on handling situations for customers more effectively? Is training an option?*

Chapter 20

A Ten-Thousand-to-One Sales Call

"Baseball is a lot like the Army, there aren't many individuals. About the only difference is that baseball players get to stay in nice hotels instead of barracks." —Bill Lee

This is about being intrepid and creative in our approach to selling. It's also about getting that one little shot that opens up so many more opportunities for business down the road. It's about making sure your organization can back you up.

One of the markets I wanted to open up for us during my sales days at the Parc 55 was the sports business, specifically Major League Baseball teams coming to the Bay Area to play the San Francisco Giants and the Oakland A's. I knew it was good, solid business, but the challenge was that the teams were currently ensconced in various other "bigger brand" hotels in the city. They had them and I wanted them. Game on.

So I met with my friend Dirk Smith, the travel manager for the Giants at the time, and asked him what it would take to get the teams to my hotel. Over several lunches and phone calls, I asked for Dirk's experience to help me plot the points to understand the things I should know, and what I would need to do. He helped me with key insider's information, "inside baseball," as the term applies, and I started reaching out to various teams.

Timing is everything

During that summer, I was taking my family on vacation to Michigan for a visit with my wife's siblings. I've always checked the Tigers' home schedule in advance of my visits to Detroit because I love seeing my favorite boyhood team play when I am in town. They were hosting the Houston Astros in an interleague series that week. An idea hit me like a home run ball whacked over the fence.

I had been in conversations for several months with Barry Waters, the travel manager ("traveling secretary" as they were called) of the Houston Astros. We had discussed the prospects of hosting his team when they came in to play the Giants the next season.

I called Waters and he was thrilled to hear that I was going to be in Detroit at the same time as his team's series at historic Tiger Stadium. Barry picked some sweet seats for us in the Astros' family section right behind the dugout, just a couple of rows from the field. I've made some very unique sales calls in my time, but this had to be near the top considering the location, the company, and the atmosphere. Getting paid to do things like this as part of my job was something I never took for granted.

"A hot dog at the game beats roast beef at the Ritz."
—Humphrey Bogart

Waters came down to the box seats from the visiting clubhouse to join me and we quickly settled into watching the action amid gorgeous summer sunshine, friendly chatter, and a couple of hot dogs. That's one of the things that makes watching baseball so great—the easy banter with friends, family, or customers. If you can't carry on a "chill" conversation in conditions like this without being salesy, then you don't belong in sales.

The conversation casually turned to his plans for next season's travel and some questions he had about the specifics of my hotel such as rates, check-in procedures, handling their baggage needs, etc. I could sense that we were on the cusp of verbally making a nice agreement for both of us right there in the ballpark.

At that moment, there were two Detroit runners on base, threatening to score. As we turned to face each other to discuss a point, there was a loud, thunderous crack of the bat at home plate. We simultaneously snapped our heads forward. Right in front of us—unfolding in fast-forward on that verdant green field—was a triple play, baseball's rarest play. The odds against a triple play in any given baseball game are ten thousand to one!

Bang-bang-bang, just like that, three outs for the Astros and three Tigers jogging back to the dugout. One swing of the bat and the inning was over. The hometown Tiger crowd was stunned, as were we. One could attend a thousand games in their life and you'd never see a triple play. It's the kind of thing where you ask yourself, "Did I just see that?"

I groaned and waved my arms. "Aw geez, can you believe that?"

Waters was grinning ear to ear. "Hey Gary, we'd better sign that contract now after *that* play. You bring us good luck, buddy!"

It was almost like that mystical epiphany that Kevin Costner and James Earl Jones had while watching a baseball game together at Fenway Park in the film *Field of Dreams*.

We shook hands on it.

Today's apple seed is tomorrow's apple tree

I wish I could tell you in Hollywood style that I got Waters' signature for a deal on my hot dog wrapper that day, but we took care of the official paperwork the following week. Waters became a good friend and also my "gateway" advocate by talking me up to the other MLB traveling managers and helping to introduce me so that I could present my case. He helped give me and my hotel legitimacy.

One by one, I pursued the other baseball clubs and they began to peel away from their host hotels and come on board at the Parc 55. By the time I left the hotel, I was proud of the fact that I had signed nine MLB clubs to a contract with us, the most of any single hotel in all of baseball. And our performance and reputation with the baseball clubs really helped me when I went to pursue and book other big-time sports business; quite a nice chunk of revenue for us over the years.

It's definitely a team game

Although I had planted the baseball "seed" and nurtured it through my continued sales efforts, the actual yield from the "tree" was also due to a sustained group effort from my hotel teammates and the great communication and camaraderie between us. Without our dedicated operations folks keeping my sales commitments to the teams, we would not have had much success in this sector, or in any other sector of our business for that matter. As in baseball or softball, even a pitcher with a great fastball needs eight other players on the field to back them up. I had some real all-stars backing me up.

As we've discussed, it's all about two teams—*the get 'ems and the keep 'ems*—pulling together. It takes hard work, cooperation, commitment, and focus. Just like with any business that has both a sales and operations component to it, a lot can happen between what the salesperson promises and what the operations team delivers.

"Baseball is ninety percent mental and the other half is physical." —Yogi Berra

As fractured as Yogi's statement sounds on the surface, I think it has a lot of merit in business. Often, organizations spend inordinate amounts of time designing, thinking, and overthinking some kind of procedure or program, only to have it get all tangled up when it is rolled out. We often find it hard to get out of our own way in the execution of plans.

We complicate the uncomplicated and it sometimes mucks up the works.

Businesses with many moving parts would do well to pay attention to Yogi here. Speaking of hotels as an example, they are often ripe for overthinking something and then the rollout doesn't quite match up with the plans. Hotels that talk about going after teams and sports business *must* have the support, cooperation, and service delivery of their operations staff. They must also be ready for the quirky nature of teams business.

Sports groups and teams bear little if any resemblance to "normal" corporate groups. From rooming lists to security needs to dining habits, teams from the major leagues to youth sports present special challenges. Hotels have to be flexible in their operations or they shouldn't pursue that market.

The same holds true of any organization. Be willing to twist the familiar of how you normally do business if you are going to pursue customers with lots of quirks.

Our Parc 55 employees were enthusiastic about hosting the teams and loved taking care of them. They were fun for many of our employees and they enjoyed going above and beyond their normal routines. The teams reciprocated by staying with us every season; we never lost one of them to another hotel while I was there.

You can't always count on magic, but it helps

As a salesperson, think about how you can twist the familiar and set up a unique atmosphere or circumstance for you and your prospect. So much today is done via emails, Zoom calls, phone calls, etc., and I get it. Those are certainly convenient and I use those same tools quite a bit, too. But I'm always thinking of how I can change things up to be unique. If you do something creative, it will stand out among the noise, and that's what you want—to do something your competition isn't doing.

I can't guarantee that you'll have the magic of something like a triple play right in front of you to set the proper aura and excite your prospect into saying "yes," but you'll never find out if you don't put yourself in a situation where that can happen.

Build it and they will come.

Building Your Playbook:

- *What's the most unusual place you ever made a sales call? How did it turn out?*
- *How important is your internal support team to your ability to get business rebooked?*
- *Is your business positioned to pursue new markets or quirky business with special requests that your other customers don't require?*
- *How can you position your clients to help introduce you to other clients or to act as your advocate, such as Barry Waters did for me?*

Chapter 21

Don't Let Quacking Ducks Kill a Creative Idea

"Innovation distinguishes between a leader and a follower."
—Steve Jobs

This is about overcoming the loud quacking of ducks. Of people "quacking" about progress, innovation, change. And the lesson here can easily be translated to any business where ideas get shot down before they ever take flight.

People who think small and always see a problem in every opportunity really rankle me. I prefer to see an opportunity within a problem. I see it as a challenge—even a game or a puzzle— to try and figure out what I call a *Rubik's Cube* issue for a client, colleague, or friend.

**"Power comes from sharing information,
not withholding it." —Keith Ferrazzi**

While on a sales trip to the Washington, D.C. area, a hotbed for headquarters of national associations and one of my major territories for business development, I was calling on one of my accounts, the Club Management Association of America, in the quaint town of Alexandria, Virginia.

I had an appointment with one of my good friends in the business, the late Nancy Clare, meetings executive for the CMAA. I took the elevator up to her office and when the door opened, I was immediately greeted with a big sign in their reception area. The heading read, "CMAA Welcomes" and underneath it were a few names on a marquee-type sign, including mine: "Gary Hernbroth, Parc 55 Hotel, San Francisco."

I was immediately impressed by that. It was unique to any office I had ever visited, and I had made sales calls to hundreds of clients' headquarters over the years. The sign looked terrific and it felt great to be welcomed in that fashion—simple yet personal. It's not every day we get to see our own names "up in lights" in some way. I thought it was a touch of class and a gesture of warm hospitality that befit an organization like CMAA.

Clare came out to greet me with a big smile and a friendly hug and I commented on the sign, thanking her for it. "That's something we do for our visitors. We're club managers, and after all, we're in the hospitality business," she said.

Whoa. Wait a minute. I was a salesperson calling on *them* to get *their* business, not the other way around. And they made *me* feel like their customer or guest. What a great twist.

While riding in a cab back to my hotel after the appointment, I was reflecting back on that CMAA sign. It got me thinking: Why couldn't we do something like that to greet our own customers in our sales office reception area back at the hotel? I couldn't imagine any reason why we couldn't make that happen. I jotted down some notes while in my cab.

Too many people want to complicate the uncomplicated

In our sales meeting the following week, I related the story from my trip to CMAA and explained the sign, throwing the idea out on the table for us to do the same thing. I knew of no other hotel anywhere that was doing such a thing, including our competitors in San Francisco, and the idea of twisting the familiar and being a trendsetter greatly appealed to me. Let the other folks copy *us*. Heck, I was copying CMAA. Good, creative ideas get passed along.

Sure enough, a member of my sales team said, "Well, I don't know how we would manage that."

I thought, uh-oh. Here comes the old "it sounds like a lot of work so let's not do it" song, a big hit with the mythical singing group, *The Cynics*. The quacking ducks were circling the pond. I silently counted to ten to keep my blood pressure in check and responded with an easy way to get this accomplished, or so I thought:

"We buy a nice-looking sign and each day we put our visiting customers' names up there. Whoever is coming in for a site inspection, a meeting, or if they have an in-house group going on in our hotel, they get their name on the sign. They'll feel great seeing their name up on the sign, just like I did in Virginia, when they walk into our offices."

Not exactly like designing the space shuttle, is it?

Another of my salespeople raised their hand: "Who is going to put the names up there each day?"

"Well, the salespeople will be accountable to put their own customers' names on the board, of course," I responded. "You each know the people with whom you've set a meeting or visit each day, right?"

"Well, what if we get busy?" was another response. Quack, quack.

I had a hard time believing my ears. I was proud of my sales team. They were overall tough performers and worthy sales competitors in a very competitive city at that time.

They won a lot of business with chutzpah and creativity. We didn't have the most recognizable brand name among the national hotel chains, so as I liked to say, "We have to jump higher, run faster, and leap taller buildings in a single bound." We carved out more than our share of business in all market segments with hard work, and we were a fairly tight-knit team. But this display of pushback was alien to me.

"And another thing we have to be careful with," said one of our assistants, "we'd better make sure we spell their names right." *I would certainly hope so.*

Our sales team included a great group of hard-working professionals, and in many ways we were like a family. But that day it might have been easier to explain the Pythagorean theorem to them. I had never really seen them in such a dither over what I thought was a simple thing. With the body language around the table, you would have thought that I had just told them that we were now going to send out our sales proposals in Latin.

I wasn't inclined to give up on the idea because I knew we would be doing this for all the right reasons. I was convinced that it would be a nice touch and add something special to our customers' experience. And to me, the benefit to our customers far outweighed a little bit of extra motion for the sales team.

Doing what is easy is not always doing what is best

When you know that what you want to do is the right thing to do, and that you're doing it for all the right reasons, you've got to quell the quacking if you want to succeed. You've got to lead and not cave to the quackers. Trust your intuition that your convictions are correct, and then get ready to sell the idea.

It can sometimes be tough sledding to sell ideas to other salespeople, like the way doctors can make for poor patients. But not *everything* in life can be put up for a vote, either. Only weak leaders call for votes on everything, pushing decisions off on others instead of making the tough calls themselves. Lots of great ideas and innovation throughout history would never have come to fruition had they been voted on. This was an office sign, for crying out loud.

I gave them opportunities to add their input for a few minutes, and still I hadn't heard one good reason for not bringing this idea to life. No one came out and actually said this was an awful, impossible idea. So I made the decision to go forward with the sign. I said something like, "OK, let's find a way to make this work. It's a simple thing and it will be a big hit, well worth the little extra effort. You've got this."

"Letting worries win is like letting pollsters decide elections." —INC. Magazine

The same magazine revealed a study in an article titled, "Always Anxious?" that should ease the worry for some people: 91.4 percent of worry predictions do not come true.

Leaders, managers, and owners should factor this in when considering their options on initiatives and ideas. There will surely be naysayers to some degree, the folks that ask "why?" vs. those who ask, "why not?" I don't believe that peoples' worries should be trivialized, but I recommend that they be discussed in a helpful, pragmatic way. The ability to calm other peoples' fears can be a valuable trait for a leader to have in their tool kit.

In this case, I don't think it was truly worry about the sign program as much as it was reticence to take on the responsibility and extra effort to make it work. Dare I say, a bit of laziness had wafted into the room?

We found an attractive-looking sign and put it up in our sales office reception area. I explained to the sales team that it was their responsibility to get their visiting customers' names up there before they left for the evening, spelled correctly, so we were ready to go when I opened the office the next day. Accountability was expected of everyone.

How did it turn out? We heard many wonderful comments from our customers, and it was pleasing to witness them regale in seeing their names on the sign. One of our most loyal event planners came in the sales reception door and said, "I've never seen this in any other hotel, this is such a nice touch." Bingo!

The quacking ducks went silent.

Building Your Playbook:

- *Have you had an idea come forth in your organization or team that was shot down before it even took flight? What was the reluctance? Was it overcome, and how so? What was the outcome?*
- *Persuading others is a sales function. What steps can you take in getting your next innovation or idea across?*
- *Draw up a list of questions that you can ask those who come out against innovation and change in order to get to the crux of their issues head on.*

Chapter 22

When the Corporate Office Doesn't Consult with the Frontline Team

"That hotel was a dump. They had a postcard, and on the picture the room wasn't made up." —Rodney Dangerfield

Have you ever encountered something that goes amiss when one level of an organization designs or purchases something that another level has to deal with? Sometimes, what looks and sounds like a great idea in a high-rise boardroom or designer's computer screen doesn't actually play out that way in reality. Use this story as a calling card for your own organization to be aware of, because this is one of those times.

Have you ever checked into a hotel room and within a few minutes of unpacking you find something that needs fixing, and the last thing you want to do after a long flight or drive is repack your things and try to haggle with the hotel on changing rooms?

On occasion, I've had to call for a hotel engineer to fix various things that were wonky in my hotel room, such as air conditioning/heating malfunctions, smoke smells, noisy fans, and running toilets, just to name a few. Especially late at night, those engineers can be your heroes when there aren't any other rooms available to move you to, or you just want to stay put for the night if possible. I salute hotel engineers—it isn't easy with some of the things they get called to guestrooms to handle. And in this instance, I felt sorry for them.

I was on a training assignment in a large metropolitan area and staying in a national brand suite hotel. My room clock didn't work properly; the time was annoyingly off by an hour. They say that even broken clocks are correct twice a day, but that doesn't help when you are moving around the room and want the convenience of glancing at the clock to check your time instead of constantly searching for your cell phone.

I put my hospitality degree to work and gave it the ol' college try. I found a lot of buttons on the clock, but for the life of me, nothing that enabled me to change the time. I turned it around in my hands several times, inspecting it like a Rubik's Cube. It also worked as an iPod base and probably could launch a rocket into space and navigate a drone, but all I wanted was for the clock to work. I felt like an idiot. I mean, how hard can it be? I had changed hotel clocks many times before when the time was off. This one was something off of a space lab, though.

"Customers don't expect you to be perfect. They do expect you to fix things when they go wrong."—Don Porter

So I called housekeeping to ask for help. They had absolutely no idea how to change the time on the clocks, either. That says a lot, too. So they referred me to engineering, and a friendly engineer knocked on my door in fifteen minutes. I briefed him on his mission and he grabbed the clock and began turning it in his hand, just like I did. After a couple of minutes, he announced that he would be right back and he left my room.

He returned fifteen minutes later, armed with a clock manual and a screwdriver, plus a fellow member of his engineering corps. My clock issue had been elevated to a two-engineer alarm!

After both engineers turned the clock over and over again, discussing something in whispered tones, the first engineer grabbed the screwdriver out of his pocket. They discovered that you have to take the back off the clock with a screwdriver to change the time.

I asked him, "Do you guys like these clocks?" He replied in monotone that they were "bought by corporate." Read into that as you like.

The seasonal time change to "spring forward" was approaching on the weekend. I asked him what that would mean for the engineers of that hotel. He smiled at me with resignation on his face and said "You're looking at it. We are going to have to go into all of our 250 rooms and unscrew the backs of all these dang clocks and change the time."

I wondered how many guests, housekeepers, and supervisors had been in that room and just settled for the time being wrong? And did it also mean that the clocks weren't ever changed at the autumn "fall back" six months ago? That told me a lot about the hotel's management. Was the quality control check-and-balance program on autopilot, and the employees just floated along with it, too?

As the engineers were leaving my room, I jokingly suggested that their general manager ought to have the people at the corporate office who bought these clocks travel to the hotel twice a year to change them all. He spun around with a serious face and nodded, "Sir, that's one heck of an idea. I'll tell him today." I wonder how that conversation played out.

Building Your Playbook

- *In your organization, can you think of a situation that mirrors this story, where "corporate" made a buying decision without first checking its practicality or viability? What happened?*
- *What happens in your organization when the upper level has no clue what the other levels do, or what they need?*
- *Could the engineers have handled anything differently or said anything differently to help or mitigate the situation?*

Chapter 23

The Flip-Flops Flopped

"Two things remain irretrievable:
time and a first impression." —Cynthia Ozik

How many times have you heard the expression, "You only have one chance to make a first impression"? Researchers have found that a first impression is made within the first seven seconds after you meet someone new, and they can form eleven impressions about you. That can be a bit daunting, right?

When you meet someone for the first time, they are taking a rapid inventory of how you present yourself. It's the critical moment when much about your personal brand is on display. You have one opportunity to get this right. First impressions are lasting impressions, so we need to make sure that the initial interaction is a positive one.

It's easier said than done. Many of us have said something in the initial seven seconds of meeting someone new and it came out so wrong that we wanted to pull the words right out of the air and put them back in our mouth. I know it's happened to me. Some people will forgive you and you can overcome it.

But not always . . .

One of my event planner colleagues in Michigan, Kathy Krajewski, related this story during one of my meetings industry programs that had salespeople and customers alike roaring in laughter. It brings with it an important lesson on impressions and how important dressing for success can be.

Her story can be related to any industry:

"One spring I was visiting a luxury resort in Michigan to do a site inspection because I was considering the property for a meeting I was planning. What happened next was tragically comical.

First off, they put me in a horrible room that was actually a condo. It didn't have any closets that were open for me to use. I think it was a secondary part of a larger living unit and the owners had locked the closets.

In getting prepared for my appointment with the sales rep for the resort, I was steaming my business suit in the shower and polishing my business heels. I'm always so concerned with how I look as a professional. I came down to the lobby to meet my sales rep in my business suit and shoes and to my horror, she was standing there—in a dress—with flip-flops on! Bright pink flip-flops.

She started walking me around the property and talking about what a great high-end resort they had. I just couldn't get beyond her flip-flops."

The fifty or so meetings industry professionals gathered in the room were in stitches when Krajewski mentioned the flip-flops. However, no one was ready for the next cringeworthy detail of her story:

"On top of that, she sorely needed a pedicure! And I kept looking at her toes. They weren't nice. They were chipped and some of the nail polish had worn off.

She was younger than me, and I know sometimes younger people are more casual, but she was much too casual, especially for the type of resort she was selling.

"Along with her toes that badly needed a pedicure, her flip-flops weren't nice, either. They were plastic and worn out, like something you'd wear on the beach.

Overriding everything that she was showing me and telling me about the resort were those awful flip-flops. I just couldn't shake it. And I didn't end up booking with her."

While the salesperson felt it was OK to represent her high-end resort in worn-out flip-flops, it wasn't the proper look according to her prospective customer. Krajeweski's tale is by no means the only fashion faux paus involving flip-flops. Phil Anderson shared his own tale of woe with me, too:

"I was general manager of the Whiteface Lodge in Lake Placid, New York, an upscale Adirondack resort. We were the eleventh rated resort in the country at the time, running an average room rate of over $500 a night.

We had a contract salesperson out of New York at the time. We had a familiarization trip of very influential meeting planners in the hotel for the weekend, and we were really rolling out the red carpet for them. We spared no expense. Our sales rep unbelievably showed up to host the group and give them a tour wearing flip-flops! There were some other things she came up short on, too, but the flip-flops were the frosting on the cake. She didn't see any problem with wearing flip-flops in that setting. We ended our contract with her the very next week."

This isn't about dissing flip-flops; I've got a couple of pairs myself — for the beach and the pool. This is about being self-aware of time and place enough to know how to dress for success. Especially for salespeople, they must have the good sense to know how to dress and represent their product.

Both of the salespeople cited in these examples were representing upper-tier luxury resorts. But they gave little or no thought to that. As Anderson later told me, "If we had been putting on a beach party for the planners on our beach and everyone was wearing them, that would have been fine. But showing up to give a tour of our resort to New York prospects in flip-flops was a no-no."

Dress for success, whatever appropriate level that is. Business has gone much more casual during the past decade or so, but as these two recent vignettes illustrate, not everyone agrees on the rules, and lines can still be crossed. When in doubt, ask.

After all, you've got your first impression—*and maybe your job*—to protect.

Building Your Playbook:

- *Have you or any of your colleagues ever been in a similar situation? What happened?*
- *Do you have an understanding at your place of business on dress codes and making the appropriate first impression on customers?*
- *Do you have written guidelines?*
- *Think of a time when you were the buyer of something and the salesperson left a less than wonderful first impression on you. What about them was lacking? Did it affect the way you viewed them or the brand? Did you buy from them or walk away?*

Chapter 24

Your Reputation is Precious:
Don't Play Loose with Your Principles

"Character above all. Character is what matters."
—Doris Kearns Goodwin

It seems that almost every day we hear of an ethics breach or personal brand-crushing incident of one kind or another, whether it's in the business world, education, politics, or entertainment. Celebrities and politicians are often the low-hanging fruit of knucklehead moves, though plenty of other people can fall into the abyss of lost reputations, too. It seems some folks get away with things for years—until *BAM!* When they goof up, their world often explodes and things usually come crashing down quickly. Gone is their good name, tarnished is their personal brand. Most likely, their careers are over or at least deeply impacted.

Still, that doesn't seem to stop some people from trying to gig the game.

My good friend Donna Sue Davis, a successful sales and marketing executive for many decades including a long run for Disney Resorts in Anaheim, has a term she uses for people who portray themselves to the world in one way, yet operate in a darker manner when they think no one is noticing. She calls it "fans and feathers."

Davis holds herself to high standards and throughout her career of leading teams, she also held her staff to the same. She's always led by example and she treats people like family. Thus, she gets frustrated by those who don't play by the rules. "Unfortunately, even in a great industry and within great companies, you have people who do not abide by our ethics and make a bad name for the ones who do," she says. "For example, they are the people who are not honest about their sales trip reports and expense accounts."

And there are less obvious ways to skimp on ethics, too. Take the employees who are sent by their organizations to represent them at conventions, trade shows, and sales trips, with all expenses fully paid by the company, of course. While many people properly represent their firms and do the right things, there are always a few skulkers who game the system for their own benefit. Davis gets agitated thinking about it:

"Those people do not faithfully attend the educational sessions offered at the conferences. They are sent there to represent their company, to learn new tools and trends in the educational sessions, and to network with customers. They should be taking advantage of the registration fee their company paid for, which usually is not cheap. Instead, some of them silently steal from their company by sleeping in late, going down to the lobby for a luxurious late breakfast, and all the while the convention is happening just outside the door."

> **"People who value privileges above principles soon lose both."** —Dwight D. Eisenhower

Resumes and online profiles can also be breeding grounds for puffed-up accomplishments and outright lies; plenty of "fans and feathers." I knew an overly slick salesperson that left an entire job off his resume because he screwed up and was terminated, and then he lied about the empty gap in his resume with a made-up story of some glorious charity work he never did.

Some people also stretch their booking numbers, revenue accomplishments, job titles, and their actual job scope. I saw someone claim they had "extensive leadership experience in the food and beverage industry." When pressed, they later admitted that they were a head busboy as a teenager in a small mom-and-pop diner. I guess this person honed their *extensive leadership skills* by telling another teenage busser to hurry up and clear off table six.

This kind of thing happens more often than you may think. Some folks infuse fakery into their past, tell tall tales of immortal deeds, and stretch their accomplishments just like the busboy did. I suppose people just don't think they'll ever be found out.

Davis has come across the same tactic:

"It's been my own experience and also that of my colleagues to discover that some people will go to drastic lengths to embellish their accomplishments, their previous positions, and their years of employment. They never consider that others who worked with them know it just isn't accurate. That saddens and enrages me. Do they think we are stupid and won't find out?

"I discovered a particularly egregious action by someone through a colleague that left me speechless,"she recalls. "In checking his background, I found out that there was another person holding the exact same position and title he claimed to have had at a company, over the exact same years. It was a boldfaced lie by a fraud. Adding to my frustration, this person later landed a terrific-paying job because the hiring company did not check his true employment background to find out he was not telling the truth. How lax is that on their part?"

"Integrity is doing the right thing, even if nobody is watching." —Unknown

People who abide by ethics and honesty have benefited personally and professionally by taking the high road. "Do the right things and do things right" as my mom and dad taught me and my brothers, "and good things will happen to you." Like other families, we weren't perfect by any means, but we didn't buy into the idea of fake it until you make it.

As a person of integrity and character, Davis gets understandably passionate when talking about people who are the essence of "fans and feathers," the veritable bad actors that can talk or show a good game, but outside of the lens of others they play quite another role. "I just don't choose to be around those phony people anymore," she reveals.

Davis would much rather recognize the good in people, those that she can trust to be real and above-board: "We are fortunate that the kind of dishonest people I've described here are in a small minority. I love working with stand-up people who I can count on to be honest, and who follow through and do what they say they are going to do. But I caution that people need to constantly hold each other to high standards of ethics and honesty. We must hold people accountable to maintain the integrity of our chosen industry, our organization, and most of all, ourselves."

"Being honest may not get you a lot of friends, but it'll always get you the right ones." —John Lennon

Once tarnished, a personal brand is difficult to repair or replace. There is no guarantee on that score. Not only can a breach of ethics knock someone down personally and professionally, but if allowed to fester, it can have deeply negative effects on a team or organization, too. People see things, people hear things, and an ethics breach is a hard secret to keep tapped down. It can also creep into the fabric of the team as an accepted behavior. That's not good.

I spoke on ethics at a conference for the Society of Government Meeting Professionals at their annual conference. One of my messages was that a "Harvard Business Review" revealed that "less than 50% of workers admit that they report misconduct they see from co-workers." I asked the audience to opine about why they thought that was: Fear, apathy, not wanting to get involved, or maybe they didn't want to be the whistleblower? Their answers essentially boiled down to "all of the above."

In that same session, I also cited a recent "Barron's" report that "85% of people said no amount of cheating was permissible on their taxes, leaving 15% saying that it was OK." Fifteen percent is still a lot of people who favor breaking tax laws!

One of my major points in the SGMP workshop that day was to recommend that their organizations have a thorough Code of Business Ethics (COBE), with clearly defined expectations and practices that the C-Suite must also abide by. Three major components of an effective COBE are:

Take a broader view of ethical behavior, not just a legal one. Have a values-driven program;

Help your staff understand not only what the rules are, but how to comply with them;

Have ongoing COBE reviews and discussions with case studies, etc. to make the elements relatable and understood by people on all levels of your organization.

Build a culture of ethics and trust
– but don't trust auto-pilot

If you are a team leader or owner I'm guessing that you want ethics and truth to be your True North for your business. You'll want to have a culture strong in three key areas (somewhat like KPIs/Key Performance Indicators): trust, honesty and responsibility.

Those essential elements don't usually run on autopilot or by osmosis, though. You'll need solid, sustainable systems and the right people in place to lead by example and hold others accountable, not allowing the "fans and feathers" folks to clog up the works. This isn't about catching people doing something wrong as much as it's about the better mantra of *catching people doing something right!* Create a workplace where doing the right thing is the norm, not the exception.

When you come across someone on your team who breaks the rules, you can—depending on the severity or circumstances—try coaching them out of their ethics lapse. If you don't feel equipped to do so, seek professional intervention of some kind.

And if you are the owner, leader, or manager, your ethics have to be squeaky clean, too—above reproach, no gray areas, period. Once you pull a back-alley deal with your ethics, it's a slippery slope and it generally leads to no good.

Leaders have to set the example and take the high road on all of this. Try starting with a credo such as "Do the right thing." It's simple and it's a great place to start. It leaves no wiggle room. Ethics are either right or wrong, there's no "kinda-sorta" about it. And the axiom "Rules for thee but not for me" (anonymous) are the ruin of many, and can rip the heart out of your organizational culture.

Your reputation is what others think of you. Your character is what you truly are.

Building Your Playbook:

- *What are some ethical dilemmas you have had or been exposed to? What happened?*
- *Have you reported unethical behavior, theft, etc., to your management? What was their reaction? Did you suffer any repercussions?*
- *What areas on your team or in your firm are most exposed to ethics breaches? What can be done about that?*
- *If you caught your best friend doing a "fans & feathers" routine, what would you do?*
- *Does your firm have a COBE? If not, draw up some areas to include as a starting point to get something going and set a deadline for a finished project. Involve others on the team, consult your legal department, etc.*

Chapter 25

How to Write an Email that Actually Gets Opened

"The single biggest problem in communication is the illusion that it has taken place." —William H. Whyte

Email is as much a part of our world as breathing air. And anything that voluminous is bound to be either very, very good, or very, very bad—and a whole lot of everything else in between. Insidesales.com claims that the average B2B email open rate is a paltry 16.72 percent.

In this section I will share with you my very simple report card for writing effective emails and improving your "open rate," the number of people who open your email rather than bang their finger down on the *delete* key.

Understand that there are no guarantees. Different people look for different things in emails—who sent them, how compelling the subject line sounds, how much time or interest they have, their mood at the time, or any number of factors. But these keys I'm sharing here are tried and true from the "School of Hard Knocks," in the trenches. Use them properly and you'll be sending better emails.

Measure twice, cut once

As a youngster, I used to love to pull up a tall stool at my grandfather's basement workbench and watch him construct something. He was quite a builder, carpenter, and painter, a jack-of-all-trades who loved to work with his hands and make things for us at his workbench. It seemed to me that he had every kind of craft-building accoutrement and tool in his basement shop.

As he was drawing a tape measure across a two-by-four piece of wood one afternoon, I asked him why he was measuring on the wood. He explained that, "You should always measure twice and cut once." It was the carpenter's credo. Always take an extra measure of something as a precaution before you cut or saw a piece of wood. He taught me that once the saw gets hold of the wood there is no turning back. So spend a few extra seconds to make sure your measurements and lines are good before you cut.

I apply the very same concept to emails.

Craft your email, then read it, check for typos, grammar goofs, punctuation, syntax, everything. Be aware of run-on sentences and gobbledygook words that muddy up the meaning of what you are going to say. Write clearly to be understood. Don't say in fifty-five words what you could say in thirty.

Take a critical look at your screen: Is your email pleasing to the eye? That means crisp, short paragraphs and bullet points with spacing in the middle that let the eye know that it will not be a tiresome slog to read through three or four l-o-n-g paragraphs. Easy on the eyes means that white space is good. Your email should have a balance to it—not too top-heavy and not too heavy at the closing, either.

If it sounds like I'm giving an art class here, I suppose I am. The more artful your email looks to the eye, the better the odds it will get read.

Now what? "Measure" again—yes, reread your email again. I'll bet you will find something you missed or something you want to change. Then give it another reading. Measure twice (or more), and cut (send) once. Because once you hit the send key, it's bye-bye birdie. You can't get it back. That's a bit scary, isn't it? Haven't we all had that hot flash on the back of our necks and the blood rush to our face thinking we might have just accidentally sent an email to someone that we didn't intend to send it to? It happens a lot, someone we should have taken off the cc list. So do like my grandfather told me to do.

We have shorter attention spans than goldfish

Relating to another chapter in this book, people form a first impression of you in just seven seconds. Same thing for emails, maybe even less. People have a shorter attention span than a goldfish, which is nine seconds by most research. Humans clock in at eight seconds before they get distracted.

So make your email compelling, attractive, impactful, and include a clear WIIFM (what's in it for me?) and not look "spammy," or you and your email will be g-o-n-e like a goldfish.

Choose your words carefully, too. I think the worst use of words I've ever received in an email were so out of left field they left me scratching my head. I just couldn't give anything else he wrote any credibility. The email came from a hotel sales rep who wanted me to come to his hotel for a tour. He was offering me choices of days to meet when he wrote: " . . . so presuming we're not all nuked by then . . ."

Huh? Where did that random thought come from? It is so disconnected from the rest of his email that I have no explanation for it other than him trying to be glib. But his choice of words was poor to say the least. Use this as a lesson: your idea of a joke or off-handed reference may not go over with the receiver as well as you intended when you sent it. Don't get too cute with your words or phrasing. Customers don't want to—nor should they have to—work that hard at reading emails.

I declined his offer of a hotel tour.

Looking for a better open rate?
These six tipping points will help you get it done

Irresistible attraction. Curiosity. Immediate attention.

I'm not describing the light-headed feeling of a new romance here. I'm describing three of the most critical elements that the subject line in your emails should contain in order to increase the chances that your email will be opened.

Just how important is the subject line? *Very.* Techjury reported that the average number of emails we receive is two hundred each day, with approximately 50 percent of them being spam. Alarmingly, 69 percent of email recipients report email as spam based solely on the subject line. That's how important the subject line is.

Your first and foremost task for any email is **to get it opened**. Ask yourself, "Would this subject line make ME want to open this email?" If you're not enticed to open your *own* email, then who will be?

Referring back to our goldfish, think how your email stacks up among the volume of emails people get, and what kind of time they give each one. It can feel like a never-ending waterfall that keeps coming and you're out of sandbags. If you are in sales, you are fighting just to hang on past those critical eight seconds of goldfish time.

Watch how people seem to be mindlessly swiping their cell phone screens as they scroll through their slew of email messages. Swipe, swipe, swipe. Are they swiping past yours, or are they opening it?

Here are some proven subject line techniques that will get more of your emails past the moment of truth, that critical tipping point between open and delete:

Use their first name: People like to see their names in print

Brevity: Suggested length is fifty characters or less; using five words or less increases your open rate by 50 percent.

How does it read: Is it urgent, important, or both? Is it spammy, salesy, or specific?

Offer a hint of value: Get the recipient to ask, "What's in it for me?"

Snag their interest but avoid amateurish overkill such as triple punctuation like !!! and ??? This isn't high school.

Build trust by not misleading the recipient. Make sure the body of your email relates to and delivers on what your subject line describes.

On the last point, "getting it opened" may be the first task of an email, but it isn't the endgame. You ultimately want someone to read the body of your email in order to take action, but you don't want to trick anyone.

I once got an email from an ad firm rep that I knew, with the subject line of "We're ready to send the new golf clubs you've just won." Well, being a golfer and knowing him I took the bait. Then I read the email: "Aha—Gotcha! There are no free golf clubs but we want to know if you would be interested in our . . ."

That infuriated me. My trust of him and his firm was undone by the trickery. Sure, they got me to open the email but they didn't get my respect or my business. It wasn't cute or funny. It was contrived and cheesy.

This goldfish didn't bite on the cheese.

Building Your Playbook:

Take a checkup of your emails and samples of those your team is sending out. I developed this report card-style checklist to score an email to determine its essential quality. Simply assign a point value (1 = low, 10 = high) for each of these criteria representing the different elements of a reader-friendly email or letter; 100 points possible:

1. **Effective/honest/accurate subject line**: "Why should I open this?" Be clear: No trickery such as "Your new set of golf clubs is on its way," like mentioned previously.

2. **Proper greeting**: Correct titles & name of the person and organization. Don't be casual with people who don't know you.

3. **Readable font size and type**: I use Calibri 14. The goal is to be easy on the eyes. Avoid cursive, it's awful to read.

4. **Short paragraphs**: Two to three sentences max.

5. **White space**. Double-space between paragraphs.

6. **Bullet points**: Breaks up the page & gives sensible order for main points. Use three to five. People remember more in odd numbers.

7. **Have a beginning, middle, and end to your message**: Sensible order, explain their WIIFM, give them the hook, don't ramble or jump around, craft a compelling call to action.

8. **Compelling reason for the reader to be interested or take action**: Don't bury the crux of your offer in the middle—it's too hard to find.

9. **Strong closing**: *What is the next action step? Own the follow-up. Do not end it with, "Please call me if you have any questions" — it's the all-time weakest closing.*

10. **Email signature**: *Include first and last name, phone number, and other pertinent contact info (website, social media links, etc.).* **The whole idea is to be easy to do business with.**

Chapter 26

The Duality of Leadership

"Leadership means trusting your own judgement above anything else. Great leaders don't lead according to words on a page. Great leaders lead with their heart."
—From the CBS TV series *Blue Bloods*

L eadership is a tough gig. And one truth shines above all others on the topic: *Leadership is a behavior, not a title.*

And behaviors determine actions. You likely already know this from your own firsthand experiences if you've ever been in the "tornado" associated with leading. Being responsible for a group of people in any setting—sports, school, family, armed conflict, business, church, you name it—is a challenging proposition with varying degrees of danger, excitement, and accomplishment. Try as we may, no one gets it right 100 percent of the time. There are just too many variables. In my own leadership development experiences, I've made both good calls and some others where I wish that I could have taken a do-over.

If you are a newly-minted manager or about to assume such a position for the first time—or, if you are a veteran leader who feels like you need something like a "shot in the arm," I'm confident you'll find this section valuable. Leadership and managing others is a wide, sweeping topic, worthy of many volumes. For our purposes here, I'm breaking that elephant into a few choice pieces over the next few chapters that will help you in several meaningful ways.

Leaders have to be comfortable being uncomfortable

This chapter introduces you to a concept I've developed that will serve you well as a team manager or an organizational leader: the duality of leadership.

Simply defined, the premise of this idea is that leaders should embrace two related missions that are at the root of being successful. One is responsibility to their organization/ team, and another is to themselves. First, they have the responsibility to help insure that their team members keep learning and evolving so they can continue to grow and develop in their work. Secondly, they have the same responsibility to themselves, to also keep learning and expanding their own skill set.

It sounds a lot easier than it is. Indeed, much is made about leadership executives needing to pull their teams up the hill by motivating, coaching, and directing them to get the desired results. *But who pulls the executives up the hill?*

"Never stop learning, because life never stops teaching."
—Anonymous

The genesis of the idea behind the duality of leadership came to me while working with many different organizations and observing all types of people in team leadership roles. And at the center of this is lifelong learning.

In recent years I've been observing an alarming trend— people getting positions and promotions with leadership and management titles who fall into two very different categories. One, those who assume that with their new title they have "arrived," and they allow their egos to tell them that they no longer need to develop their skills. Others are new managers who want or need further learning but are not provided any real coaching or management development by their organizations.

These very people are often thrown into the fire and expected to know how to get themselves and their team out without getting burned. After all, it's likely that most people in an organization are going to assume team leaders know what they are doing because of their rank on the organization chart, derived from the title they carry.

But in substantive terms, do they really have the necessary chops to develop people effectively and also develop themselves? Does a title ensure that? Of course not. I've seen a number of these folks get burned out or chewed up by the demands of the job, unable to handle the stress of the responsibilities inherent to leading and managing.

If you are a newbie manager or a veteran who needs a refreshing or refocus, and you face the dual task of managing both your team's learning and development in addition to your own, don't go it alone; get some help. And don't ever get to the point where you believe that your title gives you license to stop your learning journey. Attend workshops and webinars, read books, talk to mentors, listen and observe—soak it all in. Doctors and airline pilots have to go through continuous training on new innovations and changes in their professions—why not you, too?

Never get too big for your britches and think you don't need continued coaching. Ridiculous. No one knows it all. Smart leaders keep their eyes and ears open to new lessons no matter how long they've been at the game.

Be careful — titles don't always match the talent

What's in a title, anyway? It's no guarantee of a certain level of knowledge, is it? Hang around in the business world for a while and you'll know this is true.

Certainly no single industry owns this issue, which is often referred to as a *talent gap*. But *Hotel News Now* zeroed in on this topic as it pertains to the meetings industry and it also speaks to industries across the landscape: "Training is an area that is under disruption . . . It is clear that employees who stepped up during the pandemic are now supervisors or even managers and many of them have received limited to no training; it's a top trend to watch."

As an example, the Covid-19 peak years of 2020-22 brought about massive hemorrhaging and furloughing of jobs across thousands of industries. Plenty of salespeople have been promoted in the post-pandemic recovery to directors of sales teams because they survived the purge or put in a few years of frontline selling. The open secret is that the bulk of their sales bookings in the pre-Covid boom were *reactive*, not *proactive*. They learned to be farmers, not hunters. Thus, they are finding the sledding a bit rough in places now, proving that they need to evolve their learning in order to succeed in the next economy.

What about the customers in all of this? Certainly, they feel the pinch of trying to work with sales directors who are thin on leadership experience. It can result in a mountain of missed opportunities and tangled negotiations because some of the new team leaders just don't know where to look for the answers. As customers have frustratingly stated many times, "They don't know what it is they don't know."

Adding to the challenges, today's managers/team leaders

have very limited authority to make certain decisions compared to their predecessors of several years ago. That makes the buyers' jobs tougher, too. Sure, all of this may not be the newbie sales team leaders' fault, but they are nevertheless in the tornado and in need of some help. Management companies should invest in developing real leadership skills for those people and not simply trust luck or osmosis.

> *"Once you stop learning, you start dying."*
> *—Albert Einstein*

While that's a pretty stark take on the subject, I strongly believe it is true. I'll often add this related point for my audiences: "We're either getting better or we're getting worse; there is no in-between."

With the duality of leadership stressing the responsibility of management executives to evolve their team's skills and their own, there are times when the going gets tough or even grinds to a halt. That calls for stick-to-itiveness and creativity, including from outside resources.

Helping teams that are "stuck" to break through

Recently, a coaching client of mine, a very frustrated sales director, confided in me during our initial conversation that her team was becoming satisfied with mediocrity and that she had somehow fallen into the trap of accepting that behavior. She felt it was happening either out of weariness on her part or maybe the Peter Principle was kicking in.

I offered her this premise to start with:

"Your goal as a leader is to help your team break through where they think they can't."

To that she replied, "That's a perspective I've never considered."

I then asked her, "Who helps you when you think you can't break through something?" She looked into her coffee cup for the answer. It wasn't there. After a moment of thought, she looked at me with forlorn eyes and confessed, "Seriously? No one does. I'm kind of on my own. It's my team to manage and they [the business owners] just assume that I know everything I need to know for every situation. After all, I have the title, right? It's overwhelming. I feel like I'm on a hamster wheel at times." She's not alone.

Team leadership can indeed be an overwhelming, lonely place. But no one should work in a vacuum or feel alone. No one said that pulling a team or oneself up the hill of learning has to be a solo endeavor. Smart leaders know to check their egos and seek help where and when they need it, as the story from one of the greatest leaders in our nation's history will illustrate.

Even the greatest leaders need help sometimes

Let's go back to the doleful winter of 1777, as the Revolutionary War to decide the fate of the American colonies was raging. It was truly a pivotal moment in that conflict as the ideals of forming a new nation hung in the balance. Our story occurs some eighteen miles outside of Philadelphia, where General George Washington and his twelve thousand poorly-equipped and ill-fed Colonial troops set up their winter encampment in a place called Valley Forge, Pennsylvania.

It was also a very dire time for the colonial effort. The British Army had taken Philadelphia and forced the Conti-

nental Congress to flee. Washington's troops had scant medical and food supplies, and hadn't been paid for their services in some time. The general's pleas to Congress for money
and provisions were going untended. Desertions from the
Continental Army's ranks were in the hundreds on some
days as men as skinny as scarecrows seemed to melt away
in the snow, heading back to their homes and thus giving
up the fight.

Founding Father and Revolutionary War writer/pub-
lisher Thomas Paine famously described the perilous situation facing our colonies at this crucial stage in one of his
motivational pamphlets that was circulating among the
colonies:

"These are the times that try men's souls. The summer
soldier and the sunshine patriot will, in this crisis, shrink
from the service of their country; but he that stands it now
deserves the love and thanks of man and woman."

Thus, after a series of battlefield defeats, George Washington was barely keeping his fragile Continental Army
together as a legitimate fighting force that winter. They were
being bested by the better-trained and superbly equipped
British troops of King George III, and our fledgling American Revolution was losing steam.

Victory looked out of reach without help of some kind

At Valley Forge, Washington was deeply affected by the
woeful condition of his troops and very frustrated at not
being able to do more for his loyal men. He knew that he
had hit his own "wall" as their commanding officer, too. He
realized that he needed help.

Washington's life ring came in the person of Prussian

military officer Baron von Steuben, an extremely tough taskmaster whom he brought to Valley Forge after learning of him from Benjamin Franklin and the French minister of war. He engaged von Steuben to implement a drastic new training regimen that would hopefully turn the ragtag troops into a fighting force by the spring, when the British Army would resume their attacks.

The Baron's tactics were tough and relentless. Inexorably, the troops came to see the value in the training as they were steadily becoming better soldiers. They knew that von Steuben, by being tough on them, was nonetheless improving their chances to survive the upcoming battles. As his men got stronger, Washington himself gained confidence. His spirits were lifted as to the towering tasks that still lay ahead.

The mentor allowed himself to be mentored. It was no time or place for ego to get in the way.

Through hard, steady work, von Steuben instilled much-improved order, confidence, and discipline into Washington's troops at Valley Forge. He transformed a tattered army of demoralized volunteers into a coordinated fighting force that turned the tide of the war. As prohibitive underdogs, the Continental Armies ultimately prevailed in a war that assured our country of its independence from England.

Get help—there is no glory in failing alone

The duality of leadership that Washington faced, recognized, *and acted upon* should be a beacon of inspiration to modern-day leaders who face learning challenges for their teams and themselves. Know where and when to get help.

Remember, your goal as a leader is to help your team

break through where they think they can't. Indeed, great leaders need to foster their own growth and continually hone the skills of their team. That's the duality of leadership.

And like George Washington, it's perfectly OK to seek help in that department.

Building Your Playbook:

- *If you are a leader or manager of other people, what do you do to help your team break through where they think they can't?*
- *Are you seeing any tendencies among your team members of being satisfied with mediocrity?*
- *Where do you find your own sources of help, development, and motivation?*
- *Which areas of your own professional development do you feel you need to address immediately?*
- *What areas of improvement are most critical for your team members at this moment?*

Chapter 27

Leadership Lessons Forged in Harm's Way

"If you are going through hell, keep going."
—Sir Winston Churchill

It's not every day you get the chance to meet a member of our country's Greatest Generation, an eyewitness to history, a full-fledged participant fighting for his country on a day that changed the course of the world. His humble story of courage under fire is a lesson worth sharing.

I met Michael "Mickey" Ganitch quite by chance, and lucky for me. As my dad and I were leaving the Alameda County Fairgrounds racetrack from a day at the races, this affable man with an ear-to-ear smile pulled up driving a golf cart and asked us, "Do you guys want a ride back to your car?"

Ganitch (1919-2022) was shuttling people from the horse racing stands to the parking lot that day. He was proudly wearing a pristine "Pearl Harbor Survivor" baseball cap. Being an American history enthusiast, I felt compelled to make mention of his cap. The veterans I've encountered proudly wear their caps signifying their past service. I was banking on the fact that if he minded a comment about his participation in the iconic battle, he wouldn't have worn the cap.

I needn't have worried. Ganitch was pleased that I had noticed. "I see from your cap that you were at Pearl Harbor. Thank you for your service," I offered him from the passenger seat in the cart. He smiled and announced that he had served on the battleship *USS Pennsylvania* (BB-38) in Pearl Harbor during the Japanese surprise attack of December 7, 1941. He seemed willing to tell us more, and my dad and I were willing listeners as his passengers on our short ride to the parking lot.

Ganitch proclaimed with enthusiasm that he was "ninety-six going on ninety-seven," but his vitality made him seem much younger. In the span of less than five minutes he opened up to my dad and me, total strangers, with a riveting conversation about his former ship and shipmates. He sketched out a few details of the Japanese strike and his ordeal on that memorable day.

I was awestruck with this man, so I mentioned that I was writing a book, and that I would love to share his story with others as an example of surviving chaos, thinking on one's feet, and adjusting actions out of necessity. He enthusiastically agreed to a phone call.

While doing my homework prior to our call, I learned that I had met a celebrity of sorts in Ganitch. He had granted interviews to several organizations including the Smithsonian Channel, the History Channel, the National World War II Museum in New Orleans, and various TV spots for news agencies doing stories on Pearl Harbor.

"I'm not a hero"

Ganitch made it clear right off the bat on our phone interview that he did not consider himself a hero of any kind.

"I'm not a hero. I'm one of the lucky ones," he said humbly.

He proudly mentioned that he was a member of the shrinking local Pearl Harbor Survivors group, where the youngest member was ninety-three years old. When I asked him what his secret to a long life was, he gave me a pragmatic answer, surely right out of the Greatest Generation handbook: "Just keep breathing, because the alternative isn't so good."

He expressed to me that he was both happy and honored to help with this story so that others could learn something from it. He added that no one else had asked him about his Pearl Harbor Survivors cap the entire weekend he drove the golf cart shuttle at the fairgrounds. My thought was that it was their loss.

"Now hear this: this is no drill!"

In December of 1941, Ganitch was the quartermaster of what he referred to as "The Big Pennsy" or "The 'Big P" (the *USS Pennsylvania*), which was in dry dock in Pearl Harbor, Hawaii. The battleship was in need of repairs for a damaged propeller.

He recalled waking up early on Sunday, December 7, to get dressed into his football uniform, of all things. He was a member of the ship's football team. "I loved football and I joined the ship's team right away," he proclaimed. That fateful day, his team from the Pennsy was scheduled to play the team representing the *USS Arizona* for what he called "The Super Bowl of the Navy" to decide the Pacific Fleet's championship football team.

"We were pretty darn good," he explained. "We were 9-1 and had played the University of Honolulu team to a 0-0 tie. We were scheduled to leave ship at 8 a.m. to practice for the game at 1:00 p.m. We never played that game. We had a war to fight. They [the Japanese] spoiled our weekend."

Ganitch, twenty-two years old at the time, recalled that the first wave of Japanese attack planes arrived over a sleeping Pearl Harbor at 7:55 a.m. "We didn't have time to change clothes," he said. "We had our entire football uniforms on except for our helmets and spikes."

Ganitch's job was to climb up into the battleship's crow's nest, which towered some seventy feet over the deck. It was easier said than done that violent morning. Encumbered by the extra bulk of his shoulder pads, he had difficulty shimmying up the ladder through a small opening. The space was built for a man in a shirt, not a man in shoulder pads.

Since there was no time to stop and remove any clothing, Ganitch followed his instincts and focused on his responsibility to get up into that crow's nest as quickly as he could to help defend his ship. "You didn't have time to be scared," he recalled of that harrowing moment. "You just did what you were trained to do. I had to pull myself up with my shoulder pads on."

He was armed with only a radio and binoculars; no firearms. His Job One was to report on enemy planes and their locations in the sky as the harbor's loudspeakers were proclaiming, "This is no drill!"

As Ganitch struggled to get into his battle station, the desperate fight was already beginning to heat up. Japanese pilots were buzzing overhead in their Zeros and bombers, dropping their deadly payloads and firing their machine guns, strafing the decks of U.S. ships that were just beginning to spring to life from the shock of the violent surprise attack.

Ganitch scanned the smoke-tinged early morning Hawaiian skies with his binoculars, still clad in his football gear, desperately looking for incoming terror. He related seeing "our ships in the harbor beginning to burst into flames from the deafening explosions all around us." His ship was "stuck in dry dock like a sitting duck" as he framed it, a stationary prize for the Japanese pilots to line up in their bombsites.

Suddenly, he spotted an enemy plane bearing directly in on his ship. "I called in a plane coming in. You had to call it in when they were out there a ways because if you called it in too late, they would buzz right by without us getting a shot."

The ship's gunners got the message and adroitly fired their anti-aircraft guns, blowing up the attacking plane on its deadly approach before it could do any damage. "It was the only plane we shot down that day. I felt good that I had a bit of a hand in that," Ganitch said proudly.

The *USS Pennsylvania* is credited with being one of the first ships in the harbor to open fire on the Japanese. Her fifty-caliber machine gun crews had their guns in action even before general quarters was sounded (per the official reports).

To Ganitch's recollection, the second wave of Japanese attack planes came in from the overcast skies at about 8:10 am, just fifteen minutes after the first attack. There was hardly time to breathe. One of the planes dropped a five-hundred-pound bomb aimed at obliterating his ship and all aboard it (a crew of approximately fifteen hundred men), and it came pretty close to doing just that.

As Ganitch somberly relayed it, "That bomb passed right by me in the crow's nest, and missed me by forty-five feet. It went through two decks of armored plates. The bomb struck on the ship's starboard side and damaged one of its gun casemates and wiped out the entire gun crew."

Training made a big difference in saving lives

In Ganitch's mind, solid training and plenty of practice was a big part of why there weren't even more losses that day: "We all had our jobs to do and we knew where we needed to be."

Ultimately, in America's opening battle of World War II Mickey's ship suffered fifteen crewmen killed, including her executive officer, along with fourteen missing and thirty-eight wounded sailors.

Ganitch offered me a wistful reflection on Pearl Harbor and his unwavering pride in his fellow crewmates and football teammates aboard the Pennsy: "If the Japanese had not attacked that day, we would have played that fleet championship game against the Arizona and we would have beat them, no question about it."

After just four months as a crewmember, Ganitch had survived his first battle and his first brush with death. It wouldn't be his last.

Beware of forgetting past lessons

Ganitch had one more slice of the war that he wanted to offer as a lesson about responsible management: the need to follow protocols and to never take things for granted. He also wanted to make a point about remembering the lessons from the mistakes in our past, lest we be doomed to suffer them again.

At Pearl Harbor, the U.S. Navy and Army were surprised. They disregarded certain warning signs and let their guards down. It turns out that the cruel fates of war offered a final lesson on this for the officers and sailors aboard the *USS Pennsylvania*.

On August 12, 1945, as World War II entered its final days, Ganitch's *USS Pennsylvania* lay at anchor in Okinawa (Buckner) Bay with other U.S. ships. The war with Japan was drawing to a close. "We were just trying to stay afloat while they were negotiating the peace," he recalled. "Nobody wanted to be the war's last casualty."

He pointed out that, "Even though the war had been decided by then, there were still desperate Japanese attempts to keep fighting rather than surrender." The United States had just dropped two atomic bombs on Japan on August 6 and August 9, trying to bring about an end to World War II. While Japanese Emperor Hirohito and his military leaders haggled over the decision on whether or not to surrender to the Allies, "there was no cease-fire of any kind declared in the Pacific," Ganitch recalled regretfully.

That night, his battleship was tragically struck by a single Japanese plane.

I asked Ganitch how a rogue enemy plane managed to slip through the radar screen of the ships in the harbor. It turns out that it took a certain amount of creativity and pluck on the part of the Japanese pilot, coupled with U.S. Naval officers who made assumptions about the incoming aircraft and let their guard down. They operated without accurate information and took something for granted.

They guessed wrong.

"We were out the farthest [of any ship] in the bay and the Japanese plane picked us," Ganitch remembered. "He [the enemy pilot] came in after dark with his lights on. He was smart to put his lights on as everybody thought it was a friendly plane because of those lights. The thought on our officers' part was: 'Who would be flying at night with lights on but a friendly aircraft?"

The Japanese torpedo plane penetrated the air space over the anchored ships and launched a torpedo at the Pennsy. "It hit the ship aft [rear], causing extensive damage," Ganitch sadly recalled. "The torpedo's impact ripped a hole of approximately thirty feet in diameter in her stern. We lost twenty out of twenty-six crewmen in my group during the explosion as the compartments flooded. It was awful."

The following day, the damaged Pennsy was towed to shallow water where salvage operations ensued, earning the battleship the sad designation of being the last major U.S. warship to be damaged in World War II.

The business parallel here is that when protocols, procedures, and training are not followed, and assumptions are made based on partial information and guesswork, the outcomes can be bad.

Japanese Emperor Hirohito gave a recorded radio address across the Japanese Empire three days later on August 15, 1945, announcing the surrender of Japan to the Allies. As Ganitch somberly reflected, "Unfortunately, for those twenty poor souls aboard our ship, the emperor's announcement came three days too late."

Applying what we've learned, no matter the circumstances

Thankfully, unless our jobs require perilous work or we are in the armed forces, we aren't typically facing life-or-death dangers such as dodging enemy fire in our daily jobs. But these experiences from Mickey Ganitch can still offer some very valuable lessons and parallels that we can relate to our own stressful and challenging situations. Scale them to fit your own situations of dealing with lightning fast decision-making and overcoming adversity.

Building Your Playbook

- *How well prepared, mentally and physically, am I (or my team) to deal with a sudden dose of "shift happens" so that we bend but don't break?*
- *How strong and effective is my (our) training?*
- *Does everyone on the team understand their Job One and responsibilities?*
- *Do we practice how to do things properly so as to stay sharp?*
- *Do we learn from our mistakes so that we don't repeat them?*
- *Do we analyze our available data and information so as to make informed decisions?*
- *Do we improvise and twist the familiar when it's called for?*
- *Do we huddle to discuss situations where we are unsure as to how to handle something?*

Chapter 28

A Leader's Respect for Others Fosters
Credibility and Results

"Leadership is not about being in charge, it's about taking care of those in your charge." —Simon Sinek

I try to never miss an opportunity to glean wisdom from others who have been there, done that. In our world where there is so much fakery and not as much authenticity as we would like, it is refreshing and awe-inspiring to learn from others who have achieved great heights and remained humble about it.

Another member of The Greatest Generation who shared valuable leadership lessons with me in addition to Mickey Ganitch was bomber pilot Second Lieutenant Walter F. Hughes (1922-2020). I met Lt. Hughes during one of his Memorial Day visits to the Livermore, California Airport. Restored WWII planes were on display and open for people to climb inside and examine them up close or even take a short private flight. Several veterans showed up in uniform to talk with the public, answer questions, and enjoy the limelight a bit.

Hughes was only too glad to answer my questions and discuss with me his leadership experience as a pilot during World War II. He had a very profound tenet to share with me as the lead officer in his aircraft, one that I think you'll agree can certainly apply to today's business practices.

Hughes was the pilot in charge of a B-24 Liberator, carrying a weight of 66,000 lbs. with a bomb load of 6,000 lbs.

He commanded a crew of ten airmen and flew thirty-five successful missions over war-torn Europe during WWII.

For me, the idea that anyone could successfully pilot a huge warplane and a crew through thirty-five missions through terror-filled skies is almost incomprehensible. Imagine all of the frightening moments, the quick-thinking coordination, and the unwavering cooperation among the crew that took place during those missions. They took off from the runway each time knowing that they had jobs to do and orders to follow. Still, Hughes and his crew bucked the trend for survival in a WWII aircraft.

For a bit of context, consider the odds of survival during WWII in Europe. The Allies lost 12,000 heavy bombers to the Germans. According to The Mighty website, nearly 71 percent of a bomber's crew were either killed or listed as missing in action during the war, which accounts for approximately 100,000 service members. Thus, the odds of survival in the skies over Europe were terribly low.

I respected the man before I even shook his hand. *This was someone I really wanted to talk to!*

"Always do everything you ask of those you command."
—George S. Patton

Dressed impeccably in his flawlessly crisp uniform and medal-adorned jacket, Hughes was patiently answering questions from the patrons while standing outside the bomb bay door of a restored Liberator parked in the viewing area of the regional airport.

He greeted me with a firm handshake and a friendly smile. After a bit of small talk and thanking him for his service, I asked him about his approach to being a captain; I asked him if he could share any leadership lessons from his wartime experiences that might apply for people in business today.

"Yes, I'd be glad to, thank you for asking," he replied affably. His personable smile told me he enjoyed sharing his history with others. Indeed, he wrote an excellent autobiographical book about his career and experiences titled *A Bomber Pilot in WWII*. It's a great read on training, camaraderie, and the importance of teamwork.

"As the pilot, I wanted to know what every man on my plane had to do," Hughes began. "They each had a job to do and I wanted to know how each duty was performed. So I worked every single job on that airplane during training flights so I could know what the guys had to go through and what each position entailed."

This particular outlook on leadership by Hughes translates very well to today's business landscape. Effective managers must know and understand the different duties, responsibilities, and challenges that their team members face every day. This approach helps team leaders manage different situations, empathize with their team members, make decisions based on knowledge instead of ignorance, and recognize opportunities for improvement when people or systems begin to falter.

It also makes it abundantly clear that knowing the mission and receiving proper training is paramount to success. "My crewmembers and I had to execute our duties with precision for the good of each other and the mission," he emphasized. "I never asked them to do something that I hadn't done myself."

That kind of leadership thinking fosters credibility, cooperation and respect—so very crucial for someone in a position of authority, no matter their line of work.

> **"People don't care how much you know, until they know how much you care." —Theodore Roosevelt**

I'm betting that Hughes' crew members never had the sinking feeling some people in organizations experience today that "management has no idea what we really do, nor do they care."

Hughes' approach is the antithesis of leadership elitists who have little or no clue about what their people do or how they produce what they produce. When managers take the time to care and learn what goes on in the front lines, it gets noticed and appreciated by the team members.

To be clear, let's not confuse the act of the leader taking a turn at each job with micro-managing. The idea that Second Lieutenant Hughes expressed is that it's not the leader's job to do the crewmembers' individual jobs. Let people do their jobs. But leaders need to understand what those jobs encompass. And actually experiencing those jobs—taking a physical turn at the wheel, so to speak—goes a long way to increasing the leader's understanding of the operation.

To Simon Sinek's point at the top of this chapter, Hughes *took care of his crew* through his commitment to learning every crew position. That act of empathy and familiarity wasn't missed by the crew, either. That intimate knowledge of the aircraft's various duties had to have come in handy when enemy planes approached and anti-aircraft flak burst outside their fuselage, trying to knock them out of the sky.

There was a similar, albeit much less dangerous version of this idea in the popular TV show *Undercover Boss*. High-level executives would go on undercover missions to work in the rank-and-file positions of their own organizations to examine the inner workings of their company. They inevitably found eye-opening revelations about things that needed attention or were just plain bad, and positive changes would ensue. The incognito executives often had no clue that some of the things they uncovered were happening every day under their noses.

There is no substitute for solid experience

I also experienced the benefits of a thorough, firsthand cross-training approach coming right out of college. I was recruited by the iconic twelve-hundred-room Westin St. Francis Hotel in downtown San Francisco. I was among a small group of ten fellow hospitality business graduates selected from schools across the country to enter the company's "MDP" or Management Development Program.

We spent a year or so rotating every few months in the various departments of the bustling historic luxury hotel. Our MDP experiences took us to the front office, reservations, housekeeping, food and beverage, security, banquets, night audit, and convention services. It was a real eye-opener and an effective way to understand the many moving parts of the hotel.

We trained on all levels as staffers, supervisors, and ultimately managers. If you had an ego problem about earning a hospitality business degree and having to learn from the ground up, you didn't make the cut.

We were sponges, soaking in all of the various procedures, techniques, and responsibilities. It was a massive "learning lab," and not without its challenges. Days with five hundred to six hundred check-ins or check-outs were common for us. We experienced just about everything—from the wondrously glamorous to the seedy side of hotel life, too. Our duties took us from elegant dining outlets to the basement corridors that included a police holding pen for perps apprehended for some type of crime.

The frontline folks, many of them long-time veterans of the hotel, taught us MDPs the ropes by drawing upon their many years of experience. And being exposed to the styles of the different managers around the hotel was also extremely valuable. I learned from those managers who were really sharp and effective team leaders and also others whose management style left a lot to be desired. It's important to learn both sides of what to do and what not to do.

My three years at The Westin St. Francis taught me invaluable lessons about the luxury hotel business from the ground up and inside-out. Ultimately, the experience made me a better salesperson a few years later. And it was monumental in the short-term when I was promoted to a front office management position there. I knew the systems, the people, and what was expected of each team member.

Effective leaders understand that the whole is greater than the sum of its parts

In its own way, my hotel cross-training experience resembled Walter Hughes' outlook on what he thought was critical as the bomber pilot in charge of his plane. Like Hughes, many successful leaders today know all too well that *the whole is greater than the sum of its parts.*

What about your organization or team? Committing thorough cross-exposure training for people builds familiarity and understanding that never goes wasted, especially in times of stress and crisis. It also helps to be a leader who has strong principles and a keen sense of self-awareness to pull it all together.

When he finished his pilot training, Walter Hughes proudly reflected on his accomplishments. As he wrote in his book, "I was a B-24 pilot. I could fly this biggest of Air Force bombers, and I did it with confidence, humility and pride."

If you are looking for a great foundation upon which to build your leadership journey, Hughes' three timeless traits mentioned above would be a terrific place to start.

Building Your Playbook:

- *If you are a team leader or owner, how well do you know what your frontline team members actually do, what they put up with, how they solve issues, accomplish their tasks, or overcome obstacles every day?*
- *How well do your various department managers or supervisors know and understand what happens in other departments?*
- *Why do you think that is important?*
- *Cross-exposure training is critical. What training do you currently offer for your organization/team in that area? If you don't have a formal, focused training initiative, what's standing in your way? How do your team members improve?*

Chapter 29

Don't Let Clunky Procedures
and Poor Etiquette Kill Your Business

"There are no secrets to success. It is the result of preparation, hard work, and learning from failure." —Colin Powell

The worst sales phone call I ever received? This is an easy choice:

Them: "Hey, we're a janitorial service. Gonna be in your area. Want an estimate?"

Me: "Ah, no."

Click.

What can we learn from this? It's wrong on so many levels, not the least of which is that he jumps right in with all of the subtlety of a sledgehammer. He didn't ask me about my business to see if there was a match. He didn't ask me if I have a need for his service. He didn't tell me even a little bit about the benefits of his service. None of that. What was his name? What was his company's name? I don't know, he never said!

It was over in five seconds.

When I declined, he suddenly hung up. He apparently had little or no meaningful training or didn't care to try another approach or ask a qualifying question. Good luck to that guy.

What about *your* business? Are you 100 percent sure of what your people are saying to prospects and customers on the phone, with both outbound and inbound calls?

Driving customers away is easier than you think

My friends and colleagues often share their good, bad, and ugly sales and service experiences with me, knowing I am always looking for coaching moments that I can turn into a lesson of some sort. Here's one from my colleague Richard Rue, an executive recruiter in the high-tech industry. If there ever was an example of a business having a *Customer Prevention Department*, this is it.

Rue is a good customer of a fine wine shop near his home, and he called them to order wine for a holiday dinner. He asked for the wine buyer whom he usually deals with for his orders. The person answering the phone responded, "What's this about?" When Rue explained, "I'd like to buy some wine," the person responded, "You'll have to call them back. They're all too busy right now."

"It was really off-putting, "Rue explains. "I was treated like a Joe Blow, it was denigrating. I was in a buying mood, too."

Always strive to make your enterprise easy to do business with

Could the wine shop rep have been any more standoffish with Rue, making him feel like he was an imposition to the shop? It's not recommended to have your customers feel that way. Since when does "What's this about?" resemble anything close to a professional, customer-friendly response on the phone? It sounds awful. I can't resist thinking how my sarcastic self would have responded to the clerk: What do you *think* this is about? You're a wine shop and I want to buy some wine!

And what about the rest of the answer: "They're too busy; you'll have to call them back." That's not a response, it's a command! While I totally understand a business being busy at a given moment, that's neither the customer's fault nor their concern. Don't make it their problem or inconvenience, either. Telling the customer—and not even asking—just *telling* them to do the work by taking an extra step of calling back later? Not in my store.

I've heard this myself many times as the customer. Asking if the manager is in, I'll often get something like this over the phone, much like the response Rue received: "The manager isn't in right now. You'll have to call them when they get in." Now think how silly that sounds. How in the world's end would I ever know when the manager gets back in? Is she or he wearing a tracking device that I can find with an app on my phone in order to detect their return to the store?

So, the response "you'll have to call back" is a farce. Customers could call back an hour later or more and the shop might still be busy. Should they just keep calling to try and get lucky with a lull in the store's activity? Ridiculous. The proper response would be to take the customer's name and number and commit that someone *will call them back* by "X" time. After all, Rue called to buy something for crying out loud! He wanted to do business, not check on the weather forecast.

"We're too busy"

Entrepreneur Magazine weighed in on this topic of businesses that tell customers they are too busy: "Customers who don't want to get poor service or have inordinate wait-times go elsewhere and you're left with a clientele that is the appropriate size for your capacity to deliver. Not exactly a solid growth strategy.

You'd better hope that this clientele size matches up with your ability to make a profit or you will 'too busy' yourself into bankruptcy.

Not having time to follow up (with customers) is akin to saying you don't have time to be successful. You make time to be successful, and if that means biting the bullet and hiring more staff or weeding out the low performers, then that's what you need to do."

Don't put up walls that customers have to climb over

A similar anecdote comes from tour operator David Rubens, illustrating how some people and businesses build veritable high castle walls surrounded by moats in order to stay insulated against dealing with customers:

"As instructed by someone at the front desk of a recognized national hotel chain, I sent the general manager an email inquiry to book a group," Rubens explains. "Two-and-a-half weeks later, there was still no response. I called the hotel back and was told to send an email to the GM because 'that is the only way the GM will respond.' What, no voicemails or calls allowed in this hotel?"

Oh, it gets better.

"Then, when I asked for the standard rates over the dates I was interested in for my group, the desk agent said, 'We aren't allowed to give out that information or any information connected to a group since the GM is the only one allowed to deal with it."

Well, what do we have here, a lack of empowerment,

trust, initiative, or all three? The hotel certainly didn't show any interest in capturing this customer's business. No courtesy. No care. No follow-up. No salesmanship. In this case, the GM built the hotel's castle walls fairly high, forgetting that they are in the *hospitality* business, and that sales revenue actually keeps the lights on.

How can this hotel, or any type of business, insulate itself from customer contact like this, especially with a prospect that has raised their hand wanting to buy, *and still expect to be successful?* What about the unreturned message from Rubens to the general manager, the chief executive in the organization? What kind of example and tone does that set for the hotel staff? Why aren't other people in the organization empowered to check availability and offer rates? It sounds like a lack of trust is a huge issue there. Make a note of that for your own business.

Here is a chilling thought that a business like this one fails to comprehend: From a customer's viewpoint, if I have this much trouble jumping through hoops to give you my group's business, what kind of bigger hoops will my people have to jump through when my group is actually onsite?

How can you deliver better customer service in your own business?

Picture these kinds of similar walls in your own organization. Should you make your customers or prospects try to climb over your walls to hear from you, to do business with you? I wouldn't make a bet on that being a winning ticket. Few people have the desire, time, or bandwidth to deal with all that nowadays.

In your own experiences, can you see how easy it has

become in some places to prevent sales and to drive customers away? These examples are the direct opposites of the immortal concept of *being easy to do business with.*

> *"In the world of internet customer service,*
> *it's important to remember your competitor*
> *is only one mouse click away."* —Doug Warner

Sadly, each example cited here was easily preventable. It takes a real desire and commitment from the top to get better. It may take some financial investment. It takes training. It takes wanting to care about customers. It takes attention to detail. It takes practice. It takes management. It takes accountability. It takes owning the follow up. No autopilot allowed, no letting the chips fall as they may.

The good news is episodes like these can be fixed without having to build a rocket ship to the moon. Give your phone etiquette program, for both outbound sales calls and inbound customer calls, a healthy checkup, and be diligent about how you want things handled with your customers. What do you want them to hear and how would you like them to be taken care of when they call on your business?

Some say "scripting" works best. But I'll offer that it's not just scripting by itself that is the panacea. I see a lot being made about scripting from some customer service consultants, but almost no attention is paid on voice tone, pacing, sincerity, or friendliness. Scripting certainly helps, but only when employees can deliver it in a natural, believable way, not sounding like perfunctory robots just going through the motions. It takes practice. A scripted response or call delivered without authenticity falls flat on the listener and can actually do more harm than good.

Start your campaign for improving phone etiquette by observing what the customer experiences. See and hear the process through their eyes and ears. You may have the system that allows you to hear recorded calls for evaluation and coaching. Put them to use!

Design your phone protocols and etiquette program; then train it, practice it, implement it, and manage the process. Then retrain. Ask your customers how you are doing in this area. If need be, go back to the drawing board again until your business shines in this important area. It will be worth it.

Building Your Playbook:

- *How are the phones answered in your organization? What are your frontline people saying to your customers on the phone and in person?*
- *Do you provide them with scripted phrases, proper greetings, and answers they can give to customers?*
- *If empowered to make decisions when dealing with customers over the phone, has your staff been trained in the parameters they can use?*
- *Are there communications protocols set up internally and managed?*
- *Has everyone who speaks to customers in your organization been properly trained?*
- *BONUS: Check your customer care policies. You can have great phone manners but lousy policies.*

Chapter 30

Customer Service is an Attitude, Not a Department

"Every company's greatest assets are its customers, because without customers there is no company." —Michael LeBoeuf

Customer service sure is a wonderful thing to experience when it's clicking, isn't it? It feels great and the ROI meter goes way up when the service you receive is A-plus. But alas, no two organizations are exactly the same in service deliveries. What it really comes down to is one-on-one attention, courtesy, and a bit of soft salesmanship as your frontline people interact with your customers. It sounds simple, but some people make it so complicated and difficult that it seems to be a vanishing talent these days in many places. Here is one story of a simple yet effective approach that you can apply to your own business:

The Golden Rule still works!

When I pulled my SUV into my local Ford dealership's "Quick Lane" for a routine oil/lube/inspection, I wasn't expecting much. I was thinking about my last trip there six months prior. It was the customer service nightmare we've all faced at garages, repair facilities, and the like. You know the deal: They quote you "about an hour," and I was left on the hook waiting for almost three hours because someone assigned to my car didn't get the paperwork, so it sat there until I rattled enough cages. The manager emailed me an apology and a freebie rain check.

Still, my expectation dial was near zero.

Boy, did I get a different experience, and it was a jolt. A smiling gentleman in a clean uniform approached my car immediately, introduced himself as Jack with a nice hand-shake, and asked in a genuine voice, "What can we do for you today?"

In a matter of moments, we were having a casual conver-sation about my car, lifting the hood, doing a few pre-checks (they never did *that* before!), and I was answering a few gen-eral questions about how my car was running. I gave him a quick thumbnail of my visit to the dealership back in the summer, just to see what reaction that would bring. Too many times, the employee either pretends not to hear such a comment, or shrugs it off and says something innocuous such as, "Sorry, we get busy like that."

Jack turned to me and said, "Gary, I've been in this busi-ness for forty-two years and there is one thing I know. If you treat others the way that you want to be treated, they'll come back and do business with you again."

Wow. There it was, the mother of all service credos, the Golden Rule. Think back to the last time a frontline em-ployee quoted the Golden Rule to you. I couldn't recall if that had *ever* happened to me. It's such a pure, honest, and straightforward axiom for business and life.

He quoted me a time for when my car would be finished, and he got it back to me with time to spare. Under-promised and over-delivered—hooray! Additionally, he offered me a complimentary car wash. "I want you to come back again," he proclaimed with a smile.

The trepidation I felt when arriving at the "Quick Lane" was long gone when I drove out of their facility an hour or so later. My entire orientation to their operation at that Ford dealership had flipped 180 degrees. Friendly, honest, and caring customer care, backed up by results as promised, will do that to you.

"It takes 20 years to build a reputation and five minutes to ruin it. If you think about that, you'll do things differently." —*Warren Buffett*

A company's brand and its employees' individual/personal brands are on display every single time there is a customer interaction. Those are called "Moments of Truth." I cannot overemphasize the importance of MOTs. They happen online, on the phone, and in person. Everything a company does and commits to doing is up for scrutiny in the court of customer opinion. And every customer interaction and transaction counts.

That's a lot of pressure on performance, and that's why companies—yours!—need to stringently focus on customer care efforts. Every new day brings with it opportunities to make new customers who are looking to buy, dine, travel, etc.

And every day, your customer care will be tested. You can't ever really say, "We're there, we're finally happy where we are," regarding your customer service levels. It's always a work in progress because every day things change; it's all on the line again with a new set of customers. After all, companies who sell goods and services are in the "What have you done for me lately?" business from the viewpoints of the customers, aren't they?

And for most businesses, it all comes down to a pretty simple equation:

Deliver on your Promises + Provide Value Satisfaction = Make Sales.

The rest is in the details. You can fill in a lot of blanks with those details to be sure, but this essential equation for success is pretty straightforward.

> **Management takes care of the employees,**
> **employees take care of the customers,**
> **and customers take care of the bottom line**

Sounds easy, right? Companies of all types, big and small, somehow find ways to make their customer service approach complicated and hard to pull off consistently. You've likely encountered firms that are just plain difficult to do business with. How long do you stay with them? Do they have something that no one else offers, thus you stay with them? Many customers flee for their competition, and it's no wonder.

These companies pay lip service to their customer service by setting up convoluted procedures. They sometimes hire the wrong people in the customer-facing positions, or offer their staff no helpful training. Essentially, they do everything to unravel the process of delivering topnotch service. Or, they have a culture that demotivates people or doesn't encourage employees to go the extra mile or care about excellence. That can submarine good customer service intentions before they even get started.

I think you'll find that with many people, if you show them a measure of trust, they will grow into that and do just fine.

And no company that I know of can successfully "memo" mandatory great customer service to their staff or snap their fingers and make it happen. They have to have the actual people, support systems, winning attitudes, and overall commitments to excellence to deliver on that. They also need to commit the financial resources to make it happen, too.

If you run your own business or manage a team in an organization, don't fall into those traps. Clunky procedures are fixable, especially if you are the boss or have some influence in the organization. Streamline things. Customers don't want to be forced to work their way up the corporate organizational chart on a long slog to get to the person who will listen to them or has the power to make a decision. By that time, customers' tempers may be on a boil and you have lost them forever. And then they go on social media and tell their side of the story. And it probably won't be nice.

Here are some data points you may find helpful in designing your approach, from *Customer Service Magazine*:

70 percent of complaining customers will do business with you again if you resolve the complaint in their favor.

95 percent of complaining customers will do business with you again if you resolve the complaint instantly.

Reducing customer defections to the competition can boost profits by 25-85 percent.

In 73 percent of cases, the organization made no attempt to persuade dissatisfied customers to stay, even though 35 percent of those customers said that a simple apology would have prevented them from moving to the competitors.

If you don't take care of your customers, your competition will

To help you and your team identify, build, or redirect

your customer care initiative, here are some time-tested points that I have shared with my own clients in helping them in this area:

Service = Sales and Sales = Service: When you sell something, you are providing a service. When you provide service, you are selling customers on the idea that they made the right choice and should come back again.

Think Long-Term-Value (LTV) of Customers: Instead of just focusing on the one-time sale, think about a person's long-term or lifetime value as a customer. This could mean their referral abilities, their families and friends, colleagues, etc.

The Get 'ems and the Keep 'ems: It takes two villages to make a business work, and that includes customer service. I came up with these two terms to describe what they do: The Get 'ems are the outside sales efforts to "get" the customers in. But the repeat sales and LTV of those customers are in the hands of the delivery and fulfillment team, known as the Keep 'ems. They "keep" the customers wanting to come back, making the next sale or return to the store easier, maybe even a slam dunk. The two villages of a business need each other—one without the other cannot survive.

Avoid "It is company policy:" That phrase is like nails on a chalkboard to customers' ears. It sounds like a cop-out being conveniently pulled out to just make it easy for the employee to say no, or to lean on some unseen corporate edict to back them up when they can't or won't do something. If it is policy, explain to customers why it exists and what benefits or protection it affords. Generally speaking (and this is not legal advice), you're going to be covered if the customers want you to overreach and you can site legal, ethical, or practical reasons why you can't accommodate them.

Listen: Upset/irate/disgruntled customers mostly want to be heard. Listen to them vent and don't interrupt, cut them off, make excuses, or get emotional. Give their blood pressure a chance to recede. Listen for the actual reason for their anger—it may not be what you think.

Don't let an "it" Issue turn into an "us" Issue: This isn't personal, the employee just happens to be there at that time, representing the company. Remain calm; it helps you to stay in control, and offer them a solution or ask them what solution they think would make it acceptable. Be collaborative if possible. Often, customers come up with less of a fix than the company was willing to offer.

You Can't Really Win an Argument with a Customer: Customers may not always be right (and they can be outright dishonest at times), but they are the customers. They vote with their wallets. But that doesn't give them a right to treat an employee like a punching bag. Get help from a supervisor if things escalate. And try to have the conversation out of earshot of other customers or employees. You may find that you have to let some customers go.

You'll Never Hear all of the Complaints: Only 4 percent of unhappy customers complain to the company. The others just leave or don't come back (though some do take to the internet with a scathing review). This sounds a bit strange, but it works: say "Thank you" when a customer complains. What are you thanking them for? The opportunity to know about something that needs to be fixed or addressed. It also works to diffuse those who are steamed up and getting ready for a "battle royale."

Have a formal customer recovery program in place that takes specific steps to try and mitigate a situation and turn things around. Customers who have a problem satisfactorily fixed actually become more loyal towards the company than they were before the complaint. Strange but true.

Give your employees positive feedback when a customer praises them for their work. So many times I've told managers about the great service of someone, or how they went above and beyond, only to find out down the road that the manager never passed on my comments to the employee. Shameful! It's a wonderfully positive and motivating coaching moment that was wasted.

Moving forward, my suggestion is to meet with your team to discuss their perspectives on customer service, what they experience in their interactions with customers, what they see, hear, etc. If you have the means, ask your customers, too, either in surveys, or take the bold move of bringing together a customer advisory board to get it straight from the customers' mouths. Use the feedback to craft your program.

Whatever you do, make your company's customer service energies honest, straightforward, and uncomplicated. Your employees and customers will thank you.

Building Your Playbook:

- *Map out your customer care plan in the areas above. Use the bullet points above to discuss them with your teams or your supervisor(s) as you prioritize your areas of focus.*
- *Inspect your internal delivery systems and workflows as they also impact customer service.*
- *List the areas where your Get 'ems and Keep 'ems can work together better to create a more seamless customer experience.*

Chapter 31

Bozo-isms: Did They Really Just Say That?

"Nobody goes there anymore, it's too crowded."
— Yogi Berra

People say many unintended things. Some of them are hilarious and others are cringeworthy. I was lucky enough to get to know one of the all-time revered kings of malaprops and fractured language, Baseball Hall of Famer Yogi Berra. He won the most World Series rings in baseball history, but most people remember him for his funny quotes. Entire books have been written about them.

Sure, saying wrongful or clumsy things to others can be serious business. But let's have a little fun with this, too. Admittedly, we all say things every so often that we wish we could pull back. When we hear others say goofy phrases, we scratch our heads and ask, "Did they really just say that?" As we will see here, the spirit of Yogi Berra is alive and well in businesses everywhere.

"It's time for Bozo!"

Growing up in the Detroit area, my brothers and I as kids frequently watched the *Bozo the Clown* TV show. He was funny and lovingly clumsy, both good traits for a clown. He had red, pointy hair that poked out of the sides of his head like wings, and kids in our area loved his show. When the announcer opened the show with "OK boys and girls, it's time for Bozo," we knew we were going to have some laughs during the show. And Bozo delivered with his goofy gaffes.

That endearing clown character was my inspiration for coming up with the term "Bozo-isms" to describe fractured and twisted responses in business. Maybe they aren't intended to sound so *off*, but they nevertheless come out that way. Sometimes the phrases are comically poor and laugh-inducing, unintentionally borrowing from Yogi. At other times, they are just flat-out wrong.

These phrases could conceivably cost people their jobs and certainly cost companies some customers. It depends on the situation and who is receiving the message, and also how it is received. Bozo-isms just come out, and they can't always be pulled back. Unlike the late TV art instructor Bob Ross, they're not always just "happy little accidents."

Unintentional T.M.I. sends all the wrong messages

While on a speaking trip to Vermont, I was dining with several of the hospitality folks from the local area. They recommended a particular Vermont-style, log cabin-type restaurant. I fell in love with it immediately. The homey décor, the vibe, it was all working. I love dining in local joints as much as possible when traveling. A few of us were dreaming of a nice big juicy hamburger, the local favorite. So we asked the waiter if the burgers were as good as advertised.

"Oh yes, the meat is nice and fresh. We get it from the slaughterhouse down the road."

Someone at our table spit out their beer. Most of the rest just cringed from behind their menus. "I'll be back to take your orders," the waiter announced as he turned away, blissfully unaware of the effect his literal answer had on us. You can imagine our conversation after that. Talk about being a "painter of words" in sales. Wow. Although he had given us a technically truthful answer, it was so poorly worded, that the last thing any of us wanted was meat after hearing the word "slaughterhouse." The images we conjured up in that one word were too much to overcome. We laughed it off, but we ordered the salmon.

Another memorable story of phraseology gone terribly wrong comes to mind from a Fort Worth training trip. While staying at a major brand hotel, I came down to the lobby in the morning and hopped into the hotel's shuttle van for a ride to the downtown area where my workshop would be for the day. The driver was an affable young man who engaged me in friendly conversation and got me to my location in just a few minutes.

After my training workshop, I returned to the hotel, relaxed a bit, and made my way down to the pool and patio area to take advantage of the hotel's nightly "general manager's reception." At 5:30 pm each evening, they provided some light snacks and small bites, plus cocktails for their guests. I noticed that the employee who was cooking slider-burgers on the outdoor grill was the same fellow who had been my shuttle driver that morning.

I got in a short line for the sliders and he cheerfully recognized me. "Oh, hello sir, how did your meeting downtown go today?" I replied, "It went great, thanks for asking. So, you're out here doing the grilling for us tonight, too. It looks like they keep you pretty busy around here."

The young man grinned and exclaimed proudly, "Oh yes, I do it all, sir. I drive the shuttle, unclog the toilets, then come out here and cook on the grill."

Now *there* is a visual.

I was chuckling silently at how he explained his duties and the order in which he listed them. I knew that he was innocently recapping his typical day at the hotel. It just struck me as funny, maybe because of my hotel background—I've been around hotel-speak for a long time. But how would his recap sound to other guests? They may get a visual that is TMI as they dig into their grilled sliders.

I couldn't resist putting my coaching cap on for a moment to offer him a bit of advice. He was a friendly ambassador for the hotel and I felt he would be amenable to a suggestion.

"Just a friendly suggestion here," I offered with a smile. "You might want to rethink mentioning the unclogging toilets bit, especially as the thing you do before coming out here to grill food." He took no offense but mulled my comment over for a couple of seconds. "Yessir," he replied with grin, "I really appreciate that. I can see where that would not be a good visual for guests to think about."

Be careful WHAT you say and HOW you say it

Let's take a look at my collection (it's always expanding) of authentic Bozo-isms. I've either heard these myself or accumulated them from clients and colleagues who have been only too happy to send them to me from their travels or within their own organizations. See how many of these you recognize from your own encounters:

- "I don't know." (Which is OK if you add something such as, "I'll find out for you")
- "I'm busy with a customer." (Oh really, what am I?)

- "It's company policy." (It can sound like a cop-out; explain the idea behind it)
- "Who told you that?" (Don't you believe me? Looking to blame someone else?)
- "I don't know why they sent you here." (It sounds like you don't want to help me)
- "My manager is not in right now." (Who else can I talk to; when will they return?)
- "That's not my job/department." (Passing the buck; take ownership to help me)
- "It wasn't our fault." (Confrontational; I just want it fixed, replaced, or refunded)
- "There is no way we can . . ." (Offer a solution of some kind; what *can* you do?)
- "My manager's not here. You'll have to call back." (Take my number, they should call *me* back)
- "You didn't . . ." (Sentences beginning with "you" sound like an attack or blame is coming next)
- "You should have . . ." (Same thing; it sounds like a scolding is coming)
- "Why didn't you . . . ?" (Second-guessing; Makes customer feel like they screwed up)
- "You'll have to talk to them in the morning." (But my problem needs solving *now!*)
- "You're the first person to ever complain about this." (That doesn't mean there isn't a problem; puts customer on defensive, like you think they are lying)
- "Oh, that happens here all the time." (It means your company doesn't fix the issues it is aware of, and that they "settle" instead of trying to get better)
- "The other department should have taken care of this." (Blaming teammates?!)

- "I've told them about that so many times, but nobody listens." (Company could care less about problems that need to be addressed; employees are ignored)
- "We hear that complaint all the time."(And so what do you do about it? Are you admitting that you don't care when customers tell you something is wrong?)
- "I'm from accounting and I'll be handling all of your billing problems." (Billing problems? Are we going to have billing problems? What kind of problems?)
- "We're never really that busy." (And, why not? Is there a reason I should know of? Maybe other customers know something I don't?)
- "They won't let me do that . . ." (Then who *can* do it? No empowerment/trust?)
- "The computer won't let me do that . . ." (Don't blame it on computers. Humans program computers; garbage in/garbage out)
- "I don't have a clue, either." (So how well-informed are you? Can you point me in the right direction or take ownership to follow through for me?)
- "It's been like this for years." (Complacency; the organization just lives with it)
- "That's just the way we do things here." (Offers no hope for improvement or trying to twist the familiar for a better way)
- "That's above my pay grade." (A smart-arse, flippant answer; weak pass-off)
- "I'm only an operator." (Excuse-making; lack of accountability; shows no concern for anything outside their cubby hole in the organization)
- "I don't think anyone else here knows . . ." (But can you find out or should we both just guess?)

- "Sometimes you just can't figure these things out." (So you just give up?)
- "That's the way I was trained." (Don't blame training—you have a brain to think for yourself)
- "Don't order the steak, it's always tough." (Why can't they make a good steak? Are your cooks inept? Why is it still on the menu? Why don't they get it right?)
- "That will never work." (OK, is there another alternative that *will* work?)

This sampling should give you a good idea of the manner in which people often communicate, whether it is intentional or not, and the potential fallout from such phrasing. I'm certain that you have a collection of your own to add, too.

It is one thing to make a "happy little accident" as the late Bob Ross might have referred to on his painting show on TV, such as Yogi Berra or the grill cook in my hotel example. But it's quite another to say many of the things on this list that are just plain rude, uncaring, or thoughtless.

How do we say "bye-bye" to Bozo?

Owners and managers have to curb this and nip it in the bud as soon as they hear Bozo-isms between teammates and customers. It is important to train your customer–facing teams that come into any kind of contact with customers or prospects about what they should say in certain situations, answers they should give, etc. This is essential damage control. Use professional training and role-plays if able to do so.

Bozo-isms can really impact a business and can also bring down your customer service scores and reviews on social media. No one likes thoughtless responses or flaky excuses. Let's work to *get out of our own way* and get team members using smarter language.

I work with several of my training groups to embrace a culture of "think like an owner." Suggest to employees to think like an owner when they are talking and responding to customers: *How would they answer if they owned the business?* I'm betting their responses would be undeniably better.

Stress to your team members that when it comes to avoiding Bozo-isms by properly communicating and using the right words, there really shouldn't be any "clowning" around.

"People may hear your words, but they feel your attitude."
—John C. Maxwell

Building Your Playbook:

- *Set a stage for learning, not condemning.*
- *Discuss what the scenario was: Set up a role-play to demonstrate and evaluate a proper response under those circumstances and a corrective course of action.*
- *Get behind the root reason for the comment. What is causing your customers or guests to bring this issue to you?*
- *What action on our part was being required? If it escalated, why did it escalate? Could it have been handled without the drama?*
- *What is the proper (acceptable) response in the future?*
- *How can we fix the issue so this doesn't happen again?*

Chapter 32

Moments of Truth: it's "Show time!"

"When you pay attention to detail, the big picture will take care of itself." —Georges St-Pierre

Though the exact origins of the term "Moments of Truth" (MOT) are not certain, one of the first treatments of the concept was in a 1987 book titled *Moments of Truth* by Jan Carlzon, then president of Scandinavian Airlines (SAS). Groundbreaking at the time, many of his concepts are just as valid today as when he first wrote about them.

For example, he famously declared that "We don't fly airplanes, we fly people." That is indeed an extremely profound outlook on customer service. He also used the calculation in his book that if ten million customers each encountered five SAS employees in a year, that would be fifty million MOTs "that ultimately determine whether SAS will succeed or fail as a company. They are the moments when we must prove to our customers that SAS is their best alternative."

Relate that type of math equation to your own business. It's pretty impactful stuff!

Understanding, appreciating, and managing Moments of Truth can make the difference between running a successful, mediocre, or failing business.

A MOT is typically defined as, "the moment when a customer/user interacts with a brand or service to form or change an impression about that particular brand, product, or service. Any time a customer comes into contact with a business, however remote, they have an opportunity to form an impression."

In practical terms, MOTs are happening in milliseconds every day, and the impressions they create affect our decisions such as: to stay or go, buy or don't buy, I like this, or I don't like this, etc. They happen so fast, we aren't always conscious of them.

MOTs happen primarily through the five senses: sight, hearing, smell, touch, and taste. They are also created through feelings and emotions. Let's look at the three possible outcomes that can be created from each Moment of Truth:

A positive impression
A neutral impression
A negative impression

Two of these three aren't so good. We all know what a negative impression will do. A neutral impression, while not awful, doesn't really excite anyone or make people raving fans, either. People who feel something is "meh" may stay with it only until something better, more useful, or more exciting comes along. The center target of your efforts should unquestionably be a positive impression—*aim for the best!*

Your brand, business, and team members are always on stage

Think about the million different MOTs in your store, your self-owned enterprise, or your place of business. It's exciting to think about all the things that your customers may experience when they visit your website, call you on the phone, drive into the parking lot, walk through your door, peruse your products, and encounter a member of the staff. For every one of those MOTs, there is an opportunity to shine, to deliver on your promises and knock your customers' socks off. When customers and prospects come into contact with your firm *in any way*, it's as they say in show business: "The curtain is up."

Your company's brand promise, customer care performance, and delivery of services/products are on display and squarely in the customers' sights every moment, every day you are open for business. Your marketing slogan, advertising jingle, and slick website are also on display as to their authenticity in the eyes of your customers and they judge the validity of all that by what they *actually* experience.

For that, I like to say: it's "Show time!"

In a stage production, the performers on center stage usually get all the attention. But without the director, stagehands, set-piece artists, musicians, and the many backstage team members, the performance itself would not be possible.

In terms of your business, it's the same principle: All of your frontline team members and products— everything your customer sees, smells, tastes, touches, hears, and experiences—are on your "center stage." But your "backstage" support teams and executives are part of the total performance too. These two components need to work in sync in order to pull off a winning performance that can sustain a long run on Broadway, so to speak. Everyone owns the MOTs!

*"It's the stage thing, that rush moment that
you live for . . . To be a good live performer,
you have to be instinctive." —Bruce Springsteen*

Like "The Boss" suggests here, you and your team members should feel that rush of being on stage, representing your business—excitement, enthusiasm, and the belief that whatever you are selling and providing is the best thing going among your competition. And to properly create and manage your customers' experiences, being instinctive and understanding your buying public's tendencies, wants, needs, goals, and buying habits is also extremely important.

Please don't sell MOTs short; they are not just a concept, they are real. Test this in your own life. Take one day and notice all the little MOTs you have when shopping, traveling, or interacting with others. What kinds of impressions were created with each one? You'll be amazed.

Missed opportunities don't often get second chances

It's useful to look at lessons through stories. Let's examine three short vignettes from my travels to see how MOTs were missed and how they could have been turned into positives. These sketches, while about hotels, could apply to any industry. Approach these sketches with your own business in mind.

You want change? Not here, sir!

I placed a twenty-dollar bill on top of the front desk at a major brand hotel and asked the front desk agent if she would please break the bill for me. I needed smaller bills for tipping, etc.

"Sorry," she said blandly without sounding apologetic. "They don't give me a bank out here." I must have looked a bit perplexed as she added, "You see that Starbucks over there, across the lobby? They'll make change for you." She pointed over my shoulder in the direction of the other side of the lobby. I turned to look where she was sending me.

It was morning. We all know what the line at a Starbucks looks like in the morning. Forget that. I was heading out the door to grab a cab to make an appointment on time.

This agent couldn't have gotten rid of me any faster. Obviously I was neither her problem nor her concern. Her words were very clipped, as if I had put her out by daring to ask for change of a twenty-dollar bill. I was swatted away from the desk like a mosquito.

The little MOT opportunity to show this guest a modicum of hospitality was pulverized. Most hotel front desks have banks, though this lady said she didn't have one for some reason. Her response thus sounded strange to my ears, especially as I had trained as a front desk agent as part of my management program during my early hotel days. We had banks full of money at each station behind the desk. It was *de rigueur* to have change available for people. It was part of our hospitality ethos. So, why not at this hotel?

Was it possible this staffer really was the only one who didn't have a bank? Could she have taken a few seconds to give my bill to another agent standing next to her who could have made change for me? No extra effort was expended there.

Another poor MOT was in her use of the word "they." Who were *they*? Her hotel's management? If so, I blame the hotel. I can't blame this lady for not having a bank. But I scored it a fail for her brusque nature and poor suggestion of sending me across the lobby to the long Starbucks line, thereby making my twenty-dollar bill someone else's problem.

Let's add a note for your own MOT file: When you are responding to a customer, it is very bad form, extremely discourteous, and also cringeworthy to lay blame on fellow departments or other people in your company for the lack of something.

"Limited service" is a hotel category
—it shouldn't be a customer service approach

It's off to another city, another major brand hotel with glitzy slogans and an appealing business class website. More opportunities for positive MOTs, right? But the reality just didn't measure up to the hype. Upon checking in at the front desk, I noticed the adjacent pantry had five finely polished wood shelves which are typically stocked with candies, snacks, toiletries, and comfort food items that guests want or need to purchase during their stay.

"Old Mother Hubbard" would be sad to find that this cupboard was virtually bare. I counted four mini single-serve bags of potato chips, twelve mini-boxes of detergent, eight aspirin packages, and three Slim Jim snack sticks in a box that was lying on its side. There was lots of open space on those five shelves. A sadder display I'd never seen in a hotel. This initial MOT was a big fat negative. I thought: "What else are they lacking here?"

I asked the front desk agent about getting some cookies or a snack other than potato chips. He shrugged and said to me quite matter-of-factly, "Oh yeah. They (there is that "they" again—must be the Gremlins!) usually just stock us once a month, and nobody has been able to go to Target in a while."

So, the hotel stocks its own pantry with items from the neighboring Target. Then it's a hotel fail, not the snack food vendor's fault.

So I asked, "Oh? Where is Target?"

"Right across the street," he replied. *Thud.*

He kept his head down looking at whatever papers he was shuffling behind the desk. He couldn't have cared less about suggesting alternatives for me. Was this agent, or even the hotel itself, tone deaf about the ravaged condition of their so-called "hotel amenity" pantry?

Here is an important bit of perspective. This was a busy corporate travel hotel in a business section of town, running over 80 percent in nightly occupancy during the week. The management of that hotel was well aware of their forecasted business levels, so this shortage could not—should not— have caught anyone by surprise. When doing that much business, wouldn't it be safe to assume that your pantry supplies would be in higher demand, and that you should be making more frequent runs to Target than just once per month?

One would think.

Another failed MOT for me was the reality that many hotel employees were working right next to that pantry all day and all night, and nobody thought to look or even care that the cupboard was almost bare? Secondly, nobody stepped out of the mediocrity to take the initiative to spruce it up by getting into the hotel's shuttle van and driving across the street to replenish the supplies? Third, where was the general manager in this farce? Were they totally oblivious to the depleted pantry, located right out in front of his or her lobby?

Fail, fail, fail; so many potentially wonderful MOTs blown by what? Apathy, ignorance, laziness, not paying attention, lack of hospitality? Likely it was all of the above.

Relaxing poolside: it's for the birds!

While on another speaking trip, I meandered down to the pool patio after my session to join my clients for a reception. One of the hotel lobby attendants came out to the pool deck where we were networking. She saw that none of us were sitting at any of the poolside tables, as they had been liberally used as target practice by the local winged air squadrons. The metal pool furniture was encrusted with their droppings. She tried wiping a table and chair off with a rag and a spray bottle for a couple of minutes, to no avail. The bird poop had fossilized onto the furniture.

The attendant turned to us, put up her hands, and said forthrightly, "So sorry folks. I don't think anyone has wiped these off since I did them six months ago." And she turned and went back into the hotel lobby.

I'm not heartless. I'll give this employee an "A" for being aware of the situation and for giving it "the old college try." That was a positive MOT to be sure. However, her comment about nobody cleaning that furniture since she last touched it six months prior was more than we needed to know, and certainly more than enough for me to deduct that the hotel was lax on its inspections and cleanliness. It also meant that the managers in charge of the pool area had not cared or noticed enough to do anything about it for at least six months.

This illustrates that one simple "Bozo-ism" comment can lead to many doubts in the minds of customers, and that's not what you want them to be thinking.

As you apply the components of these sketches to your own business, where do you see the opportunities lie for you to avoid the same types of mistakes? Where is your birdie do-do that needs cleaning? How can you improve upon the woeful examples above to ensure that you create positive MOTs instead of what transpired?

As the saying goes: *It's all in the details.*

Building Your Playbook:

- *To prepare for a deep-dive Moments of Truth inspection of your team or organization, do you have customer feedback that you can review that would be helpful in identifying what they think is most important—their MOT?*
- *Can you engage help from the outside such as "mystery shoppers" to give you scouting reports from their experiences with your company for additional due diligence?*
- *What experiences can you recall as a customer when a particular MOT or number of MOTs influenced your own buying decisions or satisfaction (or dissatisfaction) of a product or service? What were they?*

Chapter 33

Harvesting Your Moments of Truth
Will Make Your Organization Stronger

"Most everything that you want is just outside
your comfort zone." — Robert G. Allen

We're about to create a powerful new energy in this chapter that will make your organization better. No question about it. We're going to get your team members out of their comfort zones for the better. We're going to improve your customers' perception of your business. And we're going to increase your sales. That's where the real gold lies.

How will this be accomplished? We'll work on building upon the lessons of the previous chapter to help you get your Moments of Truth (MOTs) initiative up and running. In automobile parlance, we're going to lift up the hood and inspect the moving parts of the "engine" that makes up your company's customer touchpoints. Then we're going to perform a comprehensive tune-up to get the engine in tip-top shape.

Let's get started!

Part One: The Components

The Overall Mission: Your ultimate "MOT Mission" is to identify as many opportunities for memorable, positive impressions as possible so that more customers and prospects enjoy doing business with you. This initiative can unquestionably lead to a harvest of new sales and increased customer retention for your business. It will also help make your firm *easier to do business with*. That's the sweet spot.

The Scope: Every department or business unit of your organization should be involved in this, as no team is an island unto itself. This initiative will also benefit internally, too. It helps tear down silos among your various business units, which improves communication, teamwork and synergy.

Selling Change: Getting out of those comfort zones requires *change*, a word that excites some people, while striking fear into the hearts of others. How this is managed will determine the outcome. When organizations grow and stretch their wings to fly a little higher, it causes a degree of stress and anxiety with some people. Get your executive team to visibly support this by getting involved. You can't get results with this by just writing a flurry of top-down memos. Everyone should roll up their sleeves and pitch in.

Tough Love: To do this earnestly, you and your team will also have to make some tough decisions about throwing out or reengineering clunky, outdated, or unsatisfactory MOTs. Put the work into designing and introducing new (better) wrinkles and procedures where applicable. It may be necessary to move some people around, too. By redeploying your team members where they can do the most good, you will be managing the process with a greater chance for success. You'll likely get some pushback, so constant communication, training, and practicing will really help.

A rising tide lifts all boats—or does it?

This is not a static program. In fact, it's arguably not really a program at all. It should be a culture, a way of doing business, a company-wide breath of fresh air. Once everyone is focused on managing and improving their MOTs as individuals and teams, the organization will begin to improve and lift its customer experiences. Some refer to this as "A rising tide lifts all boats."

But I don't buy that old bumper sticker.

Here's why: A rising tide can only lift boats that are seaworthy and waterproof. If a boat is full of holes, no tide can magically lift it up from the bottom. Applied to this topic, teams that don't plan and manage their MOTs properly and don't make enough positive impressions will not necessarily be lifted when other departments lift their games. They will wallow in the surf, leaking water, and dragging other components of the business down, too. Customers don't like service inconsistences between business units. Thus, you'll need *all* of your boats to be water-worthy. Invest in the upskilling that helps make that happen.

Realistically, you'll likely need to sell the idea of a MOT initiative to your ownership or leadership, if that's not you. It's a very worthwhile spend of time and resources, so let's take a few moments here to assess this in terms of the cost vs. the benefits. Let's start with the over-arching goal *to improve service, sales and retention.* What organization wouldn't want that?

Part Two: Getting your Team
On Board with the idea of Cost vs. Benefit

"Everything in life is cost-benefit."
—Ray Schmidgall, Ph.D., CPA

As a hospitality business student at Michigan State, I had an 8 a.m. winter term class - in accounting and finance, no less. No cold-climate college student ever forgets their classes in that icy time slot. It's a true badge of honor that we earned by getting up early before dawn and trudging across the frozen tundra of our campus, with frigid temperatures entrenched in the 20s or worse. Yes, I suppose we all said that we walked two miles uphill both ways in the snow just to earn our degree.

As I settled into my seat in the auditorium, the central heating began to kick in. The feeling was slowly starting to return to my feet, face, and ears just as our professor, Dr. Ray Schmidgall, walked to the front of the class. He introduced himself to us with a warm greeting, looked over his new crop of thawing, semi-awake students, and he proclaimed a tenet that I can still hear him saying to this day:

"Everything in life is cost-benefit."

He paused to let that settle in. Boom! I didn't realize that morning how profound Dr. Schmidgall's words would prove to be, or how often I would refer to that phrase in my post-college business life. That one statement made a meaningful impact on me primarily because the idea of it goes way beyond the classroom. It drives most everything we do, every day. Cost vs. benefit. It isn't just for accounting folks. Do you want that big piece of cake? Cost-benefit. Do you want that more expensive car? Cost-benefit. Do you want to take that job over the other one? Cost-benefit. That single sentence remains the longest-lasting lesson from my college days. It will never be obsolete.

And it works perfectly as part of our quest to identify and improve your organization's MOTs.

Once your ownership/leadership has bought into the

value of MOTs, you may also need this equation to "sell" the entire initiative to your team members or front-line staffers. After all, they have the most customer-facing contact. If they don't buy into this, it won't work.

You also can use cost-benefit to apportion your resources—time, people, money, and energies—in relation to the benefits you will reap. Express the long-term value of what improved MOTs will bring to the company in the way of your original goal (improved customer satisfaction, repeat sales, and retention) and how putting in the heavy-lifting initially will help create sustainable benefits moving forward.

Keep in mind that some of your benefits of this program may be "soft" or subjective, rather than objective, such as public relations, general feel-good aspects by customers, and increased internal morale/camaraderie among your business units. Just in case the cost analyst asks.

Part Three: Charting the Actual MOTs in Your Customers' Experiences

Account for your customers' senses
—they determine quite a bit

Before we actually chart the MOTs, it's important to know that such moments are strongly influenced by our senses. It's the whole ballgame, really. Our brains are doing calculations by the millisecond to determine whether we find something pleasing or displeasing, and which ones trigger our flow, fight, or flee instinct. *Study.com* reported that "Human eyes can analyze approximately 36,000 pieces of information in an hour."

In analyzing various data sources for this chapter, I found that while there were minor variances in the ranking order of touch, smell, and taste, the overwhelming top two of sight and hearing far outpaced the other senses in terms of how people gain impressions. This ranking represents the percentage of impressions that each sense contributes to our brain:

Sight (83%)
Hearing (11%)
Touch (3%)
Smell (1.5 %)
Taste (1.5 %)

This ranking is intended as a general guideline, not a scientific or medical absolute. Remember, as you discuss your sensory points surrounding your business, it's a case of *different strokes for different folks.*

"Those moments that don't defeat us, define us, because the comeback is always greater than the setback . . . and if it doesn't challenge us, it won't change us." —Erik Qualman

Our next criteria when analyzing our MOTs in this chart is how well we engineer comebacks, the things we do to retain a customer when things go wonky. Many organizations refer to this as *customer recovery*, because you are trying to recover an at-risk customer who may be leaving you or has already left. It's a big MOT!

We've all had setbacks with customers, and how we react, recover, and fix the problem for them will affect their decision about doing future business with us, or whether they slaughter our company on social media - a reality of our times. Your comebacks and customer recovery need to be *outstanding*.

One size does NOT fit all

As we head into the actual charting of our MOTs, it's also very important to remember that one size does not fit all. Rarely will two customers see things exactly the same way, every time. Remember the point about sensory signals. What one customer likes to see, another may not. What one customer finds fault with, another will let it roll off their back. You can never be absolutely sure. My personal credo in most situations is to try and do *the best for the most*. After all, it was Abraham Lincoln who said we can never please all of the people all the time.

Guidelines for team discussions using the MOT circle diagram

CHARTING OUR
MOMENTS OF TRUTH

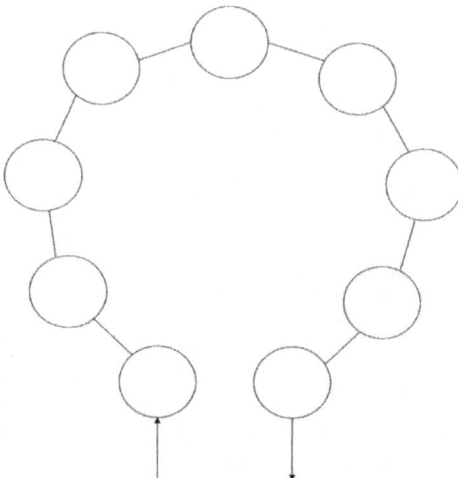

I've modeled this section after how I typically administer the MOT coaching in my workshops. To start, divide your participants into teams representing your different business units or departments. I've found that it is best to have people work on their particular section together. As a second step, I integrate their respective alliance partners.

The series of connected circles in the illustration simulates the journey of your customer with your team or organization, from start to finish, touchpoint by touchpoint. Briefly describe the interactions/transactions that take place at each circle, including what happens or what they see, hear, touch, feel, taste, or smell. Feel free to add additional circles as needed—there are no limits on those.

A typical starting point is "our customer goes onto our website" or "our customer calls us," or "a potential customer walks in our front door," etc.

Remember the 4 P's (People, Procedures/Policies, Products, and Prices)? They each play a big role in the many MOTs that your customers experience. These important touchpoints should also be part of the examination by your various teams.

Instruct your teams to discuss what they have charted on the circle(s). Are there any surprises? Any glaring deficiencies or calls for change? Anything currently lacking? What could be improved upon? What are our most immediate and also longer-term opportunities?

Begin the design phase: Decide on the most pressing priorities to begin with. Then have the teams craft their plans on improving or creating their new MOTs. This is where you can sense the "rising tide" and whether or not it is lifting all the boats.

Here are some important questions to help your team discussions:

What is our definition of success vs. our customers' definition?
Can we twist the familiar past competition with our MOTs?
Who will manage this initiative (accountability)?
What resources will we need to accomplish these plans?
What is the deadline for implementation of the new MOTs?
How will we sustain our MOT mission once it's up and running?

Part Four: It all Ties Back to Sales!

You're doing great! We're heading into the home stretch here, and that brings us to the very thing that keeps business folks up at night, the very lifeblood of our viability—SALES!

The sales department may not be your entire organization, but your entire organization is in sales

While I strongly embrace the idea that everyone in an organization *should* be a salesperson in some capacity, the cruel truth is that for many organizations it just isn't so. It takes talent, effort, and the right attitude to think and act as a salesperson. It takes empowerment and product knowledge. It takes initiative. *It's a way of operating, not a position or a title.* Developing people who have at least some sales in their DNA takes serious training and support, not just a snap of the fingers by ownership.

Identify your enablers and inhibitors

To be successful in your new MOT commitments, you are going to need plenty of internal salespeople and *enablers*, not *inhibitors*. The former helps make things run smoothly; the latter holds progress and fluidity back. Your enablers and inhibitors come in the form of your Four P's, which I mentioned in a bullet point above. Some are people-generated MOTs and others are inanimate MOTs, such as a clunky computer system or a faulty oven. Make sure you identify them accurately.

In the final analysis, it's not too bold to say that Moments of Truth can make or break your business. So challenge yourselves and your team(s) to change things for the better. Set your egos aside and admit you can do better. The more we're challenged and tested, the more we'll change. And that's a cost-benefit equation if there ever was one. I'll bet that Professor Schmidgall would give that an enthusiastic A+.

Building Your Playbook:

- *Is there a culture of "everyone is a salesperson" in your organization or on your team? If so, how is it working? If not, what is getting in the way?*
- *When can you set up your MOT exercise to begin the process?*
- *If you are the owner or chief executive of your organization, you hold the key for getting the process going. If not, how will you position this to sell it to your bosses?*
- *What intervals for the "oil changes" and check-ups will you build into this program so that it sustains and doesn't slip through the cracks over time? Evaluate the results, adjust where needed, and select another review date so it becomes a fabric of your culture.*

Chapter 34

Welcome to "Hotel Nightmare"

"Adversity introduces us to ourselves." —Duffy Daugherty

Businesses everywhere should work to excel at what they do, keep their brand promises to their customers, and not serve their customers doses of adversity for them to overcome. Staying in a hotel shouldn't be an exercise in survival.

If you've ever traveled, then it's likely that a comedy-tragedy like this one (or at least parts of it) has happened to you. Use this episode as a way to relate to your own business or industry, and how you might prevent such a series of "fails" from happening to your own customers.

When things go bad, they roll downhill fast

A business colleague of mine, Richard Rue, an executive recruiter in the high tech industry, made his way down the California coast to attend a business conference. He wanted to pace himself and take the weekend to relax in a coastal town halfway to the event. He was unknowingly headed to what he refers to now as "Hotel Nightmare," a brand-name hotel for a weekend. He made his reservation through Hotels.com, a popular online hotel booking resource.

As many travelers and hospitality veterans know, when things start to go bad in a hotel, they usually snowball and roll downhill at breakneck speed. Hang on to your roller bag.

When Rue got to his room, he flicked on the lights. The set of lights mounted over the bed blinked incessantly, like strobe lights. He turned them on and off again a few times. They kept blinking. He didn't recall booking the disco suite.

He tried to call the front desk, but the phone didn't work. It had no dial tone. He kept pressing "0" and nothing happened. He put the phone back on its base, thinking it might recharge. Nothing happened.

Almost ten minutes into his stay, he began questioning his hotel choice.

Rue decided to try the TV since there was a basketball game he wanted to watch. He turned it on and it went straight to the default movie promo channel, as usual. He held the TV remote and pressed "channel up." Nothing. Then he tried "channel down." Nope. How about the "last channel" button? Strike three.

Rather than jump out the window, he decided to calm his blood pressure by taking a nice, hot, relaxing shower. The only problem was—you guessed it—no hot water, just a spray as cold as Yosemite Falls.

After drying off and throwing on his workout clothes, he made his way to the front desk, totally frustrated and trying to maintain his composure. After all, his phone didn't work so he had to do his communicating with the hotel staff in person.

Describing his sorry excuse for a room in detail to the front desk agent, she curtly informed him that the hotel could not move him to a new guest room, as it was going to sell out that evening. After some haggling, she agreed to send an engineer up to his room to "fix everything," as she put it. Sure.

No one will confuse this hotel engineer with MacGyver

Back in his room of horrors, Rue awaited help. It arrived in the person of the hotel engineer. Taking the TV on first for a contest of wills, he grabbed the remote and went to town. Try as he might by wickedly waving and thrusting the remote in the direction of the screen like a fencer, he also could not coax the TV to change channels.

The frustrated engineer mumbled something under his breath and then pulled the TV and its dresser away from the wall. He climbed behind it and amazingly got the channels to change by waving the remote at something on the back of the TV. He told Rue that as the guest he would have to change the TV channels that way during his stay. Huh?

How convenient: Get out of bed, go behind the TV, point the remote at something on the back of the console and guess which channel you are flipping to, only you can't see the screen from behind so you return to bed. If it's not the channel you want, go back and do it again. Wash, rinse, repeat. We're talking real luxury here on the California coast, folks.

And what became of the dead phone? As the intrepid engineer discovered through his MacGyver-like prowess, the cord that connected the phone to the wall jack was missing. The entire cord was gone. Well, that accounts for the lack of a dial tone. Maybe the previous guest needed a phone cord at home. And that explains that. No replacement cord was discussed.

The blinking lights over the bed were a non-starter, too. "You'll have to just leave them off, I guess," the engineer suggested. For some reason, he never got to the hot water issue. By now, Rue didn't know whether he would burst out laughing or blow an artery. It even crossed his mind that the room might very well be haunted.

You want hospitality? Not here!

Surely, the many fails in this room go above and beyond what a paying guest should have to endure from a business that lists itself in the category of "deluxe hospitality." Rue didn't anticipate that along with his room rate, the hotel would provide a hundred pounds of adversity for no extra charge.

With few options available to him short of repacking, checking out, getting back in his car, and heading down the highway in the middle of the night, Rue ventured down to the front desk again to discuss realities. He asked for a discounted rate for that night and to be set up for a move to a different room the next day, as inconvenient as that always is.

The response he got at the front desk was so awful, it suspends reality. It might just be the worst response I've ever heard given to a hotel guest, anywhere: "You'll have to take it up with Hotels.com."

Thud.

Rue couldn't believe his ears. The front desk agent went on, sounding like she blamed him for doing something wrong: "You booked through Hotels.com. You'll have to go back to them. We can't do anything else for you." He reports that her tone was anything but sympathetic, either.

What a cop-out. What a lack of empathy. What cruddy service.

So let's get this straight. Rue was put into a real doozy of a loser room, and the hotel rep claimed that they were handcuffed from trying to make things right for him just because he used an online booking site? He was more than a bit peeved at this response.

He left the hotel the next morning, one day early, after relating his torture to a supervisor at the front desk who told him they "would tell the general manager and they will get back to you."

Rue never heard a thing.

This hotel's shoddy performance and lack of empathy simmered in Rue's brain and boiled over after his trip. He told me he had no choice but to write about this experience honestly on a social media review site. "I gave the hotel every chance to fix this right then and there, and they blew it," he said. "Other guests should be made aware of it. I hope they'll take a lesson from this."

"Success does not consist in never making mistakes,
but in never making the same one a second time."
— George Bernard Shaw

So let's take our own lessons from this episode and compress the pain points into coaching moments:

• There was no real apology, empathy, or understanding from the hotel team. Can it be that the employees actually thought that their responses were acceptable, such as the front desk agent "haggling" with Rue before she agreed to send an engineer up to his room? Take a deep breath, stay calm, and take ownership of it. Apologize and inform those who need to know in order to fix it. Assure the customer that you're working on a solution. Follow up with them on the progress so as not to leave them in the dark.
• It's on management for the lack of training of their team

members, especially in the areas of proper responses to guests, showing empathy, accepting responsibility, and applying problem-solving. *Mind Tools* say that "Saying 'sorry' takes courage, but it's far better to come clean than to hide your error or, worse, to blame others for it. In the long run, people will remember your courage and integrity long after they've forgotten the original mistake."

• The hotel shuffled off its accountability for delivering an unacceptable room product on an inanimate internet resource located thousands of miles away. And considering the time of this crisis— late at night—the last thing a guest wants (or should get) from a staffer is a scolding on what they should have done differently weeks ago. That didn't help one bit. After all, Hotels.com didn't plant all those screw-ups in Rue's room.

• It tells us a lot about the culture of the hotel and its management to think it is OK to pass off a room with that many flaws to an unsuspecting guest, and charge them the full rate for it. Then hope the next guest doesn't notice those things, either?!

• Housekeeping gets a fail here. Their checklist program apparently doesn't have any teeth in it. Lights, TV, phone, and hot water were all fails. And none of those things went out of order magically in the time between when the housekeeper left the room and Rue checked in. If that's as careful as they inspect their rooms, I wouldn't dare looking under the bed or under the toilet seat. Shabby, careless quality control—*and at full price?*

• A lack of response by the general manager, as was promised. This was a classic case of *over-promising and under-delivering*, plus a glaring lack of "the buck stops here" type of accountability/ownership of the issues by the top executive in the building. Shabby. It seems as if the GM was afraid to contact Rue. It left an awful taste in Rue's mouth that he was either forgotten or avoided.

*"Those who cannot remember the past
are condemned to repeat it"* — *George Santayana*

When you have a breakdown in service or product delivery, don't waste the moment. Learn from it for the future. Of course, put out the immediate "fire" and take care of the situation for your customer, then step back later and evaluate what happened. Take the flub as an opportunity to leverage the mistake into a catalyst for "looking under your hood," examining the elements of the breakdown, and making adjustments so those things don't reoccur.

No matter your business, here are five solid, time-tested tools for your tool kit that I have employed in work situations and often include in my management coaching curriculum:

1) **Listen to your customers**: They first want to be heard. Don't interrupt, deflect, make excuses, or argue. Respond quickly to things gone wrong. Customers want to know someone is listening to them. *Explain,* don't lecture.

2) **Tighten up your internal quality controls**: Put the extra effort into ensuring things work as you promised in the first place, just like you advertised in your marketing materials, your website, and the like. Your customers deserve something that isn't broken. After all, you're charging them enough for it.

3) **Have a customer recovery program in place and give it some teeth**: Ensure that your people involved in guest re-

covery have the ability and authority to fix things for your customers—on the spot, quickly, properly, and completely.

4) **Have your staff practice empathy and understanding toward your customers**: After all, they pay the bills. The Golden Rule works well here.

5) **Own the problem**: Accountability is a virtue. Fix the problem. Don't pawn it off on another person, unless it is someone whose job it is to pick up the ball and handle it. Make sure to follow it through for the customer. When you fix a customer's problem satisfactorily and efficiently, 95 percent of them will do business with you again.

Building Your Playbook:

- *How do these incidents relate to your own business?*
- *Do you have a customer care or recovery program? Is it working? If not, can you improve it?*
- *If you don't have a customer care program, can you create one (or help to create one)?*
- *Do you have a training program and management oversight check-and-balance tools that help improve your business model so that your customers don't have the same type of experiences?*
- *What are the three most critical customer care areas you want to focus on most urgently?*
- *Do you coach your frontline staff on their conversation and response skills with customers?*
- *What do you offer your customers when your business promises fail like the hotel's did?*

Chapter 35

Good Questions Unlock Many Doors

"The important thing is to never stop questioning."
—Albert Einstein

Young children love to ask "Why?" According to Emily Connor, writing in BGD Media's *Scary Mommy*, "As a child grows up, they realize that there are so many wonderful things around them, and thus these questions are a way of finding out more about the world they inhabit. For a little child who is still coming to terms with the world, everything is overwhelming—hence the need to know..."

Thus, parents would do well to keep cartons of patience around the house for answering all those questions.

But then something happens when we grow up. Instead of asking "why" when we want to discover something as adults, some people just assume or remain quiet. Are they too embarrassed to ask, or do they want to appear to be too smart for questions? Don't let your hubris get in your way. Although we're not children anymore, the reason for asking questions remains the same—it's still how we learn, even if many of our questions start like this: "OK Google, why or how . . ."

To me, it's never dumb to ask questions. It's the smart people who ask questions. The dumb thing is to want to know something but not ask the question. Some folks just walk away wondering what the answer is and they're no better off, are they? They are shrouded in ignorance on the matter. That's not a good thing. I repeatedly encourage questions, but I can't force them.

> *"It's better to go slowly in the right direction than go speeding off in the wrong direction."* —Simon Sinek

I believe that it's best to ask questions when the answer isn't clear or I want to learn. It drives my sons crazy when we go to a restaurant and I dare to ask our server a question about one of the entrees. For some reason it's embarrassing to them that I ask questions. I smile when the server responds with something like, "That's a great question. It's got a topping on it that lots of people don't ask about and they find it too spicy. It's better to ask about it before you order it."

Aha!

And about the importance of questioning and asking why, Simon Sinek has another great take: "In the business world, properly and successfully defining your 'why' cannot be an afterthought. It must be your forethought's forethought. It is an important element when defining your business."

It sure is! When I am helping my clients define their businesses, their culture, and their goals, I try to ask compelling questions that help bring forth invaluable insights and revealing information. The best questions act as springboards to meaningful—and sometimes difficult—conversations.

Sometimes I'll suggest to a company that we should ask questions of their customers, such as an advisory group or board, for feedback on different aspects of their business such as customer service, value, and ROI. Those exercises can be quite revealing and helpful, and they go a long way in building relationships. Customers love to be asked and will "tell it like it is," plus feel an affinity with the organization in that they cared enough to ask for their opinions.

But there are two very important things about asking questions in a customer advisory exercise. First, the company should NEVER do it themselves; always use an outside facilitator. Company reps can and will start to make defensive comments or "explain off" problems that get identified. I've seen it happen and it's not good. Customers will shut down if they think that the company is just going to make a bunch of excuses and not listen or take criticism.

Secondly, I tell my clients straight-up before we roll this project out: "Don't ask the questions if you don't want to hear the answers." Let's face it – especially when you ask customers about your business—not all the answers you get will be laced with roses and perfume. You'll hear some thorny complaints, too. Keep an open mind and check your egos at the door.

Questions—and answers—help build strong foundations

Why a chapter on questions? For one, no one knows it all. Questions get people thinking, discussing, and exchanging ideas and thoughts. Author Jack Canfield (the *Chicken Soup* books) told a group of us on an authors' webinar, "What separates a winner in life from everyone else is that they are willing to invest in something such as learning . . . We're not born knowing everything."

Thus, we ask questions.

So let's get airborne with sets of helpful questions you can use in various situations. I have utilized these at one time or another in various coaching programs and keynotes.

They can really unlock doors for sales, executive leadership, front-line teams, supervisors, etc. They have been helpful in moving people and teams forward, improving organizational culture, and uncovering opportunities. I'm betting that you and your organization will find them valuable, too.

Four pillar questions

These first four pillar questions (I introduced them in an earlier chapter) have proven to be terrific early-planning queries for executives/leaders/sales teams. They work for any level of an organization, too, from C-level to individual frontline business units. Not only do they uncover vital information, but they can also expose unforeseen issues and some real "rabbit holes" where people and teams can easily get lost. They lead to some fantastic brainstorming conversations that create actionable plans and re-directs:

Where are we now?
How did we get here?
Where are we going?
How will we get there?

Undestanding our customers

The next set of questions work well for sales applications. These enable us to find out how much your team understands their business, their customers' loyalty, and what areas they need to improve upon to increase customer retention. They also allow us to challenge assumptions:

Why do customers come to you?
Why do customers stay with you?
Why do customers leave you?

Accountability starts with me

When developing personal action plans and making strong statements of accountability, this following duo does the trick—and quickly, too! They are pretty stark—stopping and starting something, just like that. Please note that each question has three distinct applications:

To make you/the team/the organization better,
you would start _____?

To make you/the team/the organization better,
you would stop _____?

Gap selling

Understanding what your competition is all about is a key requirement for topnotch sales professionals and business owners. I developed this next set of questions to represent a simple yet effective way to analyze one's own competition. The better we know our competitors, the better we can sell against them and take advantage of their vulnerabilities. It is imperative for salespeople to know and understand the differences between *us* and *them*—what I refer to as the "gaps."

This "gap selling" exercise presents incisive questions that allow us to stack our services, people, procedures, and products up against our competitors, toe to toe. We examine the gaps between our company and the competitors, and how we can either close those gaps if we are behind, or widen the gaps if we are ahead of them in certain areas. I've also designed a fun exercise on competition analysis that is very interactive. Here is how it works:

We split the sales team into groups of two or three and have them analyze a competitor. Each team then presents their findings and recommendations of how to sell against that competitor. The learning curve on competition really soars with this exercise. Here are the questions to help you determine your all-important *competitive selling advantages*:

What do we have that they don't have?
What do they have that we don't have?
What do we do better than they do?
What do they do better than we do?
What are the customers' perceptions of these differences?

When you ask questions, you get information. When you get information, you are no longer making decisions in a vacuum. Remember: decisions made in a vacuum suck!

Building Your Playbook:

- *Are there other questions you can think of that could help reveal areas for development and improvement across your organization?*
- *What additional types of questions would you like to ask of your customers, and how would you roll that out?*
- *In which applications could you use these sets of questions in your business: executive retreats, group training workshops, one-on-one coaching, etc.?*

Chapter 36

Cleanup in Theater Six
—Will Someone Take Charge, Please!

"A person always doing his or her best becomes a natural leader, just by example." —Joe DiMaggio

From my perspective, whether someone moves mountains or they move packing crates for a living, I admire them if they try to their job to the fullest of their given ability and commitment to excellence. That in itself qualifies as a type of natural leadership, just as the great "Joltin' Joe" stated above. You don't have to have a lofty title in order to show leadership. As this episode will bring to light, leadership isn't a title, it's a behavior. And I saw this premise play out in my local movie theater. Let's see how this story might translate to you or the people in your organization.

It's likely happened to you. Somewhere, at some point, you've just needed to find a leader who will take action while others stand around doing nothing. I don't mean needing the kind of leader on par with Mount Rushmore or a C-level corporate executive, just someone who will take the bull by the horns. I'm talking about regular, everyday people who can step out of the crowd and make a leadership decision when it's called for, without wasting time, and without having to consult a stupid manual.

I wanted to enjoy a relaxing night out at the movie theater with my wife. But shift happens. We needed a take-charge person. On this particular night, I needed to find some of that leadership mojo in our local movie theater.

My wife and I were among a dozen or so people who were admitted into theater six at our local multiplex about twenty minutes before show time. It looked like a cyclone had hit it and the cleaning team had bypassed it. This was clearly an "oops" as this theater was normally pretty clean. There was a huge XXXL popcorn tub overturned on the stairs leading to the seats with what seemed like five pounds of popcorn that a patron had spilled and just left there. It had "slip and fall" written all over it, at least to me.

I gave our fellow theatergoers a minute to see if anyone would break out of the pack and go alert the theater staff of the needed cleanup. I turned on my heels and told my wife that I'd be right back. She shrugged. She knows me. She knew where I was heading. I wasn't going to just sit in my seat and start "wishing and hoping" that another patron would take the bull by the horns. You know the saying: "If you want something done . . ."

I went out into the hallway in search of uniformed staffers to make them aware of the situation and to ask them to clean our theater for us, and quickly, too—it was almost show time.

I saw three young men in theater uniforms walking down the hall in the other direction with brooms and dust-pans. It appeared that they were on their way to clean another theater and were oblivious to our poor theater six.

"Excuse me guys," I said. "We need a little help here, please." I explained what was going on with theater six. I also took quick stock of who I had in front of me. For the purpose of this story, let's call them "The Rules Follower," "The Fence Post" and "The Thinker."

The Rules Follower immediately went for the folded

sheet of paper in his pocket. I could see a movie schedule on it. "Well," he said slowly, "we're supposed to go in order." His long look at his paper schedule told me that he probably thought that would end the conversation and that I would go away.

The Fence Post apparently wanted nothing to do with this conversation. He stood there and offered nothing in the way of body language or verbalization. He wasn't rude or impolite, just quiet—as a fence post. His eyes were riveted at The Rules Follower as if to say, "You've got the paper, buddy, I'm just here to follow it like we were told to do."

The taller fellow, The Thinker, was, well, *thinking!* He was looking at me, making eye contact, listening to me, and I could sense his mental gears grinding inside his head. I was thinking that we may have a glimmer of hope here.

Time was of the essence if my fellow moviegoers and I had any prayer of enjoying our movie experience in a cleaned theater *on time*. I knew it would be hard to clean the theater with people already seated.

"Look, guys," I implored them in a kindly manner. "Can you please help us out here, or at least just call a supervisor and make them aware of the situation?" One of them had a walkie-talkie. "People are streaming into the theater as we speak," I added, "and it's a mess in there. It is not ready for prime time, guys."

The Rules Follower went to his pocket again, waving the paper and repeating lazily, "We're supposed to go in order." It almost sounded like a question.

On-the-spot leadership—a thing of beauty when it happens

There was silence in the circle for another five seconds,

nobody moving. Then all of a sudden, quite assertively, The Thinker's light bulb went off and he blurted out, "OK, you guys go into nine and I'll go with him to six, and then come over and join me as soon as you can." It wasn't a question. He took charge, even though I don't think he outranked the other two staffers.

I enthusiastically said to him, "Now *you're* someone who's cut out to be a manager. Thank you!" I think I startled him with that. I'm not sure he knew it was intended to be a compliment.

The Rules Follower and The Fence Post just stood there, looking at him.

Without waiting to take a vote, this young man turned to go into theater six with me. The other two then turned to go in the other direction, probably glad to be rid of this dilemma. Within five minutes, other theater staffers showed up and worked like busy bees to make theater six respectable again. The Thinker had used his walkie-talkie to call for additional reinforcements.

This tiny little moment left absolutely no doubt in my mind which of those staffers I would hire for my own team. As he left the theater, I thanked him again and told him that he's the kind of guy that if we ever had to go to war, I'd want in my unit because he could make a decision. He nodded, smiled at me, and said, "Thank you, sir." I also made his theater manager aware of his take-charge attitude.

Leaders can evolve when "Shift Happens"—find yours!

We all know that shift happens. And when it does, it can reveal a leader, and it can also reveal others' true colors, too. Shift happened when the ticket-taker inadvertently let us into a messy theater. OK, it wasn't supposed to happen. But it did. Now what do you do?

It's likely that your business or organization faces dilemmas like this every day. Some are more important than others; some are "oops" moments. But in each case, someone has to make a decision to move forward and take action.

Here is a primer on cultivating people to step up and take charge:

Do your people think on their feet in a crisis or dilemma? Are they *allowed* to think like an entrepreneur in order to solve a dilemma or a problem? Will you cover them — or instead smother them — if they make the wrong decision?

Proper training is very important; knowing what to do, when to do it, how to properly and effectively do it, and how to get others to pitch in. Part of it is training on empowerment, where people have permission to make decisions, make it right for the customers, and make tough calls that are ultimately backed by management.

Communication is key. Make sure your team understands its parameters and what it can and cannot do, and also what it should and should not do. Let them know that you have their backs. If they make a wrong decision through empowerment, discuss the circumstances afterwards, coach the correct application, but don't rip them for it. They won't want to ever stick their neck out again to make a decision for fear of reprisals.

Pay attention to the signs in people. Budding leaders may be flying under your radar. And as stated earlier, natural leaders don't come from a training manual and leadership is not a title — it's a way of operating, a behavior. It's in the head. It's in the heart. And, it is clearly not in everyone!

Leaders tend to think like an owner

In this revealing episode of the messy theater, one young man showed his leadership skills on the spot while the others stood around, frozen into inactivity. He made the decision to balance their rules, their orders, and all the other things that can cloud a decision against a higher purpose—in this case, customer satisfaction and comfort, all the while on a time crunch. He took charge of the moment during the "tornado" and made an independent decision.

He certainly thought and acted like an owner, like a natural leader—right out of Joe DiMaggio's playbook!

Building Your Playbook

- *Have you ever had a similar situation like this one where you or someone you know evolved out of the pack as a leader from a singular moment or activity?*
- *What kind of qualities does your organization look for in its leaders? If you are an owner, manager, or CEO, what kind of qualities do you look for in your budding leaders?*
- *Do you have a formal training/coaching program that helps develop and define leadership in your organization? Can you get one started?*

Chapter 37

A Team without Accountability
is Destined to be Mediocre

*"You cannot escape the responsibility of tomorrow
by evading it today."* —Abraham Lincoln

The good eat the mediocre. The great eat the good. And great wins.

A client of mine in the financial services sector engaged me to help his expanding firm go from good to great. His analogy was that they had been a small fish in a big pond and were striving to take the next step to be a medium fish in a big pond. After the first set of workshops, I should have muttered the line of Chief Brody in the film *Jaws*: "I'm going to need a bigger boat."

The process of enlarging his company was exhilarating, but there were growing pains, too. This showed itself during one of our early training discussions. We asked the management team to do a bit of homework prior to our workshop the next day. It involved looking up one or two of their competition's mission statements on the internet. We were going to start working on developing their own company's mission and vision statements, and the thought was to have the team bring them to the session for a comparison of phrasing, ideals, and a bit of a look into the other firms' corporate souls, so to speak.

When I asked the managers to share their findings during the next training session, I was shocked to learn that only about half of the team did their homework and brought something to share. Those that complied had searched the internet, found their assigned competitors' websites, and copied the mission/vision/core values pages as instructed to do. They were ready to dive into the discussion.

The other half of the management team shrugged their shoulders, with some saying, "I don't have anything," while others just looked at the person sitting next to them as if to say, "Your turn, I've got nuthin.'" Their blasé attitude was unsettling. Neither the owner of the firm nor I thought that what we had asked them to do was all that difficult.

> *"Accountability is the glue that ties commitment to the result."* —*Bob Proctor*

I was embarrassed for the group as a whole, and it was clear that the two co-owners of the firm were set back by what they saw, too. They remained silent, just watching the room. One of the people who ducked out of the assignment was fairly smug about it, as if he shouldn't have had to do it anyway. He was number three in the company org chart. We went forward with the discussion with what we had, and continued on with the rest of the agenda.

Afterward, I sat down with the co-owners of the firm to discuss the day. I hit the elephant head-on. When I commented that it was less than impressive to me that only half of the managers had done their homework, especially as simple as the assignment actually was, one of them looked down at his shoes and said, embarrassed, "Well, that was actually better than it usually is here." Wow. That told me volumes.

The sad paradox was that this was the group of managers

who were expected to lead the company's charge from good to great. They showed me that they had a long way to go.

High accountability should be the norm, not the exception

"Gary, how can we get better?" was the question my client put on the table. I offered that a good place to start was addressing accountability, and to start holding people accountable for things like this, a basically simple assignment. What gets measured gets done. I explained how it is an expectation level set at the top and reinforced throughout the organization, not just in pockets.

Further, I explained that you want to get to the point where the level of ownership/accountability is delivered from within the ranks as a way of doing business internally, and thus it becomes the norm and not the exception between teams. Ultimately, it becomes the culture and not a sometimes thing.

If you do not hold your team accountable on projects—especially your management/leadership team—then you will have difficulties in many areas. Having a *truly great* organization isn't possible with some departments and people failing to respond or owning their part of the follow-through.

> *"People know you for what you've done,*
> *not for what you plan to do." — Unknown*

Results talk, excuses walk. Your terrific "eagle" performers can lose faith in the organization when others around them aren't held accountable for what they say they will do, or what they are supposed to do. Double standards, excuses, and poor accountability drive top performers crazy and deplete their morale. They get frustrated, throttle down, and sometimes leave. The "quacking ducks" who claim they don't have time or are always "too busy" to get things done are not going to lift your organization to the next level.

Here are five keys for improving accountability and helping to move your organization's needle from good to great:

1. **Clearly explain expectations, time deadlines, the importance of projects, and how they impact the success and forward movement of the organization.** "Hello people, this is important to us, and it's not an elective!" A real team acts in unison. Make it a part of your organizational *culture* that this is the expectation. All hands on deck. Pitching in means *all* hands, not just *some* hands. You don't need any prima donnas walking around.

2. **Hold all teams equally accountable, and *especially* all of your managers/leaders of those teams.** Managers should set the example. When they slack off, others slack off. It gets noticed. And you can't play favorites or make exceptions by handing some people "Get out of jail free" cards without some repercussions across the other teams.

3. **What gets measured gets done**. Keeping track of results, monitoring deadlines, and doing periodic progress checks to keep things moving forward all help raise accountability levels.

4. **Explain the ramifications of not being accountable.** "Here is what happens if this isn't done or this deadline isn't met..." It's not a threat—it's a cause-and-effect conversation. Lay out what a lack of accountability costs in terms of customer service, loss of business, wasted time, overage of costs, team morale issues, etc. Sometimes you can tie a dollar amount to

it, which makes a bigger impact to some to see the fallout of their non-performance in dollars and cents.

5. **Be prepared to practice "tough love."** What are you prepared to do in case of a lack of accountability? What is the fallout? What is the penalty? You don't have to do this in a heavy-handed way, but understand that it's human nature to try and get by with things as long as there is no penalty. Some organizations I've worked with tie their incentive and salary bonuses into accountability to make it real. That tends to make people stand up and pay attention.

Focus on *what the right thing to do* is. And expecting accountability is the right thing to do. When you get tempted to bend your principles and "dumb it down" for the few who want to take the easy way out, remember this phrase from William J. H. Boetcker:

"You cannot strengthen the weak by weakening the strong."

Building Your Playbook:

- *What is the current level of overall accountability in your business or team? Is it satisfactory?*
- *When people or teams aren't held accountable, what happens?*
- *Do your team leaders hold all people equally accountable, or do some play favorites?*
- *How does a lack of accountability affect morale, teamwork, turnover, etc.?*
- *How can you improve accountability for yourself and your team?*

Chapter 38

The "Sweet 16" Attributes of Winning Teams

"A united army of sheep can defeat a divided
army of wolves." —Matshona Dhliwayo

According to the Cambridge Dictionary, an *attribute* is defined as: "A quality or characteristic that someone or something has."
Why sixteen attributes? A bit of explanation . . .

The term "Sweet 16" refers to the remaining sixteen teams still alive after two rounds of play in the men's and women's NCAA basketball tournaments each spring. Making it as far as the Sweet 16 out of an original field of sixty-eight teams is an enviable accomplishment and a barometer of success for many teams.

While watching the exciting "March Madness" play out on TV a few years ago, I was simultaneously working on a list of important team attributes for an upcoming management program I was developing for a client organization. It just so happened that my list contained sixteen critical areas for team success. Thus, my moment of inspiration centered on the idea of a Sweet 16, and here we are.

These sixteen have morphed and evolved over the years, based on my work with a diverse set of client groups. These are the most critical components of teams and business units that I see bubble up most often. They either help to make them better, or hold them back from realizing their potential or accomplishing their mission.

That's the point of this chapter—to examine our businesses and work toward high quality performance in these sixteen areas so that they truly become attributes that enable people, teams, and organizations to be more successful.

"Self-examination is the key to insight,
which is the key to wisdom." —M. Scott Peck

Please bear in mind that these attributes aren't on islands. They are extremely interconnected to each other. Try doing without one, or have one of them performing poorly. You will inevitably see breakdowns happen along the line to one or more of the other areas, too. A line of standing dominoes falling one by one comes to mind.

And while I don't pretend that my list is the "be all-end all" on this subject, I believe with all my heart that this collection is an extremely strong place to start. I am confident that if you focus on these areas for your business, they will have a great cumulative impact on your internal teams and external customers.

But you have to be willing to look inward and analyze these areas with a critical eye. Look at things as your customers look at them or you'll be wasting your time with a half-hearted gloss-over. As motivator and former coach Art Williams says, "I'm not telling you it's going to be easy. I'm telling you it's going to be worth it."

The attention given to these sixteen team components has paid off for many of my clients in the form of increased proficiencies, fewer redundancies, greater camaraderie, improved customer service and retention, lower turnover, and increased sales. You can do this, too!

And this isn't a flavor-of-the-month club project, either. If done right, it can foster a better long-term team and organizational culture, too.

After all, *everything starts with having a strong team.* Can you imagine achieving success in your business without one? It's a ridiculous thought. Creating a strong team is at the center of an organization's universe.

Just ask Bob Ladouceur, the coach we met earlier in this book, the man with the all-time longest consecutive winning streak in high school football history, how important a strong team fabric is. As he writes in his book *Chasing Perfection,* "Creating a team is bigger, tougher and more elusive than any opponent we will ever face." The very same thing holds true for businesses, too.

The Sweet 16 Attributes of Winning Teams

1. **A smart, participative, decisive, and supportive leader**
Such a leader is not afraid to make decisions, including the difficult and unpopular ones; fair with discipline; shows tough love when needed; believable and inspiring; celebrates the wins and allows for some fun and letting off steam; has the ability to marshal the efforts of all units toward the goal; smartly utilizes available resources; inspires, challenges, and appreciates the contribution of others; earns and gives trust; leads by example; shows good ethics and honesty; creates an inspired team; has a strong moral compass.

2. **Aligned on the "true north" and the rules of engagement**
Teams must be aligned on a common purpose and a unified ultimate mission: where are we heading, and how will we get there? Create clearly defined goals, roles, and responsibilities that are understood by everyone.

3. Show commitment and care of others throughout your team

Thoughtfulness, respect, empathy, and rapid response will increase camaraderie and cooperation among teammates.

4. Focus on fundamentals

Master the basic blocking and tackling across all channels and include training, preparation, and practice as part of the culture. What are the "little things" that absolutely have to be done correctly to ensure our quality and success?"

5. High-touch communication levels and protocols

Clear, constant, and consistent verbal and written communication should be understood and practiced by all business units and periodically reviewed for effectiveness. No "silos" or isolated islands of communication allowed.

6. High trust levels

Very little can be accomplished if there is a lack of trust among stakeholders; this is something that must be earned, often by deeds and actions.

7. Accountability

Must be equally shared and respected among all business units and channels. Taking ownership and assuming responsibility should be the standard expected across all business units.

8. Accuracy

There's no such thing as "almost" or "close enough" when accuracy is needed. Expect and manage accuracy across all channels.

9. Timeliness

Deadlines and target dates are set and met, with periodic reviews of efficiencies and checkpoints on progress. Constant communication and updates recommended.

10. Creativity and innovation

Let's twist the familiar where we can, as these elements are important to evolving our team/organization and moving forward. People should feel encouraged to stretch the boundaries, take chances, and challenge the status quo. Innovation means change, so expect some pushback that can impede progress.

11. Quality-driven

Strive to be great vs. just good enough. Commit to a unilateral effort to producing top quality performances across all channels and not just settling for mediocrity. Identify and address enablers and inhibitors. Develop an alliance partners program to help bolster teamwork, processes, and quality across units.

12. Ability to overcome times when "shift happens"

Practice adaptability, flexibility, and patience. Don't be brittle; bend, don't break. Have the ability to handle "shift" on a timely basis with a minimum of damage, delay, or loss. Swift recovery for each other and our customers is the goal. Review causes of the shift. It could it happen again and what can we do to prevent it or deal with it better?

13. No blaming allowed

Create a culture of identifying, correcting, and solving issues constructively and forthrightly. Expend energies on fixing problems so they won't happen again, instead of "the blame game." Blaming can tear teams and people apart.

14. Handle conflicts and failure/setbacks

How do we work things out? Can we survive, overcome, and ultimately learn from our failures, conflicts and mistakes? Do we let little conflicts grow into bigger ones? Let's not turn "it" issues into "us" issues.

15. Focus on tangible results and "Job One"

Keep your eyes (and the team's) on the prize by zeroing in on what really matters—the results! The two most important jobs a business has to do to survive are the acquisition and retention of customers. And that really can't be done without the acquisition and retention of strong employees.

16. Have an elastic culture and a "three-way vision"

This refers to the ability of a team or person to be adaptable, depending on conditions. Flexibility can mean survival in business. In basketball, "triple threat" defines a player's ability to be flexible at any point in a game, and to be ready to dribble, pass, or shoot. For business, that type of readiness is important as conditions, customers, and priorities can change rapidly. Team leaders need to develop a flexible three-way vision of remembering the past, managing the present, and planning for the future, as all three will play a role at one time or another.

As the basketball saying goes: "The ball is in your court now—what will you do with it?"

Building Your Playbook:

- *To begin an improvement project, list the Sweet 16 on a spreadsheet and make notes for each one from your own business or team, identifying any issues or key points that should be addressed. Note the good, the bad, and the mediocre, and the declining and the improving pieces, too. Don't worry about capturing every single thing, as you'll be tweaking your list throughout the process.*
- *This is a good exercise in which to involve the entire team or organization. Others can and should be helpful in examining each attribute, turning over the rocks, and identifying opportunities for improvement or change.*
- *Draw up the game plan for strengthening each area: Who, what, when, where and how?*

Chapter 39

The Sweet 16 Revealed in Moments of Leadership

"The one thing in life you can control is your effort, and being willing to do so is a huge competitive advantage, because most people don't. It's a rare quality. Putting in effort means going beyond what's required to solve problems, even when you aren't asked to . . . You take the initiative and exhaust every possible option to find answers." —Mark Cuban

You've likely learned by now that running an organization or leading a team is rarely, if ever, a cakewalk. Oh sure, there's cake. But you have to make that walk first. And sometimes that walk can be a bit of a challenge. Think shards of glass and no shoes. Yet you've got to put in the effort to lead and succeed, as Cuban so forthrightly suggested.

But you shouldn't make that walk alone. So let's look to the Sweet 16 to help you make that walk. If you've got the sixteen attributes working well and in sync with one another, then you've likely got healthy sales and a healthy team, too.

The vignettes that follow are intended to help illuminate many of the Sweet 16 attributes that we learned in the previous chapter. They have been specifically curated to help drive many of the lessons home for you. Think about how these scenarios run parallel to your own business situations. Given that the inspiration for the Sweet 16 idea was drawn from basketball, I've featured impactful sports episodes that can easily translate to any business.

Part One: The Upset

It's not the size of the dog in the fight,
but the size of the fight in the dog

March 16, 2018, will likely never be forgotten by college basketball fans, especially those who had meticulously plotted out their NCAA men's basketball brackets and settled in to enjoy the opening round of the tournament. That evening, the cow jumped over the moon and a dish ran away with the spoon, because fairy tales really did happen.

For the very first time in men's college basketball history, a lowly 16 seed team, the University of Maryland-Baltimore County (UMBC) Retrievers, knocked off the high-flying number one-seed team in the entire 64-team tournament and also the top-rated team in the nation. The heavily favored (by 20.5 points) 31-2 University of Virginia (UVA) Cavaliers were thrown from the "Big Dance" in unceremonious fashion and with relative ease, 74-54.

This David vs. Goliath matchup wasn't even close.

As in business, the biggest don't always win the prize. How did this small school team accomplish this feat? To start with, they played loose in their underdog role. UMBC player Joe Sherburne summed up how he and his teammates felt with this pregame comment: "We know we can go out there and have fun and play hard, and we really don't have anything to lose, so it'll be, we go out there and play loose."

UMBC came out fast from a tie game at halftime and took control of the pace of play, and the Cavaliers were unable to find a higher gear to stem the tide. They got outhustled by the Retrievers.

Losing UVA head coach Tony Bennett showed humility, honesty, and leadership after the shocker: "That was not even close. That's a credit to the job Ryan Odom [UMBC head coach] did. Their offense was very hard to guard. They shot it well. We kept getting broken down and did a poor job . . . it was a thorough butt whipping."

Bennett showed class, accountability and added some terrific leadership perspectives from the shattering loss, in what would be a prescient foretelling for his team in the following year's NCAA basketball tournament (more on that in a minute):

"This is life. It can't define you. You enjoyed the good times and you've got to be able to take the bad times. When you step into the arena the consequences can be historic losses, tough losses, great wins, and you have to deal with it. And that's the job."

Winning and losing are temporary imposters, proven every day in business. We win some and we lose some. As we touched on earlier, don't let a setback define you because failure isn't permanent. Conversely, don't get a big head from winning either, as success doesn't last forever. People and organizations have to know how to handle success. UMBC couldn't follow up the success of their epic performance as determined overachievers. They fell back to earth quickly, being bounced from the tournament by losing their very next game two nights later.

On the other hand, the Cavaliers and Bennett, no doubt driven by their embarrassing showing in 2018, achieved the all-time worst-to-first story the very next season. They bounced back from the historic UMBC defeat on a meteoric journey from the outhouse to the penthouse, putting the hard work in to overcome all challengers and become

NCAA champions over Texas Tech in 2019.

Part Two: It all starts with the fundamentals

"It's the little details that are vital. Little things make big things happen." —John Wooden

Hall of Fame basketball coach Wooden won a record ten NCAA men's basketball championships in twelve astonishing years at UCLA, including a record seven in a row. He often told about how a major key to their success was focusing on the little things. In their preparation, no detail was too small.

Wooden was a staunch believer in fundamentals, the so-called "X's and O's," the very basics that successful businesses and sports teams are built upon.

He claimed to have built those championships one brick at a time. Those detailed little things that he and his athletes did in practice day in and day out over many years—"the boring, repetitive fundamentals" as he put it. That approach paid off in their multiple championships. Of course, they had plenty of talent every year (every business needs that, too) but they also consistently outworked their competition.

How much time and effort do you or your organization spend on the fundamentals so that they come almost naturally to teams across your org chart?

None of us is as strong as all of us

To me, this is not just a bumper sticker, it's very real. Why? Because it's true; *a team is the sum of its parts.* It's essentially 1 + 1 = 3 personified. No matter how much of a superstar anyone is in their own right, they are inevitably stronger as part of a team.

Wooden had plenty of superstars—he coached eighteen All-Americans. But he never coddled them or strayed from the fundamentals and the importance of the "team." Business units with superstars usually do very well when those top performers help make their fellow team members around them stronger, thus elevating the entire team rather than preening like peacocks.

Phil Jackson, another Hall of Fame coach who won eleven NBA championships with the Chicago Bulls and Los Angeles Lakers, also had his share of future Hall of Famers (such as Michael Jordan and Shaquille O'Neal) and prima donnas on his teams, too. But he was able to get them to play together within a team framework in order to win all of those rings. No superstars could have won those titles by themselves.

O'Neal says the players bought into Jackson's methods based on his experience in winning championships: "He had that resume. He knew what he was talking about. The guys really, really believed in him."

Believability and credibility are key traits for a leader to have. And in turn, Jackson said this about the idea of group strength outpacing individual glory: "The strength of the team is each individual member. And the strength of each member is the team."

Selflessness— and a bit of "Magic"—can help teams win, too

One of the most unselfish players in the history of team sports can still teach us valuable lessons for our business teams. Former Michigan State Spartan and Los Angeles

Laker basketball Hall of Famer Earvin "Magic" Johnson was a famously selfless team player. He elevated others around him at every level and is still doing that today as an extremely successful business mogul.

I was fortunate to be attending MSU when Magic played there. I fondly recall how he lit up the entire campus during his two years as a Spartan. He was the team's floor leader and co-captain, earning All-American status as a sophomore. In addition to his own accurate touch on shots, he became noted for dishing out eye-catching passes and a record number of assists to his Spartan teammates so they could take open shots. Magic didn't care who led on the stats sheet, he just wanted to win the games.

Magic's style and personality made others want to be around him to learn from him and catch his spirit. With his leadership and game management skills, he elevated his teammates' games by encouraging them and pushing them to elevate their play. He made other players wearing the green and white significantly better.

Think of those traits and how valuable someone like Magic would be on your own business team. Having people who have the "game" to dish off to others and not worry about getting the credit, ultimately making others around them better. That person is highly-valued in any organization, worth their weight in gold! Anyone who shows excellent selfless leadership "chops," whether or not they have a management title to go along with it, are truly special.

Remember—leadership isn't a title, it's a behavior.

With his tremendous talent and infectious ear-to-ear grin oozing confidence on the court, Magic led the Spartans to the 1979 NCAA National Championship over Larry Bird and Indiana State. Fittingly, at the very beginning of that championship season, the team chose its own theme for the year: *"Potential."* Short, sweet, powerful. How prescient of them! They backed it up. They went out and put the hard work into fulfilling their destiny and reaching their potential *together.*

Are you and your organization doing what you can to help your entire team achieve its *potential?*

Building Your Playbook:

- *How proficient and focused are you (or your team or organization) on the fundamentals? Is there room for improvement?*
- *Regarding the NCAA upset, what lessons can you take away for your business from both UMBC and Virginia?*
- *Is your team or business unit the sum of its parts? How do the big egos blend with the rest? How do they work together?*
- *In what ways can you develop your own potential and that of others? Does your team have a floor leader like Magic Johnson?*

Chapter 40

Beware the Arrogance of Success

"Success is a lousy teacher. It seduces otherwise smart people into thinking that they cannot lose." —Bill Gates

Now that we've got the spirit of good coaching, fundamentals, selflessness, and cultivating our "assist leaders" to elevate our team, let's spend a few moments on something that can cause real problems for teams if it's not nipped in the bud. And it can adversely affect the attributes of the Sweet 16:

I call it "The arrogance of success."

Arrogance is a dangerous emotion, "seducing us," as Gates suggests, into engaging autopilot and assuming we'll keep our successes rolling, and maybe taking our competition for granted just because we kicked their butts last quarter. Does the anesthesia of winning start to dull our senses and put us to sleep? It certainly could.

Essentially, we get too big for our britches.

And then it can get dangerous. Things change. People change. Conditions change. Remember Covid? That was change enough for ten lifetimes, wasn't it? A lot of what we used to do, we could either no longer do or we couldn't do in the same ways. The pandemic was a raw lesson in the idea that *past performance does not guarantee future results*.

Championship football coach Nick Saban has a warning signal for teams or organizations that get a bit heady from previous glories: "You have to earn success all over again. The future and legacy of a team will be determined by what happens ahead of them, not what happened before." Remember, he also said, "There is no continuum for success." That means you've got to earn your reputation and results over and over again, and reprove yourself to your customers, one at a time.

"To handle yourself, use your head; to handle others, use your heart." —Eleanor Roosevelt

My Sweet 16 has helped business owners, leaders, managers, and team members at various stages of their development. It is especially important for newly minted managers to grasp the power of these attributes because it can be very overwhelming to suddenly be responsible for the results of a team. It's a lot to handle and it takes a different set of gears, as Mrs. Roosevelt opined.

For illustration, here is a short story about a star player in their own right, who had to find a very different gear as a leader of others after his playing career was over.

At the same time Magic Johnson was playing basketball as a Spartan, another talented All-American athlete was on the Michigan State campus, too, playing football and baseball. Kirk Gibson went on to a memorable baseball career with the Detroit Tigers and Los Angeles Dodgers, winning the 1988 NL MVP Award and hitting all-time dramatic home runs to help both of those clubs win their respective World Series championships.

Gibson was a very tough competitor who, like Magic, played to win. But where Magic wore a wide grin on the court, Gibson wore a scowl on the baseball diamond and football field. He preferred to run right through opponents rather than try to go around them. It wasn't personal with

Gibson, it was just business. He was referred to as a football player in a baseball uniform. "There was a perception of me, and I earned it because I was really intense, really gruff," he recalls.

When Gibson retired as a player, he pursued a career in coaching in the Major Leagues. He had to develop an entirely different set of perspectives when he was promoted to manager of the Arizona Diamondbacks. His days of crushing home runs and running through catchers at home plate were over. He had to learn to jostle all the duties of keeping a team of quirky individuals in top mental and physical shape in order to win baseball games. It was an entirely new gig. He knew the game, but did he know how to *lead*?

As manager, Gibson was responsible for the performances and results of twenty-five players and assorted staff members. It was his locker room, his show to run. He was voted NL Manager of the Year honors in 2011 but his run as the team's field general wasn't easy.

The change Gibson experienced in his transition from player to boss is very similar to what happens in business with people who get promoted from staff positions to supervisors and managers/directors. There is a whole new set of rules and expectations on their shoulders; thus, an entirely new skill set is called for, too.

Let's face it, you can't just bring your "skill set A," those traits that made you successful at your previous level, over to your new management position and call it a day. You'll need an added "skill set B" as your goals and responsibilities have drastically expanded from "me" to "we."

You have to develop those new skills and care about others in ways you never had to worry about as a lone-ranger performer. You can't play favorites or be buddy-buddy like before. You have to find that delicate balance between ca-maraderie and discipline. Some people can make the adjust-ment, others cannot. Often, people think they can make a successful transition into managing others, only to find out that being the boss isn't everything it was cracked up to be.

Time and again we'll see that skills at one level do not necessarily transfer to the next level. For example, star base-ball players don't always make it as successful baseball man-agers, and star salespeople don't necessarily make it as successful sales directors, either.

As Gibson learned, leaders must develop a managerial presence while holding personal emotions in check: "If you're a manager you can't get frustrated and be emotional. You have to continue to steer the ship. You can't let go of the wheel because who knows where it [the team's direction] will go then."

Humility can be an effective teacher, too

An earlier chapter started with Gibson's quote about learning lessons from "being schooled," important for not getting too full of ourselves.

Nobody really wants to get "schooled," but wake-up calls happen in businesses all the time, too. We need school-ing and some humbling experiences every so often. We would do well to learn from those moments and pick our-selves back up off the floor, and thus be better informed, bet-ter equipped, and better prepared to deal with what comes next time.

And there will always be a next time in some form or fashion. But success is never guaranteed. We have to take advantage of the opportunities that come our way and also keep our heads from being hung up in the clouds of arrogance.

"Alone we can do so little; together we can do so much."
—Helen Keller

Building Your Playbook:

- *Do you sense any signs of the arrogance of success in your organization? Where? What can be done about it?*
- *Can you recall a time when you were "schooled" and learned a valuable lesson while making the transition to a new role?*
- *Have you ever been in a situation where the "arrogance of success" caused trouble for your team or organization, or you personally? What could have been done to forestall that?*
- *What challenges have you faced, or will you face in the future, in getting a promotion with more responsibility and having to develop a new skill set? Have you seen this happen with others? How did they succeed or fail?*

Chapter 41

Calling all Leaders: It's Time to Shine in Times of Change

> "If you don't like change, you are going to
> like irrelevance even less." —Eric Shinseki

Think back to where you were in the late winter of 2020. In late February/early March, I was first in Memphis and then in Brooklyn doing a sales training program for a hotel company. The hotel in Brooklyn had set up a couple of Purell stands in the ballroom where we were doing the workshop. I recall a few conversations during our breaks and dinners involving comments about "some really bad flu-like illness" over in China and Europe that was getting mentioned in the news, and the hope of everyone in our group that it wouldn't reach the shores of the U.S. It seemed to be a faraway thing.

Still, most of us fist-bumped and kick-bumped with each other instead of shaking hands, and we hit the Purell dispenser a few times during the day, just to be sure. It almost seems silly to think of that now.

Like many other people, I had a business plan for that year. It was working very nicely for the first three months or so. I had one of my busiest starts to any year that I could recall. Then *WHAMMO!* A veritable meteor hit the earth. COVID-19 was thrust upon us quickly and violently, sweeping across our lives like a gigantic cloud cover, changing our lives almost entirely.

My playbook was now obsolete, like a lot of other people. It was time to draw up a new one.

Let's face it—certain ways of living and doing business have been altered forever; some for better, some not so much. Shift happened. Shift is still happening. And it will continue to happen, because shift is change and change is constant. But that's only the half of it.

Change is constant, progress is optional

I did a management training program for a client who shared with me his current state of affairs with his management team of twenty-five people: "Gary, it's like this in our company. We're restructuring our team and renovating our facility, lots of change happening. Many of my managers have been here awhile and don't like change so much. There is lots of grumbling going on. I want you to help get the message across that the 'change train' is leaving the station, and they need to get on the train and find their seat."

What a take-charge general manager!

For people in management and leadership positions, steering through change can be a difficult proposition. Part of the reason is the talent gap now being realized in our business landscape. In many industries, good, solid, "battle-tested" mid-management experience is harder to come by than in previous times. Covid didn't help by decimating the experienced ranks of many industries such as hospitality, for one.

The shift we saw on such a massive scale from the pandemic makes it even harder for inexperienced managers and leaders to handle today's challenges without solid training.

Thus, this chapter will give you five valuable steps to solid footing for new managers or managers in new situations.

"The universe likes change. All that appears solid and substantial is built on the shifting sands of ceaseless transformation . . . that's the one steady factor about the universe—it is always changing." —Ilchi Lee

Trying to manage through shift can feel like the sand under our feet, such as when you are standing in shallow water on the beach. You begin to feel the sand inexorably pull away as the ocean recoils and sucks the water back. All of a sudden you're not as sure-footed as you were just a few seconds before. You have to move your feet to find solid footing again, until the next wave coils back. You can never stop it, just like the change in our lives. It keeps coming, and it's all a matter of how we adjust and deal with it.

It can be maddening. We make plans and then later we have to throw out our existing playbook and change it all again many times over, as conditions dictate. Many people had to do that in 2020, and some did it better than others.

Leaders need many talents and characteristics in order to be considered *great*, but maybe none more so than having wisdom, strength, and calm under fire while the storm is raging. And it seems like some kind of storm is always raging somewhere. I refer to this as "shifting sand leadership," and it requires a special breed of person.

Firefighting is not a long-term strategy

Have you been asked to step up and be a leader or to develop your leadership skills more fully since the days when the pandemic was raging? Maybe you are the last person standing from the team a few years ago, or among a fewer number of people running around having to constantly put out fires.

Under those conditions, in any business, where is the time to plan, the time to learn, the time to upskill?

While emergency firefighting is necessary at the time of the proverbial fire, leaders and managers need something more sustainable long-term. They aren't really leading if all they ever do is fight fires.

I see it often in all sorts of businesses—managers and supervisors running around firefighting and never seeming to plan ahead or anticipate things. It's all they can do just to keep their heads above water. Some of that is staffing, but much of it is being properly trained.

Managers have to learn how get out in front of things and assess, plan, and execute. Smart leaders learn to deploy their teams wisely and not try to do everything themselves. In your role, spend time and efforts finding out what conditions tend to cause your team's "fires," and work to prevent them from happening and causing damage before it happens. Anticipation certainly works better than reaction.

Where is the playbook for that?

"Those who become true leaders inspire tremendous loyalty because they care, because they feel responsible for others, because they want others to succeed, and because they want to contribute to the common good, a cause beyond their own basic human needs." —Chesley Burnett "Sully" Sullenberger III

Here is a short course in five critical areas that I've developed to help you get out in front of situations as best you can. Consider these your top priority areas when assuming a new position, taking over a new team, stepping into a new job with a new company, or assembling your team to begin an initiative or mission. These five are a great place to start and establish your base of operations.

1) Clearly Communicate the Mission: What gets measured gets done, and what is understood gets done quicker. People want to know: What is the overall goal here? What are we expected to do? How do you want it to look when it's finished? When does it need to be completed by?

Clear, concise and constant communication saves people from running off in different directions, wasting efforts, wasting precious time, and a whole lot of other unfortunate things.

2) Prioritize: Do first things first. Define what "Job One" is. And remember that not everything can be "Priority No. 1" at the same time. Make lists: What is most immediately important for us and our customers? What will give us the best momentum? What is achievable, at least initially? Small victories at the start really add up.

As a leader, you should be your team's pathfinder. Clearly defining and communicating new priorities will help get them accomplished sooner.

3) Gather Your Necessary Resources: Even the best of leaders can be hampered by a lack of resources. It happens to generals who lead armies. Think about your mission and what you will need. Start by categorizing your needs into what I call "The 3 Ps" that are found in every organization/team: People, Products, and Procedures.

The job at hand becomes easier to see when the greatest needs are identified in each area: People (staffing, team deployment, human resources); Products (what you produce, hard goods, software, equipment, etc.); Procedures (the way you do things, processes, policies, etc.).

Remember my earlier point about throwing away the old playbook? You may need totally different resources thanks to the new realities of your business during recovery times and beyond. Great coaches adjust to game conditions and redeploy their resources to their best advantage. You should be willing and prepared to do that—and quickly—if need be.

4) Show Confidence and Courage: You'll need to have the mettle to make tough calls, to show confidence and conviction in your decisions, even when you have your own doubts. Confidence is admirable but cockiness can be a brand-killer. Know the difference. Being courageous is about taking risks, which means that you'll have to ask people to stretch themselves, to do things differently, and to challenge the status quo.

And while you can't win them all, if your risk-taking is based on solid factors and you have a team that believes in you and supports your efforts, then you have greatly increased your chances for success. Remember—leadership is not like winning a high school popularity contest. You'll never please everyone, all the time, about everything.

5) Be Consistent: The great writer Rudyard Kipling once penned: "If you can keep your head when all about you are losing theirs and blaming it on you . . ." Kipling may not have been specifically referring to business management, but I absolutely think it applies here. Never let your team think that you've lost your head in a crisis (or any other time). While all people are emotional creatures, those in leadership roles are expected to be even-keeled, especially in rough times. Leaders should strive to set a calming, confident example, especially as the tornado swirls about the place.

"If you always do what you've always done, you'll always get what you've always got." —Ms. Jessie Potter

For the foreseeable future, as we continue to rediscover the "new normal," and the new wrinkles brought about by the biggest event so far in this century, things can still be surreal and a bit off-kilter in your business, such as staffing shortages, less products to offer, higher prices, longer wait times, supply chain issues, shifting customer buying patterns, etc. You can't do what you've always done and expect a different result.

You've got to find that delicate balance between changing up your game when necessary, and also staying true to your strengths, foundations, and principles that have made (or are making) you or your business successful.

Managers or owners who can lead while change swirls around them and then turn those changes into advantages— to twist the familiar—will be the next generation of prosperous leaders.

As I like to tell my coaching proteges who are just getting their feet wet in their roles as managers and are going through tough, challenging times:

The brightest leaders shine in the darkest times.

Are you ready to shine?

Building Your Playbook:

- *Do you have moments of shifting sand management, or where you are putting out fires in a reactive mode?*
- *What can you do to be more proactive and get out in front of things more effectively?*
- *Is turnover a problem for your organization? Which areas experience the highest turnover? Are there reasons why?*
- *Jot down some starting plans and ideas for the five points in the short course to implement them for yourself or your team. Use them as a starting point for your short-term plans.*

Chapter 42

Risk-Reward Lessons from Two Giant Icons:
The Beatles and Coca-Cola

"Without risk, there is no growth." —Robert J. Hernbroth

My dad sprang this phrase on me when I was in high school. We used to kid him about it at home. As a lifelong educator and administrator, he was full of lots of little nuggets like this for my brothers and me while we were growing up. Not that we always listened to him, but he sure was right about this one.

Distinctly challenging times bring risk-reward front and center to much of what we do. Sometimes it's by our choice, sometimes not. To me it's about letting go of something in order to try and gain more of something else; essentially letting go of one thing for something riskier in pursuit of a greater reward.

Leaders and innovators who initiate risk-reward actions put themselves out there just by deciding to take the risks in the first place, as there may be no blueprint or past performances to rely on. That's called living on the edge. Some folks live for that.

Conversely, when conditions are thrust upon them that are *not* of their choice, leaders must rise above and be strong enough to navigate their teams through the rough water, sometimes just to survive. Indeed, it's a paramount leadership decision to know when and how to let go of something for the prospects of a greater gain.

Innovation via entirely different roads

Let's examine this two-sided coin through the lens of two ubiquitous brands that at first glance may not have a lot in common. Actually, the pairing of The Beatles and Coca-Cola is not as random as you might think.

In its early days, the band posed for photos while sipping from Coca-Cola bottles, although there is no clear evidence that they were paid for doing so. The band's favorite drink in the early '60s was reported to be a blend of rum, Scotch, and Coca-Cola, dubbed as the official "Beatle drink." Paul McCartney confirmed in an interview with Rolling Stone magazine that "You look back at the early Beatles concert programs, and there were Coke ads..." And The Beatles mention Coca-Cola in their 1969 song "Come Together", although the beverage company had no legal grounds to object because it was a whimsical reference.

Though by different routes and in very contrasting ways which I will draw out here, both The Beatles and Coca-Cola offer powerful examples of achieving substantial risk-reward success. One road traveled was voluntary, the other was by necessity, and both can offer valuable lessons to businesses and industries today, including yours. Let's take a look . . .

"The Long and Winding Road" of brand evolution

The Beatles became the first truly global mass culture phenomenon, a tour de force. They skyrocketed to world-wide fame, achieving a record twenty number one hits on the charts, and still have number one selling products to this day, a truly remarkable achievement considering they broke up in 1970.

The beloved group was always striving to innovate and experiment, never wanting to repeat themselves. They accomplished something very few enterprises in any industry can do successfully. They willingly moved away from a winning formula that created a hugely successful world phenomenon (known as "Beatlemania") and subsequently progressed into a significantly different style of their own making. In doing so, instead of losing their early fans who loved their original style, they actually grew their popularity and took their fans along on their journey, gaining even greater success in the process. As The Beatles' music evolved and essentially "grew up," so too did their ardent admirers.

How did the "Lads from Liverpool" accomplish this?

They were bold, brash, and confident in their musical abilities. They didn't follow any Top 40 formula. After their initial slew of hit records scorched the charts and established them as worldwide pop culture icons in music, art, and fashion, the Beatles decided to risk their early sound in favor of evolving into more sophisticated music.

Band members John Lennon, Paul McCartney, George Harrison, and Ringo Starr bravely wrote and recorded terrific new music that bore very little (if any) resemblance to their initial work. It was a pretty risky move in its day, cutting across the grain of the time-honored entertainment axiom: "Don't screw with the formula."

The Fab Four wasn't interested in being stuck in their musical past. As an older Lennon famously said in a TV interview, "I didn't want to be singing 'She Loves You' when I'm thirty."

The Beatles gave their fans a new musical experience with each successive album, constantly taking artistic chances and thus challenging their own status quo. They didn't wait for the music industry to change them. They got out in front and changed the industry. They were innovators who flipped the music world on its ear.

The band's risk-reward gamble paid off handsomely. Regarded to this day as the most influential band of all time, The Beatles still reign as the best-selling musical act in history, more than fifty years after they disbanded.

Most people are risk-averse —it's a time for true leaders to step up

While The Beatles willfully brought about their own measure of risk, it was quite a different story for the rest of us when Covid-19 turned our planet upside-down. We didn't get a choice—risk suddenly enveloped much of what was around us. Since early 2020, we've all had to let go of certain things in the way we live, work, and cope. And the waves of change keep coming, pushing the need for innovation and risk-taking.

As we examine the risk-reward episode of Coca-Cola, we will see that out of crises true leaders and serious innovators can evolve. They know that in order to survive in tough times or create positive change you need to take risks, as painful as that sometimes may be. And that magnifies the idea that leadership is not a title or a rank. It's more a way of thinking, operating, and grasping emotional intelligence.

Risk is clearly not for everyone. A recent study by the University of Chicago revealed that as many as 99 percent of people are risk averse. That's not a typo.

"Have a Coke and a Smile!"

Remember that line? It was once Coca-Cola's marketing slogan. But there weren't a lot of smiles around the company when Covid hit. We can learn a valuable lesson here from the beverage giant in how embracing huge risks seriously tested—*and also revealed*—true leadership amid the pandemic. A recent business channel interview of CEO James Quincey offered an intriguing look into the elements of risk-reward, change, and innovation:

"The biggest risk was riding that pandemic moment of the lockdowns, the second quarter of 2020," explained Quincey. "We started to focus on 'OK, this crisis is going to end. And when this crisis ends, do we want to be known for just managing through the crisis, or do we want to be known for having emerged stronger and being ready to have much more growth when the crisis ends?'"

Subsequently, Coca-Cola made the tough decision to drop one-half of its portfolio ("the weakest half," as Quincey called it). Yes, you read that correctly. Fifty percent of Coca Cola's product lines were lopped off. They also changed the ways in which they worked, letting go of many longstanding procedures. They shifted almost immediately into the future, unknown as it was.

Quincey also coined a veritable battle cry for risk-reward thinking:

"All that [eliminating the weakest products] has given the organization more belief that risks CAN be taken. We tend to over-research things and hesitate because something could have gone wrong. We forgot about the idea that something could have gone RIGHT!"

"We humans are programmed to over-weight, by far,

things we lose versus things we might gain," the CEO continued. "Risk-taking and innovation is not to let the fear of what you're going to lose obscure the possibilities of what we might gain."

We can't be so afraid to move forward
that we freeze in place

While there is no guarantee that you'll hit gold with every risk-reward effort like The Beatles and Coca-Cola did, resilient innovators pick themselves up from setbacks. After all, what's the alternative? Sometimes there isn't a good one. Trial and error is a big part of taking risks for the sake of progress. Remember risk-taker Thomas Edison from an earlier chapter? He held over 1,000 patents and explained his temerity this way: "I have not failed 10,000 times. I've successfully found 10,000 ways that will not work."

Risk-reward, however, isn't recommended as a "close your eyes and jump off a cliff" move. Such decisions shouldn't be taken lightly. Analysis and consideration of the collateral fallout and the up-side/down-side potential is critical. There are hurdles to overcome and levels of acceptable risk to be calculated. The road to innovation is rarely just paved with roses and lavender. For example, naysayers in organizations are often extremely tough customers when it comes to selling risk-reward propositions. This can lead to internal struggles between the opposite factions of "We can't" vs. "Why can't we?"

Innovation comes with a price. There are vitally important factors on several sides of an issue that need to be carefully considered such as people, planet, and profits.

Decisions affecting those elements can be far-reaching and must be a part of an organization's *innovation equation.*

The element of change can be a cruel teacher as much as it can be a breath of fresh air.

Don't make risk-reward decisions in a vacuum

I've mentioned that "decisions made in a vacuum suck." That's why smart leaders make it a habit to seek honest, straightforward input from trusted advisors and other resources, such as frontline team members and customers. Ask your own set of "Round Table" advisors questions like these:

What are we actually risking?

What rewards (goals) are we ultimately trying to achieve?

Let's have a reality check. Does it make sense to do this? Plus-minus equation.

What will we need to do or have in order to make this happen successfully?

Be careful, however, not to become frozen into inaction with so much scattered input that it ceases to become helpful. I once heard a brilliant line in a *Blue Bloods* TV episode: "No one's idea of what is right is everyone's idea of what is right." That is a beautiful way of saying the ol' bumper sticker of *one size does not fit all.* Can we ever really hope to please all of the people all of the time?

While input from others can be helpful to a point, it is leaders alone who must get the group off the mark and moving forward in the innovation/risk-reward department.

And what can get in your way of doing all this?

Procrastination, of course, as expressed in this tongue-in-cheek way: "Procrastination isn't so bad—you'll always have something to do tomorrow."

No doubt that at some point you've heard one or more of these in your office meetings:

"We've heard about that."
"We were wondering about that."
"We've been thinking about that."
"We've been talking about that."
"We've been looking at that."

I've seen this kind of talk drag down all kinds of innovative ideas and risk-reward opportunities. Blast past these excuses, dig in, and get the ball rolling. Don't get mired in drawn-out debates or paralysis by analysis.

After all, windows of opportunity close quickly and change waits for no one.

Who owns the risk-reward decision?

It depends. In the case of The Beatles, their band dynamics were such that all four members shared the decision and the responsibility to evolve their artistry and songs. They each wanted to expand the boundaries of music and experiment with new material. With Coca-Cola or any organization or team, the buck stops with the CEO, owner, or team leader. Authentic leaders accept responsibility for the decisions and results. Advisors' input is great, but it's the leader's neck that is on the line.

It's very much like a professional golfer whose sport is all about risk-reward. The golfer consults with his or her caddie before each successive shot in order to get their input on the nuances of the hole: the distance, the wind, and any hazards. Though they value their caddy's strategy tips in assessing the situation, the golfer knows that the actual execution of the swing—and the result—is all their own doing. They must step up, hit the shot, and live with the consequences, good or bad.

Let's apply this to your organization or team

You don't have to be The Beatles or Coca-Cola to make a successful go of this. The risk-reward concepts expressed here can be scaled and applied across a diverse array of organizations, large or small.

Everything needs a starting point, a "true north" as Stephen Covey used to say. Let me draw your attention to one of my Pillar Truths, what I refer to as my "Rule 1 and 1A of Business": *The two primary goals of a business are the acquisition and the retention of customers.*

Everything else you do is the "stuff" that must support those two functions, because without one or the other you can't have a successful business. It's that simple. If your risk-reward initiative doesn't somehow improve or solidify these two goals, then why are you doing it?

Whether out of necessity for survival like Coca-Cola or the innate desire to evolve like The Beatles, embracing risk and letting go of something for the prospects of getting more of something else is really a process, not an end.

And as John Lennon famously said: "Everything will be okay in the end. If it's not okay, it's not the end."

Building Your Playbook:

- *What risks do you think need to be taken in your business or organization, such as ways of doing business, delivering your products/services, customer care, employee engagement, etc., in order to innovate and thrive moving forward?*
- *Have you assessed those risks in an analytic way such as best-case/worst-case scenarios? What level of risk are you willing to accept to achieve your goals?*
- *What elements of your organization do you have available that will enable this risk or pursuit of innovation to actually happen? Can your infrastructure, technology, processes, and team members (your "bench strength") handle the new changes that are expected to take place?*

Chapter 43

Smart Leaders Keep their Eyes
on What is in Front of Them

"In the business world, unfortunately, the rear-view mirror is always clearer than the windshield." — Warren Buffett

To Buffett's point, hindsight is 20/20, or so the saying goes. Often in business, hindsight is too late. The lucrative customer, the valued employee, or the financial opportunity is long gone. This section can be very valuable in helping you anticipate, prepare, and lead your team so that you notice things out in front of you through your windshield, giving you time to do something about them proactively instead of reactively; it's about planning vs. firefighting.

If you are new to managing or leading a team, or you need some fresh inspiration as a veteran of team leadership or ownership, here is my short list of fundamentally critical areas to help your efforts. I developed these "X's and O's" to help give my clients a kick-start in their business planning, and I believe you'll find great value here too:

1. As a business, try to stay out of your own way: Providing service as a product can be a grinder. Let's not make it tougher on ourselves by making fundamental mistakes that could have been avoided with some clear thinking and by paying more attention to the details. Let's stop saying the wrong things to guests and customers, such as those dreaded Bozo-isms. Be more self-aware. And please — let's stop complicating the uncomplicated. Life is too short!

2. Think like an owner: Everyone on the service team must understand their part of the bigger picture as a stakeholder, and be empowered to think and act as if they owned the place. It is the role of management to make this clear and encourage people to feel comfortable and assured in the role of an "owner."

3. **Accountability:** Everyone owns a piece of this. No departments or individuals on the team can be excused from being held accountable for their deliverables to the customers or each other.

4. **Communication:** This is often the catch-all of things that go wrong. Why? Communication means a lot of things—verbal, written, person-to-person, virtual. It must be clear and understandable both internally and externally. Some of my clients have implemented "no email Fridays" as a place to start, to get people talking to each other again. Easier said than done, but this battle to overcome poor communication is one worth fighting.

5. **Collaboration**: Everybody pitches in; if one of us is in trouble, we are all in trouble. We believe in having all hands on deck to help fix an issue or make special things happen for customers. Idea-sharing and working on solutions together with our alliance partners is the norm. Working in silos is *not* welcomed here.

6. **Camaraderie:** Create an environment and culture where people honestly care about each other enough to give a darn to pitch in, create success, and figure things out together. It's OK to cross departmental lines to plug a hole. Encourage problem-solving, showing mutual respect, and celebrating victories together; have some fun together and work to pull off impossible feats for guests and customers.

7. Have a sales and service mentality vs. a transaction mentality: When you are selling solutions to someone, you are providing a service to them. When you are providing a service to someone, you are in effect selling satisfaction so they will come back next time, too. With excellent service, you will solidify and justify the decision to buy in the customer's mind. And guess what? They come back!

When you lead with service, you show a higher level of care and concern for your guests and customers. Being friendly, treating people nicely as individuals, and committing to helping someone never goes out of style. That is the root of creating longer-term relationships and customer loyalty. Conversely, the transactional approach is nothing special — perfunctory and forgettable. It doesn't make people loyal, raving, fans when your staff just goes through the mechanical motions in a dull manner. Think of the LTV (Life/Long Time Value), including the important math of how much incremental business that could represent from your customers over time, and you'll take your customer care program a lot more seriously.

8. Protect your brand fiercely: Everything that happens at your business is "on stage" to guests and customers: Everything that is said, heard, seen, done, felt, and experienced, counts as a moment of truth. While not all social media reviews are truthful, fair, or just, everybody's ability to be a critic with their mobile device in their hands is here to stay. That fact has forced many businesses to clean up their act and polish up their services and products, which is a good thing. Remember: It can take years to build up your brand and seconds to have it crushed. Everyone in the organization owns a piece of this. *Protect your brand with all of your might by doing the right things, and doing things right.*

9. Hold "Time" in highest regard: According to leadership authors Jeffrey McCausland and Tom Vossler in *Battle Tested!*: "Time may be the most important resource that a leader manages."

The leader of an organization (and in a smaller scale business, the team leader) is the ultimate manager of the clock. And of all the components of an organization such as resources, people, programs, commitments, etc., time is often the most inelastic of all. You only have so much time to accomplish things. How leaders manage the "move-through" of projects within the time available is one of the most important skills they can have.

Building Your Playbook:

- *How would you grade your team or organization in these eight areas?*
- *Where do you see opportunities for improvement and focus?*
- *Rate these keys in order of importance, and then ask your teammates, fellow managers, and executives to do the same. How similar or divergent are the rankings? That may tell you quite a bit.*

Chapter 44

Necessity is the Mother of Invention
—and Wine was a Necessity!

*"Don't ever tell me about starts. Don't ever tell me
about middles. There's only one thing that matters:
do you finish the job? Period."* —Tom Izzo

Have you ever had one of those times in your business life when you double and triple-planned for an event, had a crisis thrust itself upon the scene, and you or others had to think fast to avert a disaster? And then, lo and behold, things actually worked out for the better? This was one of those times.

To Coach Izzo's point, thank goodness it wasn't how we started, but how we finished that really counted.

I recall at the Parc 55 Hotel we had a few instances where something went wonky. No place is perfect. When there are a lot of moving parts and teams of people going in different directions, things can sometimes get crossed up and go sideways. When your best-laid plans take a crazy detour, you do what you have to do behind the scenes to produce the magic moments, hopefully without your customers being any the wiser. The idea to "never let them see you sweat" comes to mind here.

We were planning to host a group of influential meeting planners/decision-makers at our hotel for what the hospitality industry calls a "familiarization trip" or simply a "fam." The premise is that potential customers visit the hotel for an all-expenses paid weekend "show-and-tell," experiencing all we have to offer. This affords them an up-close look at our operation so as to evaluate us as a potential site for their future meetings and events. We really expended our energies on even the smallest of details for these folks.

On this particular occasion, we triple-checked everything. Our entire hotel team seemed poised and primed for showtime. We were a four-star hotel and accustomed to delivering topnotch service to our guests, but even so, everyone in the business knows that shift can happen.

"Wine is win with an e on the end" —Anonymous

We wanted a "win" that weekend with our fam group, so we planned to put a classy bottle of wine in each planner's room as one of our welcome amenities. I knew that any other hotel could, and often would, do the very same thing, so I looked for a way to twist the familiar in our own unique way. The thought crossed my mind that each bottle could be artfully customized with the person's name on it, making for a fitting keepsake of their time with us. I called upon a man in our room service department who I knew did beautiful calligraphy work for us.

I asked him to personalize each bottle with the planner's name on it, including the date, using a gold calligraphy pen. That way, the wine bottle would possibly end up displayed in their homes or offices as a keepsake. This room service guy was beaming—he loved to show off his artistry and he was flattered. I returned to my office to check on that night's welcome reception for the group.

Our calligraphy artist did a wonderful job on all thirty bottles, but in his exuberance, he placed them all back in their special wine gift boxes, label side out, and set them on a cart for delivery to the fam guests' rooms. The next shift was to deliver the bottles. All set, right?

One teeny weeny little detail was missed.

Instead of looking at each bottle for the corresponding name and matching it up on the rooming list with the guests' assigned room numbers, the delivery folks just grabbed the list of room numbers and delivered the bottles to all thirty rooms without any regard to the individual names meticulously painted on each one!

Crisis management — it's wine-thirty right now!

I found out about this little goof when I got a phone call from one of my fam clients who had checked into their room. I welcomed her to the hotel and we chatted for a minute about the night's reception coming up. Then she asked me, "Gary, by the way, who is Ray Miller?"

I replied, "He's one of the other customers here with your fam group. Why?"

"Well," she said, "I have his wine bottle."

Gulp. My face went flush. My heart leaped. I knew immediately what had happened. But was it just her bottle that was wrong, or all thirty of them?

I exhaled and told her that I would call her right back; I needed to buy a bit of time. I called the room service manager and my worst fears were confirmed: "Yeah, Gary," she said in an exasperated and apologetic voice, "I guess they didn't see this rooming list by names sitting on the desk down here and they didn't notice the different names on the bottles. I'm really sorry."

Geez, they were written in bright gold pen across each bottle! OK, I thought, I'd deal with that later, it wasn't the time for blame. I just needed to find a way to "MacGyver" this, and quickly. The welcome reception was starting shortly.

"In any moment of decision, the best thing you can do is the right thing, the next best thing is the wrong thing, and the worst thing you can do is nothing." —Theodore Roosevelt

A lightning bolt idea hit me, literally out of thin air, but I couldn't do it alone. Thankfully my assistant, Mary Mackres, was still in the office. She was a gamer who had bailed us out of a few other crazy-close calls over the years. She heard the phone call and asked what had happened. I looked at her and said, "Shift happened. And I think I know how we can turn this into a save, but I'm going to need your help with this plan, please."

Mary and I made a good team. She loved my offbeat ideas and colorful projects—the bigger the challenge, the better. She perked right up in her chair, smiling, and said, "OK, what are we going to do? I'm ready!"

I sat down and jotted a note for her to format into our card printer that went something like this:

"You have been delivered a bottle of wine with someone's name on it from the group. This is your 'buddy.' Please bring this bottle to our opening reception tonight where you are to find your buddy and make a new acquaintance by giving them their bottle, and then finding out whoever has your bottle, too."

Mary loved the idea as an icebreaker/networking device and told me she had full confidence that this spur-of-the-moment plan would work. She whipped the notecards out on our stationary and ran them over to our head bellman to have them quickly slipped under the guest room doors. I held my breath thinking: *This just might work.*

As Mary was leaving for the day, she wished me luck for the weekend, gave me a little smirky smile, and ever the baseball fan, she gave me a high-five and said, "Nice ninth-inning save, Hernbroth." I loved her confidence. "I sure couldn't have done it without you," I told her. We were the only two people to know how this plan came to be hatched. I have to admit, I was quietly optimistic that this would indeed work.

The ploy worked like a charm. People had fun exchanging their bottles and seeking out their new "buddies." It was a terrific icebreaker, much better than we could have imagined. These were customers who had seen it all and done it all, but never this. They loved the idea of trading bottles so that everyone could mix and meet each other in a unique way.

Sometimes you get lucky with an idea. Still, you have to have a support team to go into instant motion and help you pull it off. We incorporated the same "wine swap" into our subsequent customer groups, too, with equal success each time.

Quite by accident and necessity, we indeed had found our "win" with an "e" on the end of it!

Building Your Playbook:

- *Can you think of a time when you were thrown a curve ball such as this, and you had to come up with a solution on the spot? How did it turn out?*
- *Is your support team built to come to life when shift happens so as not to have everything come to a screeching halt?*
- *Have you ever had an innovation born out of necessity that succeeded and then became your company's new S.O.P.?*
- *How can you encourage your team to stay on the lookout for additional opportunities?*

Chapter 45

Never Waste an Opportunity to Learn from Good —and Bad—Bosses

"Failing organizations are usually over-managed and under-led." —Stephen Covey

As even a modicum of business experiences will attest, we can learn as much about what *not to do* from a bad boss as we can learn what *to do* from a great boss. I've had both varieties.

I worked for some really smart people, but they weren't necessarily great bosses. Here's a take on that from the book *Making a Difference* by Captain Chesley "Sully" Sullenberger III, the brave pilot best known for his heroism as captain of US Airways Flight 1549. He safely and famously ditched the plane in the Hudson River in 2009 after both engines were disabled by a bird strike. All 155 people aboard survived:

"Leadership can be learned. You don't have to have the highest IQ or the most charismatic personality. You just have to be willing to work incredibly hard, and you have to care about the welfare of everyone around you. Traits including competency, courage, integrity, empathy, determination, trustworthiness, respect for others and concern for the greater good are all values that can be taught and learned. The ability to apply those values can be honed by those striving for continuous improvement."

My best boss ever was Diane Shields, the pre-opening director of sales and marketing who brought me onto her sales team with the Renaissance Parc 55 Hotel in San Francisco.

She was a brilliant marketer— bright, witty, and sophisticated, with a sense of humor, too. She was precise with details and expected the same from us. She taught us to do things with class. And she could get her tough points across with forthright words and a subtle delivery.

She also knew something about motivation. I had been on Diane's sales team for a year of crazy-busy, pre-opening efforts. A few weeks after our 1,005-room luxury hotel had its gala grand opening, I was sitting at my desk in my office, writing up a contract. Diane walked into my office and sat down in my guest chair across from my desk, not saying a word. I was in the middle of a thought and I assumed she was being polite and respectful so as not to interrupt my writing, waiting for an opening. I looked up at her and she was smiling, but not saying anything. So I said, "Yes, Diane?"

"Gary, I just wanted to let you know how glad I am that you work for us and not for any of our competition." With that, she rose from the chair, turned on her heels, and walked out of my office.

I was stunned. I had received compliments before, but never one like that, delivered with such simplicity and suddenness. I was bursting with pride. You could have knocked me off my chair with a feather. I let what she said rattle around in my brain a moment or so. All I could muster was a smile and a "Thank you."

At that moment, I would have boarded a plane and flown to the North Pole to make a sales call if she would have asked me to do so.

In one simple, uncomplicated yet profound sentence delivered in fifteen seconds, Diane had lifted me up and given me my most memorable motivational feedback moment ever.

Part One: "But we've already printed the posters."

My son Michael learned several important lessons about bosses and business while working his way through college. He had a job on campus all four years as a member of the campus escort system (no, it's not what you think!). The name refers to the shuttle service that transports students around the campus.

During the last few months of his senior year, he approached his supervisor about some redundancies on the bus routes. Two buses, each from a different organization on campus, were scheduled to pick up passengers at the same locations and had the same two stops within minutes of each other. Thus, while the first bus loaded up with passengers, the next bus pulled up minutes later to an empty stop. Michael concluded that schedule was wasting time, gas, and expenses.

He made note of this redundancy, especially in the context of the budget restraints being applied to this department at the time. It just didn't make any logical, practical, or financial sense to him.

He approached his supervisor with his concerns, and also with ideas of how to better streamline the schedules. He was met by this question: "What do you care? You're graduating in two months."

Now *there* is a real motivator of a boss.

Michael was taken aback with this response. He couldn't believe his ears. It discouraged him from ever wanting to raise his hand again and make any further suggestions for improvements. It seriously impaired his will to care anymore about the organization improving itself for the remainder of his time before graduation.

What bothered Michael was this: Why hadn't the organization done its proper research into the bus routes, even going so far as to put people on the buses to chart and observe the timing and location of the various routes before drawing up a new schedule? As a business student, he had been learning the ins and outs of how to create better business efficiencies, and he was applying what he had learned. What Michael's supervisor said to him in three seconds succeeded in ripping the enthusiasm right out of him.

Great organizations encourage and reward their people for coming forward with ideas and showing signs of "thinking." Apparently this supervisor had missed that lesson. To further her absurd response, she offered this desultory finish to Michael's idea of changing the bus routes and timing:

"Besides, we've already printed the posters."

For a campus department with the largest budget among the university's student-run organizations ($300,000), it made more sense to this supervisor to cling to a $100 printing expense for bus schedule posters than to improve efficiencies for the long term.

And some businesses wonder why their turnover is so high. Always encourage your team to come forward with ideas. Of course you can't put them all into practice for certain reasons, but those times you do, your staffers will feel invested in the destiny of the team, like they own a piece of the action. If you squelch their ideas, you also squelch their enthusiasm, and where does that lead?

Part two: Things are not always as how they were promised

Michael's department manager assured the team that she operated with an "open-door policy."

A team member of Michael's, "Chris," took the leap of faith and went in to see this manager with ideas and concerns about the operations of the department. He reported to Michael that she gave all the appearances of listening to him, for the most part.

Soon after, his direct supervisor came to Chris and chewed him out for going in to see the department manager in her office. It turns out that the supervisor himself got chewed out by the department manager because Chris had dared to come see her in her office and, as she put it, "waste my time."

Now what do you suppose the impact of this was, not only on Chris but also the entire team?

The department manager first and foremost broke her pact with the team—she did *not* actually have an open-door policy. Plus, she chewed out a supervisor because one of his frontline staff members actually took her at her word and approached her in her office with an idea.

Airing the comment "he wasted my time" was extremely inappropriate, too.

The morale of the staff member was crushed. The team chemistry, the bond of trust, and the element of honesty was clumsily fumbled, and it bushwhacked the team for some time. When you make a pact with your team, keep it. You're only as good as your word and when you break that bond, you've likely lost the team.

"A team is not a group of people that work together. A team is a group of people that trust each other." —Simon Sinek

My oldest son, Greg, worked for a mid-sized organization that had company sales rallies filled with lots of rah-rah motivational slogans and donuts. But the reality of the day-to day operation was quite different. He and his colleagues called it "top-heavy corporate this and that."

A systemic lack of trust permeated from the top. There was so much oversight it took five signatures to approve a paycheck, and several weeks more before the sales team got paid. The field offices were so skittish by the corporate "visitations" that Greg's general manager would sweep through the offices right before the corporate reps arrived.

As Greg tells it, "He would take all of our family photos and personal items off all of our desks—where we barely spent any time anyway, other than when we were writing up offers—and hid our stuff in drawers. He didn't want corporate to see those things and think that we spent all day sitting at our desks. It was demoralizing, and also told us a lot about our general manager and his lack of leadership backbone."

The irony is that most all of the corporate executives were terminated within a year or two for "cooking the books."

Some quick lessons from these episodes:

Don't stifle people on the team from coming forward with ideas and ways to improve the organization.

Even if you can't adopt every idea, make the person feel they are appreciated for coming forth and "thinking on the job."

Don't treat people roughly or discount their input, even if they are leaving soon.

Don't make promises to your team that you can't keep.

If you have an open-door policy—or any policies—keep the commitment to them.

What level of trust does upper management show the rest of the organization? Can you do anything to improve it?

Building Your Playbook:

- Have you ever come forward with an idea in your organization and presented it to your boss? What was the reaction and next step?
- What can you and your management do to encourage frontline staffers to come forward with suggestions and ideas? After all, they see it all right in front of them and are always getting customer input.
- Are they ever asked about what they see, hear, and experience firsthand?
- Do your supervisors and managers need training on proper ways to respond to other team members?
- Motivation isn't always about dishing out gift cards and pizzas. Often, a few well-chosen sincere words of support and acknowledgement delivered on-the-spot can mean a lot to people.

Chapter 46

Carving the Elephants into Small Pieces: the Four P's

"Nothing is particularly hard if you divide it up into small jobs"—Henry Ford

As I first started to grow my Training for Winners enterprise, I had the terrific opportunity to get out from under the day-to-day world of hospitality sales and management, and begin working with many diverse companies and organizations in all types of industries. It was—and still is—very exhilarating for me. I learn something new from every audience and customer organization I work with.

And as vastly different as hospitality and other industries may seem to be, they all share more commonalties than meet the eye. I enjoy bringing many "crossover" qualities and ideas to both my hospitality and business-at-large clients. There certainly are enough good attributes to go around, and no industry has all the answers. My hospitality clients have a lot of things that at-large businesses could and should adopt, and vice versa.

That's where my "Four P's" have their genesis. The more organizations I worked with and discovered through deep dives into the fabric of their businesses, systems, and people, the more I began to think categorically about their infrastructures as far as needs, strengths, weaknesses, and opportunities.

The whole is greater than the sum of its parts

So I boiled it all down to my Four P's, noticing how all types of organizations have these components in some way or other:

1. People
2. Products
3. Procedures/Policies
4. Price/Value

This way of looking at the components of an organization helps break the elephant up into small pieces. It's easier to work with that way. This can be done in a myriad of ways, and these four areas really give people a meaningful snapshot of their infrastructure—good, bad, or mediocre. I've helped my clients develop countless action plans coming from this type of examination, and the improvements have been the stuff of legends in organizations that never thought of themselves in this context.

Let's take a quick look at the Four P's in detail so that you can put them to use in your own business:

People:

This is the "who" in the equation. This is your team—your internal performers, titles, job descriptions, org chart, alliance partners—anything that has to do with people. Do you have the right people in the right positions? Do you have a training investment in your plans to keep your workforce and management continuously evolving and upskilling?

How about your human resources initiatives, disciplinary procedures, etc.? What are your motivators and employee engagement programs? What is the culture across your different business units? Do you have brainstorming gatherings, executive retreats? How about providing cross-training for your workforce?

And let's not forget the customer-facing people. They are your "on stage" performers. How do they communicate with each other and interact with your customers? Do they have a service excellence or a transaction mentality? Is your sales team trained and focused on their goals?

Products:

This is the "what" part of the equation. These are the actual hard goods that you produce or own. Looking under the hood at these include both what you produce for your customers, and the things you have on hand, such as your physical goods in the office, home offices, etc.

This element examines your software/computers, office layout/physical plant, and the like. These are tangibles. Are they outdated or are they sufficient? Are they enough? Are they overstretched for the velocity of output? Are they broken or breaking? Do they need a bit of spit and polish? Do they need a total renovation?

Saddle a team of excellent, talented, well-meaning, motivated employees with outmoded or worn-down equipment, or products that are not 100 percent, and it will drag your business down. Whether you are producing hamburgers, software, or furniture, your products and deliverables greatly impact your brand.

Procedures/Policies:

This third P is the element of "how." Examine how you and your organization do things. How are your deliverables accomplished? How do we move things around here from point A to point B to point C? How do we operate minute by minute, day by day, month by month? What kind of hoops do we make our customers jump through?

One key question I like to ask my clients is this: "In what ways do you complicate the uncomplicated?" Trust me, if you look under that hood you *will* find something that fits the bill! I'll guarantee you that when you challenge your status quo, you will come up with ways to streamline or simplify policies and procedures. No organization is perfect. No team is above finding ways to do things better and more streamlined.

Here are some effective questions to ask:

- *What takes too long to do, and why?*
- *What takes too many hands (too many people having to "touch it")?*
- *What takes the most time for the littlest return (our biggest time wasters)?*
- *What is too complicated (too many steps)?*
- *What are we consistently falling behind on, or not accomplishing?*

And, as you develop these answers, this exercise will help you draw conclusions about what to do moving forward. Here's one to start with:

What can we change, re-prioritize, eliminate/discontinue, fix, add, subtract, or create/build?

Price/Value:

This is the "how much" element of the group. I'm not here to tell you what your prices should be. You know what prices you need to charge to make a profit and keep the lights on. For our purpose here, let's just focus on price-to-value.

People buy *value*. And they rebuy due to value, too. So much so, that they often don't even remember the price they originally paid. If what they bought really came through for them, they'll likely rebuy it, even if the prices go up. Meanwhile, your salespeople might try to tell you, "But everybody wants the lowest price."

No, they don't, but remember this: Customers who think that the lowest price is always the best thing, and salespeople who believe that all customers just want the lowest price, are both wrong.

What people want is the best *value* they can get at the price that makes the most sense for that level of quality in the product they want/need to purchase. In other words, most buyers *say* they want the lowest price, but what they really mean is that they want a product that will do what it says it will do and not break down. Customers have the money to spend, but they don't want to overpay. Who does?

So it's the salesperson's job to sell the *value*. And that starts with tying into the customer's WIIFM—"What's in it for me?" That really is one of the secret sauces of selling success.

Building Your Playbook:

- *The Four P's is a worthwhile exercise for every level of an organization. Where do you want to start the process in your business?*
- *After an in-depth Four P's examination, what action plans do you see evolving from the results of the exercise?*
- *This can be an extremely valuable examination for an organization if all business units and levels take it seriously and do it honestly, with careful attention to even the slightest details. Set the tone and manage the process.*

Chapter 47

The Art of Giving Feedback: Make it F-A-S-T

"Giving honest and well-intended feedback
is often confused with being mean.
It's not mean; it's nice." —Robert T. Kiyosaki

"I've been here twenty-five years, and I've never had a performance review. I still have my job so I guess I'm doing alright," said a friend of mine who worked at a golf club.

One word came to my mind when I heard this: *unforgivable.*

My friend was relieved of his job within a year of this comment, based on a whim by a member of the golf club. It was a sad affair. Another friend, an attorney, counseled him to pursue legal action, especially with a clean employment record, with no performance reviews or reprimands to draw upon. He ultimately won a settlement against the club for wrongful termination. With no performance reviews — good or bad—the club was exposed.

Giving employee performance reviews at regular intervals makes a lot of sense for a lot of reasons, some in the favor of the employee, and some in favor of the organization. They actually protect both parties in different ways.

Reviews should be appraisals of performance and also road maps and blueprints for future actions/goals to be achieved. They need to be documented formally to have a written record of the conversation. For both the reviewer and the person being reviewed, keeping a written record of feedback is important. And just how important will become glaringly obvious if things go off the rails.

> *"Feedback often tells you more about the person who is giving it than about you."* —*Stephen R. Covey*

My experience is that many people new to management are squeamish about giving reviews. They often get skittish about giving less-than-glowing comments to staffers, even when they are called for. Tough love is a prized commodity in leadership, and it's often in short supply. I've seen numerous new managers think that giving frank, corrective feedback will make people on the team *not like them* or *not be their friend anymore*. This is an important part of developing management maturity. Stop running for a popularity contest as if in high school, and start acting like a leader. There are people on your team who will respect you more for doing so.

I attended a human resources workshop where the instructor told us: "It's not the people you fire that make your lives difficult, it's the ones you don't." While that may sound harsh, I think her point was about balancing the health of an organization or team against allowing unacceptable behavior or results from an individual. Situations that grow untenable can infect a team or organization in many ways. Your little problems can easily grow into bigger problems.

The number one problem with positive feedback and reviews

One would think that giving positive feedback would be as easy as rocking in a chair, given that there is no real stress involved. Then what is the problem with positive feedback?

Simple—*there isn't enough of it!*

For one reason or another, people tell me that although they are doing a good job and hearing compliments from customers, their managers rarely if ever give them positive strokes. That's regrettable, because those are lost opportunities for boosting morale and making people feel good about themselves.

Reviews, if done right, in a concerned and supportive manner, should actually be in both directions, too. Wouldn't it be refreshing to see a greater number of managers ask more questions rather than just giving feedback, such as, "Do you have all of the tools you need in order to be successful?" or "What kind of additional training would you like to have?" Or even better, "How am I doing as your manager?" That's a leap of faith, for sure. How many managers are brave enough to ask that question?

There is a major no-no regarding giving feedback. It's delivering "gotcha's" in a review, like saving up for a big surprise. I don't recommend it at all. Timeliness is everything here. Strike while the iron is hot—good or bad. An annual review isn't where you just bring a basket of stuff into the room and dump it all over the reviewee's head. People deserve to hear the good and the bad as they happen, not saved up for a dump in their review. If you've saved up all the praise or critiques for the annual review as a surprise, you haven't done your job properly.

One of my colleagues related that their boss brought something up that they noticed six months ago. Six months! My colleague was incredulous: *"You noticed these things six months ago? Are you kidding me? I didn't know it was even a problem, or I would have stopped doing it that way!"* People deserve better than that. Experienced managers know that *what you allow is what will continue.* It is better for everyone—the employee, the manager, the team, and even customers—to nip it in the bud.

Why let something fester, just because you don't want to rock the boat? I've got news for you—if it's been happening for six months, the boat is already rocking somewhere.

You may or may not be aware of something called MBWA. It means *management by walking around.* It refers to managers getting out of their offices to see what is happening first-hand, being visible, not being cloistered in their ivory tower. While exercising MBWA, be a leadership hero by *catching people doing something right.* That makes big impressions on people. Too many times, managers have the reputation of the opposite: walking around just to look for things being screwed up. That's tyranny, not coaching.

Here is a good self-check on the timeliness of positive reinforcement: If you cannot remember the last time you gave an "atta-boy" or "atta-girl," (a figurative pat on the back for a job well done), then it's been too long.

> ***If you manage people, you owe them timely feedback whether they want it or not***

Here is a very useful model for giving F-A-S-T feedback; it features four important components of an effective review/coaching opportunity:

Frequent: Give feedback at regular intervals, and don't miss performance review datelines. Take it seriously, as you would want your own boss to do for you. It speaks volumes as a real morale-killer and a reflection of your lack of care as a manager if you go past their review date. I've seen it tear teams down. Also, praising or corrective coaching at "the moment of impact," so to speak, has much better value than keeping it all in for a review a week or months later.

Accurate: Make sure that whatever you are critiquing or complimenting an employee about, that you have accurate information. No one likes to get gigged on things that they didn't do, or performance numbers that are incorrect. It's a reflection on your attention to details as a manager. Being accurate in praise also helps to build peoples' self-confidence.

Specific: It means much more to someone if you refer directly to a situation or give a specific example, rather than generalize. "We need you to treat customers better . . ." is *not* specific. What does a person do with that comment? It's open to interpretation; and you won't get the results you want with such generalities. People leave such conversations scratching their head, "But what did they mean by that?" Instead, offer a specific example of what "better" means in real terms.

A salesperson I was coaching related to me that in her performance review, she asked for feedback on what additional things she could be doing to be considered for a promotion. Her general manager didn't offer her anything in the way of a direct, helpful answer: "Oh, you're doing great, just keep on keeping on, doing what you're doing." What a sugary nothing burger! Don't just pat someone on the head (metaphorically) and say something like that without offering some "meat" on the specifics. The general compliment she received (which also lacked any specifics) was really just ear candy. Give people some meat and potatoes, specifics on why you think they are doing great, and what they can improve on, or what they can do to advance to their next position.

Timely: The sooner you speak to an employee after a good or bad performance, the more impact your coaching will have. Memories of moments fade after time. It also prevents employees from thinking that you never notice anything. You don't want the team to think you're asleep at the wheel or, conversely, not appreciative of their good moments and victories. Can you imagine this: "Mary, I saw how you handled that situation with our sales team eight months ago, and I thought you handled it well..." *Eight months ago?*

> *"Every human being is entitled to courtesy and consideration. Constructive criticism is not only to be expected but sought." —Margaret Chase Smith*

Performance reviews aren't a privilege; they are a necessity, for both the employees and the managers/team leaders. People often get butterflies (or worse) over giving and getting reviews. But they don't have to be feared like a trip to the dentist to have wisdom teeth removed, especially if the F-A-S-T communication approach is used throughout the year.

Team leaders lose footing in the reputation department with their staffers when they don't manage things that need to be managed, the tough situations that need to be addressed. Such negligence is seen as a sign of weakness or favoritism in some cases. Corrective coaching for someone who needs it, if neglected, can erode team morale among the other people who are performing well and playing by the rules.

Sometimes, reviews are tied into salary bumps. When they aren't forthcoming, people start to get agitated and lose faith in the organization. I once approached my boss to ask him about giving me and our team members our long-over-due reviews, which were necessary in order to get our annual raises. I got an exasperated response with the tone of *how dare you even ask*?

"I haven't even got my own review yet, and it's three months late. I haven't heard of it coming anytime soon, either. When I get my review, all of you will get your reviews." The big lead balloon floated in the air above our sales office for some time after that.

Great coaches know their players and how they operate

It is incumbent upon managers to understand the strengths and weaknesses of their team members, how they perform in game conditions, how they react to pressure, and how they interact with others. These should be components of a good review, too. Effective coaches know that no two reviews are alike, because no two people are exactly alike. Great coaches constantly reevaluate their players and monitor their progress, or lack of such. Here is a quick guide to help you understand the orientation of your own team players, as they generally will fall into one of the following categories:

Knows how and wants to (high knowledge and high desire): Your "eagles" and can-do performers; they have both knowledge of their job and the desire to perform at a high level. These people are your reliable go-to's.

Doesn't know how or can't, and wants to (low skills and high desire): Your very coachable up-and-comers. They have the desire to learn and progress, to perform well; all they need is some training and practice and they will find their wings.

Doesn't know how, and can't or doesn't want to (low

skills and low desire): There is work to do here, to develop their job skills and get to their motivational core if you want to see success. It's easier to *hire the attitude and train the skills* than the other way around. They lack drive for whatever reason, and the sooner you find out the key to unlock that door, if there is one, the better.

Knows how, but doesn't want to (high skills, low or no desire): A motivational (and possibly disciplinary) challenge here; something hasn't dialed in with them yet. They are usually the most frustrating of the four types because they have the skills or knowledge, and maybe even the empowerment to do the job, but they just don't want to do it. There is no fire in their belly. If they cannot be coached up you may need to consider separation. Bad attitudes, tardiness, and sluggish work can be contagious. Good performers will expect leadership to do something about this situation rather than ignore it and hope it goes away. The worst thing a leader can do here is nothing.

Building Your Playbook:

- *If you have a review or feedback from your boss coming up soon, what do you think will be discussed? Are you prepared for the conversation?*
- *If you have to review or give feedback to those who report to you, what can you incorporate from this chapter?*
- *When is the last time you gave on-the-spot feedback, good or bad, and how did it go?*
- *Do your teammates take feedback well, including constructive coaching?*
- *What is the culture of your organization's feedback? Is it encouraged, feared, useful, constructive? Can it be better?*

Chapter 48

Is Finding Your Dream Job Really a Sales Process? You Betcha!

"Take time daily to reflect on how much you have. It may not be all that you want, but remember—someone somewhere is dreaming to have what you have." —Germany Kent

"**W**ell, my friend," the call began from one of my longtime colleagues during those dark days of mid-2020. "It was fun while it lasted."

I was prepared for what he was going to tell me. It was happening many times every week with quite a few friends and industry mates. "Yup, after being the vice president of sales with a team of thirty salespeople and eight hotels, I am a man looking for a job. Can you help me?" he asked.

He wasn't the only one by a far cry. *The Wall Street Journal* estimated that between thirty and forty million jobs in the USA were lost in 2020 due to Covid-19 and the resulting lockdowns. Although my speaking business was initially put on ice due to the elimination of meetings and conferences—at least until virtual meetings kicked in as the thing to do—I was more than a little busy helping friends and colleagues experiencing furloughs, terminations, and recalculations of their future direction and hopes for a better work-life balance.

The work landscape has changed, and will continue to do so

Although many of the lost jobs have come back, the challenge remains much the same as always. Companies want to find the best talent that can handle their expectations for a post-pandemic recovery. And for many job candidates, they don't just want any old job, they want *the right job*. And there is plenty of competition out there. This chapter will work to illustrate sound tactics that both employers and candidates can use.

In over thirty years of successful executive recruiting specializing in the hospitality industry, Mark Auerbach has seen a myriad of changes in job applicants and the attitudes associated with job searches. "Many candidates now are very particular as to where they will go and what they will do for a job. Not that that's wrong, but it does limit their opportunities from a geographical standpoint. Many see moving from their current locations as more of a hassle and less of the adventure it used to be years ago."

Auerbach takes a consultative approach to his work, often acting as much like a mentor to his candidates as a recruiter. As a former hotel general manager, he knows firsthand what kinds of traits hospitality companies are looking for in candidates.

Auerbach notes that it's not just the new wave of college graduates in hospitality that have specific criteria: "It's everywhere. There is much more of the 'what's in it for me' now. Lifestyle and work balance plus location preferences trump career advancement, pay raises and job titles. Also, expectations are more accelerated—some think that they should be a general manager after two years of experience."

Above all, be AUTHENTIC

According to Auerbach, honesty and full disclosure are important components in the recruiting process for both those seeking jobs and the firms looking for candidates. "It does no one any good to keep their cards hidden. After all, they will be working together. It's not the time to start things off with a lie or misrepresentation."

Here are some do's and don'ts from Auerbach about interviewing and presenting a professional resume. These points also apply to video/virtual interviews, when you are truly on camera – and the camera never lies!

Interviewing Do's:

1. Show up early.
2. Answer questions directly, succinctly, and honestly.
3. Be presentable, in the appropriate wardrobe. Great hygiene is a must.
4. Be prepared to have questions of your own to ask the recruiter about the organization. Remember that an interview is a two-way street.
5. Maintain eye contact throughout the interview.

Interviewing Don'ts:

1. Don't talk too much. Long-winded answers hurt your chances.
2. Don't fidget. Sit up straight and focus on the interviewer.
3. Don't go off on a tangent and get involved in the weeds of a long story.
4. Never put the client on the defensive.

Resume Do's:

1. Keep your resume to no more than two pages.
2. Use bullet statements to define your career accomplishment. Include results!
3. Have solid references ready on request.
4. Ensure that your grammar and spelling are perfect—no typos.

"Whatever you do in looking for a new job or a promotion," offers Auerbach, "come with a positive attitude, be optimistic, bring energy, and show enthusiasm. Those are qualities employers and companies want."

Going virtual: it's show time!

Speaking of virtual interviews, they are on the rise and that presents a whole new dimension. While many recruiters say that for positions over $125K in salary, most companies still prefer in-person interviews, the use of virtual interviewing is here to stay. Be careful—you can't just throw a sweatshirt on, slurp a cup of coffee, and chat like you would in a virtual book club or school committee meeting.

Make sure you have a high-quality camera and speakers, excellent desk lighting, and proper positioning of the camera centered to your face. You never want to be looking down at the lens or have parts of your head cut off. And no close-ups of the inside of your nostrils, please. *Yes, it's happened!*

Be as soundproof as you can from outside noise interference and use an appropriate background. Don't get silly with some cutesy background that detracts from the interview or doesn't fit the setting or your personal brand. You may want to play it safe with the "fuzzed out" background.

Proper attire still goes, too—*this is your career!* If you got by during Covid doing virtual meetings with business attire on top but workout shorts or sweats on the bottom, I don't recommend it for an interview. Don't be lazy. Wear pants or business attire. You never know when you'll have to suddenly stand up at your chair to shoo your cat or the kids out of the room or close the window because someone is cutting the lawn next to your house! As they say in Hollywood, "The camera doesn't lie."

Going to that big interview could change your life: cross your T's and dot your I's

Richard Rue of The Volare Group in Scotts Valley, California is an executive recruiter in the high-tech industry. Like Auerbach, he helps his candidates prepare for what can be a very grueling interviewing process. One of his groan-inducing moments is to see a resume from a mid-manager level that is a bad cut-and-paste job.

"It's a sign of sloppiness," Rue explained, "and when it comes from someone who is looking for a job in the high six figures, it's pretty sad. I've seen plenty of them from young candidates. They'll cut and paste an old resume with an update, but they don't check to make sure the formatting, font style, or font size all match. Or maybe they don't even notice all of that because to them it looks OK. And that's even worse."

Rue offers his top three "Big Mistakes" that will wipe out a candidate's chances for an interview or a second look before they can even get started: "A hiring manager or recruiter looks at a candidate's resume for thirty seconds or less before deciding to either keep it or throw it in the trash. These three mistakes on your resume or cover letter will get you knocked out of contention immediately:

Spelling or formatting errors.

Too many short-tenured jobs in previous positions.

Spraying your resume in many different directions for a position that requires far different qualifications than your resume is showing you have."

Rue offers his list for the top five interviewing mistakes:

Overconfidence: Don't assume because of your past experience, previous related positions, or a high-level academic degree that you are the best candidate and that you will be offered the position on the spot.

Skipping your homework: Your chances can be severely hurt by not performing enough research about the interviewing company. Knowledge of where the company has been and insights into its future direction, methodology, mission, and core values are priceless.

Overactive Ego: Tone down the rhetoric on your greatness. Be proud and confident, not arrogant. Companies can be wary of candidates that think they know it all.

Dressing inappropriately: Dress for success, for both the position itself and the company culture. You are rarely penalized for dressing up, but you take an unnecessary chance if you miscalculate the company's dress code and dress down.

Lack of attention to detail: A poorly formatted resume or one with a misspelled word, misused punctuation, or bad grammar will kill your chances of getting on the short list for an interview.

Rue highly recommends that candidates make sure their resumes and their social media profiles are synchronized: "Especially in terms of past employers and dates of employment, they need to reflect the same information, since most companies now look at both resources. Having an inaccurate, outdated LinkedIn profile, for example, will stand out like a sore thumb."

"An ounce of prevention is worth a pound of cure."
—Ben Franklin

Rue also prepares his candidates with questions they may be asked by interviewers so that they don't have a *deer-in-the-headlights* look when they come up in the discussion. He believes preparation is the key to a great job interview. This exercise forces candidates to come to terms with reality. "Their chances for employment may hang in the balance, depending on how they respond," he cautions.

Think of the one question or area that could possibly torpedo you below the waterline, and how you would answer for that. Be prepared, not arrogant.

- *How would you describe yourself?*
- *Name your three most important accomplishments.*
- *What have you learned from your mistakes?*
- *What was the most difficult decision you ever had to make?*
- *What is your biggest weakness as a manager?*

"The last question is admittedly a tough one," Rue offers, "but it will show me whether they have prepped themselves properly for interviews or not. Too many just assume they can go in and just wing it. That's the wrong tack to take. Often a candidate thinks their resume is enough to sell them, but it's really only a door-opener. Resumes reflect accomplishments, but not soft skills, and those will come out in an interview. It's best to be prepared."

"The toughie"

Speaking of being prepared, I've saved this one, what I believe is likely the mother of all interview questions. It's a true revealer of how prepared someone is and how much self-confidence they have. I have seen some people look down at their shoes, out the window, fidget in their chair, and have a hard time coming up with an answer. It can truly be a deal-breaker or a dealmaker, and as a coach I would feel I wasn't being truthful to my coaching mentees if I didn't prepare them properly:

"Tell me why we should hire you."

There it is. It's similar to when a customer asks a salesperson point-blank: "Tell me why I should buy from you." It's right there, no hiding from it, and the person being asked better have "game."

When I coach people in transition or college graduates, I am mentoring their journey into post-graduate jobs, and we work on this question. I've had many of them tell me how tough a question it was, but they were glad I prepared them for it and they were ready for it in case it came up in their interview. I always want to prepare someone for the toughest path, not the easiest path.

After all, if someone doesn't know why a business should hire them, *then who should know?*

Building Your Playbook:

- *How would you answer "the toughie?" (and consider bringing it up first!)*
- *If you are interviewing, have you prepared thoroughly in the areas mentioned here?*
- *How about in reverse, as the interviewer?*
- *Do you have some short personal stories that could personalize your answer and humanize a topic?*
- *Do your homework and research your potential company. Do you have some questions prepared? It will impress an interviewer by showing that you prepare and are inquisitive.*
- *If you are doing the interviewing, what kinds of questions have you prepared for the candidate? Are they mostly "open" questions that can only be answered in more than one or two-word answers? Open questions ("Tell me about…", "Describe how that turned out…") do the job of getting the receiver/candidate to elaborate on their answers. Thus, they can reveal quite a bit more than closed questions (such as "How many years did you work there?", "How many people did you manage?" etc.).*

Chapter 49

Have you Considered Using Failure as an Attribute?

"It's fine to celebrate success but it is more important
to heed the lessons of failure." —Bill Gates

Whether you are looking for a job, being considered for a promotion, or seeking a new responsibility in your role at work, let me really twist the familiar on you here and suggest that failure—yes, failure—could actually be an ally to your cause.

How so?

In a recent conversation with Steve Lowe, one of my longtime business friends who led many successful teams in the hospitality business, we were talking about interviewing sales and management candidates. As we compared our styles, we found out that we shared a unique approach to interviewing. Our revelation was that we both liked to ask candidates during an interview: "Have you ever failed? What happened, what did you do about it, and what did you learn from it?"

Why talk about failures and setbacks? Shouldn't we all just keep things upbeat and breezy? Balderdash! Steve and I are among those that believe you can't really be truly successful at anything without having failed or suffered setbacks at some points during your life. It's how we learn our best lessons.

Whether it's sales, management, or being on a team in any role, failures and setbacks happen to everyone. I know that I've learned from my own setbacks plenty of times.

When we fail and come up short, then get up off the mat again, those times can reveal a lot about our mettle, our stick-to-it-iveness, and our character.

It's OK to fail—just make sure you learn from it

Some failures or setbacks are our fault. Sometimes we're in a group that fails, and at other times we're part of a failure that is someone else's fault—and we just get caught in the wake. There are also times when shift happens. It just does. Everyone knows that. Take a moment to breathe here. Keep in mind that nobody's perfect. Nobody.

Everyone has a few failures and setbacks in their rearview mirror, a few dings and scratches from the long and winding road of life. Just think of the experiences those afford us. So don't worry about being in an interview or new job discussion and having to sound like you're perfect in all you've ever done. The interviewer knows you're not perfect, because they aren't, either! It's a charade to act otherwise, so shelve the ego and the perfection facade.

I think of it this way: *You say you've never failed? Then you're either lyin' or you ain't been tryin.'*

If that sounds harsh, well, to me it simply means we're human. It may sound counterintuitive or even strange to talk about failure, setbacks, a job interview, or a promotion in the same sentence. But how you've dealt with failure and how you overcame it may very well be one of your better cards that you can play when talking to an interviewer. Companies don't want you to fold like a house of cards at the first sign of a setback or tough challenge. After all, it's business, and there will be plenty of those challenging times to go around. So you'd better be able to handle them.

As an interviewer or interviewee, I suggest putting these questions to work for you. They are part of a story, the "open book" of one's career. They reveal a lot about our character, attitude, aptitude, and the ability to learn from mistakes.

Using failure as an attribute also helps define one's personal brand in four other key areas: *courage* (to bring it up in the first place), *honesty, accountability,* and *learning ability.* Those are very valuable qualities to organizations. So instead of being a prisoner of your past setbacks, learn from them, make adjustments, and use them as your catapult.

Never let a crisis go to waste

Having overcome or survived "the vortex of failure" a few times, you need to gather your confidence and turn those experiences from deal-breakers to dealmakers. Don't sugarcoat your crises or minimize them into some fairytale of revisionist history. Rather, show how you've moved forward and are better for the experience. *Keep it real.* This can be very revealing as to your ability to operate and overcome challenges when shift happens.

Now here's another twist. I also suggest that as the interviewee or promotion candidate, you should be bold enough to bring the topic up as a talking point *before* the interviewer does! Yes, you read that right. This tactic can actually work as a terrific selling point in your favor. It shows a lot of bravery and bold thinking.

Tell a story to explain what happened:

What was the failure or setback?

What contributed to it?

What was your role or involvement in the scenario?

What was the result of the setback?

What did you learn from it?

What adjustments or changes did you make as a result of this situation?

Since the setback, what positives have come about because of the changes?

True leaders respect lessons learned. They've had their own fair share of them along the way. Leaders aren't mistake-free, either. I've personally had a stronger bond with someone because we shared a similar setback.

Be accountable and honest. Have the courage to explain it. Make the episode an attribute in your favor. Doing this could give you a leg up on other candidates who think it's all about looking and acting like they're always perfect. They're not.

Building Your Playbook:

- *What failure or setback (s) have you had? Apply the set of questions above to tell your own story.*
- *Have you used this tactic in an interview? How did it work out?*
- *If you are interviewing someone and they employ this tactic, how would you react?*

Chapter 50

Achieving the Sale by Twisting the Familiar

"Nothing is impossible for those who have a commitment to excellence and an obsessive will to win." —Sumner Redstone

There are salespeople and there are sales professionals. These are real stories of real people I've known in my life who used their creativity to create success in sales as *professionals*. In each case, they did things differently than the other salespeople in the crowd. Picture yourself in similar situations and think about how you can apply these same concepts to your own industry or business.

Please keep in mind, nobody in these stories cured the common cold or discovered a new planet. Everything you'll read is authentic and accomplished by regular folks doing irregular things. That means everything here is within your reach too, if you apply your creativity to twist the familiar.

ROI of six thousand to one, plus a little ingenuity at Wrigley Field

My friend and colleague, Tim Ryan, had a wonderful run creatively leading sales teams at the Pebble Beach Company for many years. He relates a story about one fantastic return on investment, proving that you don't necessarily have to spend huge amounts of money to make big impacts with customers.

"I was on a five-day sales trip to Chicago and the surrounding suburbs," recalls Ryan. "My top objective was to close a multi-million-dollar contract with a medical association, for us to be designated as the headquarters hotel for their annual convention. I completed a full morning of calls downtown and while driving to the suburbs for my appointment, I decided to check voicemails. For some reason, I had a funny feeling that my potential customer had cancelled the call."

"My intuition was right," Ryan explained. "I received a message that our appointment was cancelled. Knowing that I couldn't return home without the contract, I called to reschedule the appointment. My prospect answered the phone and apologized, saying: 'I'm sorry. I didn't realize the Cubs had a double header. I had to get to the first game." Those Cubs fans are pretty loyal, as Ryan found out.

"I asked her, 'Are you going to the Friday Cubs game?' Her answer was yes. I had a plan. I asked her, 'What's your seat number?' On Friday, I made my way to Wrigley Field for the Cubs game and purchased a ticket at the window. I headed to the concessions area and bought two beers, a hot dog, and a bag of popcorn. I bundled up the refreshments in my arms, rechecked the note I had made when she gave me her seat location, and made my way around that beautiful ballpark to deliver the goods to her in the stands. She was quite taken aback by that."

Ryan reports that during the first inning of the game, he and his prospect discussed all of the outstanding points of the contract, and she gave him her verbal commitment to seal the deal. The rest of the game was pretty chill with the business out of the way. He had made the extra effort to meet his prospect on her turf, doing what she wanted to do, seeing her Cubbies play in person. She sent the signed contract to Ryan the following week.

It's a shame so many salespeople today want the customers to do what is easy for the salespeople. Too few think to expend the extra effort to customize the experience for their prospects and set up the conditions most conducive for hearing, "Yes, I'll buy," just like Tim Ryan did in Wrigley Field.

He shared the impressive math of this sales call:

"Game ticket and ballpark food: $125;

Value of the business to my hotel: $750,000;

Return on investment for my expenses: six thousand to one."

A voice message classic

While we're on the topic of coming up with unique ways to spark sales and twist the familiar, I would be remiss in failing to mention how Tim Ryan crafted the all-time favorite outgoing phone message that I (and many other folks) have ever heard. It is the stuff of legend, known to people across the hospitality industry for many years:

"Hello, this is Tim Ryan. I hope the reason I missed your call is because I'm out playing Pebble Beach with a customer. If you'd like to be that customer, leave me a message how we might be able to work together."

One of the things that I coach salespeople to be are great painters of words. With this message, Ryan was Michelangelo.

This message was so popular, that other hotel industry salespeople have mentioned it to me over the years in random conversations. Now that is something in its own right!

Ryan tells a story about his message that really resonates. "I worked with a VP from a financial firm whom I hadn't met in person until we met in their hospitality chalet for the AT&T Pebble Beach Pro-Am tournament a number of years ago," he recalled. "I introduced myself and he says, 'I love your voicemail. I called you last week just to listen to it, and then I just hung up.'"

Ryan asked the client if he had called him the previous Wednesday, because he had noticed a lot of hang-ups on his phone line that day.

The client confessed. As Ryan tells it, "The client replied that, 'I had a bunch of brokers in my office near the trading floor, so I called your assistant and asked her not to answer your phone. I told her that we were going to call just to listen to your message.' He called my line on speakerphone so that all the brokers could listen in. He said they called five times just to listen to it, and then just hung up. They loved it."

Ryan's masterpiece of a message did a great job of placing his callers in their "happy place" at Pebble Beach where they conjured up a picture in their minds of playing the storied golf course. It was pure sales gold.

> *"80 percent of success in life is showing up."*
> *—Woody Allen*

And writer Phil La Duke adds that "the other 20 percent is following up."

My best friend since college, Chris Wagner, runs his own independent insurance agency in mid-Michigan. He shares a rare but powerfully creative approach that has worked like a charm for him over the years in getting new business. It's the most non-salesy approach I think you'll ever read about.

Quite simply, he patronizes his prospects' businesses when possible or appropriate. He spends his money with them. He becomes *their* customer. And not in a disingenuous way, either.

In other words, he shows up. And he follows up, too.

"It's unbelievable how well this works out," he offers. And it's not a calculated, planned approach. Chris patronizes a place of business, and because of his and his wife Patti's friendliness and affability, business owners naturally engage in conversations with them. After a few such encounters, they find out what business Chris is in, and they feel comfortable enough to ask him if he could take a look at their insurance picture!

Chris has an uncanny, disarming kind of personality. He treats people like they are longtime friends. And he doesn't do things for people because he expects them to give something back to him, either. He is genuine, generous, and trustworthy.

In one particular case, Chris and Patti became fans of a famous upscale restaurant in the Traverse City area. A dinner there was a staple of their trips up to their lake house on Torch Lake. Over the years, one thing led to another, and pretty soon Chris and the owners were getting to know each other pretty well. It was a small, intimate restaurant where the owners recognized who their frequent diners were. The Wagners started getting invited to private wine-tasting dinners and a friendship with the owners bloomed.

One day, the conversation about the restaurant's insurance picture came up. The restaurant had experienced some serious damage from a recent Michigan storm. With the restaurant's current insurance agent slow in responding to the claim, the owners asked Chris for his opinion. They trusted him, and he did not set out to usurp the other agent from the picture. But over time, his many appearances at their restaurant and his loyalty must have made an impression on the owners.

During this conversation, the owner's wife shared with Chris that as far as their current insurance agent was concerned, they were not exactly feeling the flowers and chocolate anymore from him. She said, "We're lucky if we see him once a year." He also NEVER came in and spent one dime in their restaurant, either.

Not a smart move.

Chris recalls the moment: "They were basically looking at the question, 'How much does our current agent spend with us?'" Coupled with that, the other agent's slow, unresponsive nature regarding a storm damage claim when the owners really needed help, added up to a time ripe for change in insurance reps. Chris, in quite a consultative manner, had positioned himself nicely without any plans for a "takeover." He and Patti had become loyal patrons of the restaurant, built trust with the owners, and they moved their insurance to his care.

The lesson here is pretty straightforward. Not every salesperson has the ability to patronize their customers' businesses, but if you do get the opportunity to do so, use it to your advantage—not in a heavy-handed manner, but in a subtle way. If it's a restaurant or store, just say "hello" to let them know you are there, spending YOUR money in THEIR business. If it's another type of business, leave them a note or send an email complimenting their service or product, or how you are putting their product to good use. Give their business a positive review.

If you are going to ask people to spend their money with you, it just makes sense to reciprocate. You could gain a loyal customer for life. And here is where the LTV equation kicks in again. The value of a longtime customer is well worth a little patronage on your part.

"I've seen this all my life, and it seems to work well," Chris offers. "People like to do business with people who do business with them."

It sure can't hurt.

Making the most of your six-minute opportunity

Clorinda Holland was flat-out one of the most impressive, hardworking, and successful hospitality sales professionals I ever had the good fortune to work with. She and I teamed up for sales calls together when she was our regional salesperson for Park Lane Hotels. I would go to New York, New Jersey, and Connecticut to make sales calls with her. She knew all the right customers like no one else did.

She has a tale of her own on sales ROI and about making the most of what you are given, even if the odds seem long: "I found my dream job as a remote salesperson representing Salt Lake City. I was working in my New Jersey home office selling SLC to groups located in the Northeast.

"I had my work cut out for me, as our destination hadn't had anyone working that territory for a long time. Part of my sales strategy was to gain as much exposure as possible in the shortest period of time. I needed a big bang for our bucks. Unfortunately, I did not have a robust budget to work with," she revealed.

"I heard of an important industry luncheon coming to my area and I jumped at the chance to secure us as the name sponsor of that lunch for the first time ever," Holland says. "It was $2,500 to sponsor the lunch. With that, I would get the opportunity to make a sponsor's pitch. I took the leap of faith and told the planning committee, 'I'll take it!' They gave me a whopping six minutes.

Holland planned her brief allotment of time carefully, hoping to strike just the right chord with the audience of event planners. Ever the veteran professional, she knew the crowd and what was likely to work in that setting.

"I showed a very short but hilarious video that we had produced. It was a takeoff on the TV comedy show *The Office*, which was different than most typical visitors' bureau videos. It was a big hit," she recalls.

When the video ended, Holland poured all of her enthusiasm into a brief presentation to the group on the benefits of SLC, working inside the time constraint with the few minutes remaining following the video. One particular event planner in attendance complimented her on her delivery and they began discussing the outlines of a $6 million group annually for three years.

"That's a 2,400-to-1 ratio for the ROI on sponsoring that original luncheon," Holland reports. "I booked them and the group represented SLC's second-largest convention booking in the history of the city. That's quite a return on those original six minutes!

"Sometimes you spend a little and get a lot back in return—it's all about being targeted with your approach, "she adds. "My story here has two main lessons: If you don't have a foothold, you have to think outside the box and create one, make some kind of memorable splash the customers will notice. You can't just wait around for customers to find you. And secondly, when you only have six minutes, you'd better darn well make the most of them!"

The $300,000 bottle of wine

Nina Ramos, a former destination sales team leader for

San Mateo County in California tells another tale of a small investment that yielded terrific results:

"During an industry tradeshow, partnering with our local convention and visitors bureau, we displayed a special collector's bottle of thirty-dollar wine we were using in a drawing as a prize to gain interest in our booth," Ramos recalls.

"For every RFP (Request For Proposal) we received, we entered that meeting planner's name into the drawing. As it happened, the wine drew the attention of a particular event planner who asked me excitedly, 'How can I get that bottle of wine?'

"After I explained the details of the promotional giveaway to her, she casually shrugged and told me that they always booked their meetings in the Midwest. When I asked her if there were particular reasons why they always met in the Midwest, she thought about it for a minute and said, 'No, not really. We've just always booked there.'

"Aha, I saw an opening! I thought I would take the opportunity to drill down a bit deeper," Ramos adds.

"I asked about her meeting details and for the biggest deciding factors for her location choice. As it turns out, our destination in San Mateo County was a perfect fit for her requirements. She loved the idea of a California destination option and she gave me an RFP for 350 rooms.

"We booked her group for three consecutive years! Her group was one of the biggest revenue-producing weekend meetings we ever booked, and it all started with her interest in that bottle of wine, which we ended up presenting to her after all," Ramos chuckled.

The moral of this story, aside from the value of a promotional bottle of wine being worth at least ten thousand times its purchase price, is to recognize and seize your opportunity, even though it may be a slim one. Instead of giving up after the first negative response by the event planner, Ramos recognized a small crack in the window of opportunity and went to work as an intrepid salesperson. She asked important follow-up questions, probing further to find an opening, like a wily chess player. And she found one. *If you don't ask, you won't get.*

With further digging, fact-finding, questioning, and reframing things for your prospects, you may get them to rethink their original situation and go in a direction they never thought possible.

And when you twist the familiar, you very well may find yourself going in a direction you never thought possible, either. As these stories illustrate, applying creativity to your sales efforts increases your odds of making an impression on your prospects far beyond that of your competition.

Building Your Playbook:

- *Describe an uphill journey you took in the pursuit of a sale. How did it turn out? What did you do?*
- *What was your most creative sale?*
- *How about your sales team? Do they use their creativity to garner sales?*
- *Do you have any potential customers where you could become their customer and start building that bridge to your pipeline for the future?*
- *Have you ever captured a client when their current vendor (your competition) fell asleep on the job and took the business for granted?*

Chapter 51

Salespeople Who Don't Pay Attention Lose to Sick Cats

"It is not your customer's job to remember you. It is your obligation and responsibility to make sure they don't have the chance to forget you." —Patricia Fripp

Some sales presentations shine brightly, and others are so bad that a customer uses just about any excuse to end the torture.

Ron Young, owner of Eagle Communications in Murfreesboro, Tennessee, relates a tale of woeful salesmanship that forced him to use a unique escape mechanism to end his misery at the hands of a poor salesperson:

"I was being pursued for two months by a company that offered search engine optimization," Young recalls. "Every day I seemed to be pushing their sales rep off. This 'never-take-no-for-an-answer' salesperson told me I could make more money with their custom plan. He promised me a customized presentation. I finally caved and agreed to meet with him. I gave him details of what I needed and was looking for. After all, I'm not above learning and I wanted to improve my SEO."

"Recipe for the perfect pitch: Be able to describe your business or product in two sentences. Be energetic, honest, informative, and brief." —Lori Greiner

From what you will see unfold here, I doubt if this SEO salesperson ever heard Greiner's advice. In fact, he broke her every rule.

The meeting was set up at his local Starbucks. When Young arrived, the persistent sales rep was sitting at a window-side table with his laptop open, waiting for him. The hot sun was beaming through the window onto the table from behind him. As great salespeople know, the setting matters. Not to this guy.

"I arrived, got my coffee, and sat down," Young continues. "He saw me but didn't offer to get me a coffee or anything else. Being in sales myself, I thought that was a bit of poor hospitality and salesmanship, as he had invited me to hear his pitch. It was not a great opening impression."

Without any real warm-up conversation, the sales guy started right into his PowerPoint presentation, with his screen facing *him*, not Young, as he began to read his slides, word for word.

"All I could see was the back of his laptop, so I got up and leaned over the table to see the slides on his screen. He was oblivious to that, never offering to rotate his laptop for me. He tried to show me a canned video, but I couldn't see it as the bright sun was coming directly into the window, over his shoulder, and causing a glare. He wasn't off to a great start.

"I looked for him to take a breath so as to give me an opening for a question. I asked him about how his product would actually work for my business. He said he would get to it later; he was clearly determined to parrot through his slides. By this time, we were thirty minutes into this slide slog, which lacked even a shred of any customization to my needs that I had given him in advance."

Young tried to again tap the sales rep's brakes by giving him a chance to address his specific needs. The tone-deaf sales guy reminded Young that he would "go over all that later." In his quest to administer this death by PowerPoint to his prospect, he ignored all of the hints and signals. Young doubted even a bullhorn would have worked at this point.

"Thoroughly exasperated and one hour into this bore-fest, I asked him the question that no self-respecting sales-person ever wants to hear: 'How much longer is this going to take?'" Young remembers. "He totally missed the clue. 'Just nine more slides,' was his response to me. OMG, the most clueless sales rep I had ever seen. I wanted to jump through the plate glass window!"

Groggy from the redundancy of the sales guy's mono-tone voice reading the slides and absolutely frustrated at not getting answers to things he wanted to know, Young tried to be courteous, but his well had run dry. Ninety minutes into this, frustrated, with a sore back from leaning over the table and sweating from the sun reflecting off the window, he had reached his limit of patience.

"At this point, I was ready to pull my hair out. I had to get out of there. I abruptly stood up from the table, looked at my watch, and bluntly delivered what has to be the worst-sounding reason ever given for ducking out of a sales call:

'I have a sick cat at home. And she needs her medicine right now.'

"As funny as that sounded, I *did* have a sick cat. But it was being taken care of by a family member while I was out. I just needed a reason to stand up and end that poor excuse for a sales appointment, and it just popped into my head," Young admitted.

"Beware of monotony; it's the mother of all deadly sins."
—Edith Wharton

This SEO rep could have used this quote as a screensaver. What a train wreck. Let's boil down a few of the most salient lessons from this episode to help us learn what *not* to do:

• *The sales rep failed to deliver the goods of what he promised—a customized presentation. This was nothing but a canned slide deck. A big customer letdown.*
• *He did not make the customer comfortable. Young had to lean over the table to see the screen and the sales rep did not pick up on that awkwardness.*
• *His sales etiquette was missing in action. If you invite a prospect to meet with you to hear your sales pitch, you pay for the food and beverages.*
• *He didn't read Young's body language, missing the verbal cues of a bored and disengaged prospect.*
• *Too many slides, and he read the slides without offering any questions or creating any engagement. Boring! One should never just read slides during a sales pitch or presentation. They are intended to support/illuminate your presentation, not* **be** *your presentation. This is unfortunately a common malaise.*
• *The sales rep did not ask questions or sell consultatively. Spewing factoids equals feature-vomiting. Yuck! Engage, engage, engage! Two-way conversation is a must.*
• *He didn't answer direct questions posed to him by his prospect. He missed great opportunities there. Questions reveal a lot, such as what kinds of things the prospect finds interesting or is concerned about. Prospects literally help you sell to them when they ask questions, so pick up on those clues!*

The bottom line is this: Don't be such an insufferable

salesperson that you're doomed to the inglorious fate of getting dumped by the excuse of a sick cat at home.

Building Your Playbook:

- *Review the actions of the sales rep. Are there any areas where you or your sales teams have made the same errors? And what happened?*
- *What would you have done differently as the SEO sales rep?*
- *Do you or your organization practice sales calls and proper use of support materials such as PowerPoint presentations BEFORE going live in front of prospects? I highly recommend it.*

Chapter 52

Passing Out Bad News to Customers?
Beware of Flying Donuts

"I forgot all my dos and remembered all my don'ts."
—Arnold Palmer

I was watching a video of a classic televised golf match in Hawaii several years ago pitting two of golf's royalty, Arnold Palmer and Gary Player, in a friendly match for charity. Arnie hit a rare poor shot and his golf ball skidded across the fairway, much like a ball that a weekend duffer would strike. Ever the epitome of class, Arnie turned to Player in a good-natured, self-effacing way and spoke those words above. It got me thinking. Whether golfing or doing anything else in our lives, how many times do we do the same thing?

This next story coincidentally also happened in Hawaii. It relates to how a luxury hotel also *forgot its dos and remembered its don'ts* when it came to its customers. It's a cautionary tale that easily translates to any business that practices some kind of customer care.

Hospitality sales lifer Gary W. Brown of Williamsburg, Virginia was a jovial and affable sales leader of many outstanding lodging and destination teams during his long career. Over the years, like many other hospitalitarians, he and his teammates would find themselves in a pickle every so often. He shares this episode where a situation went sideways quickly and was anything but funny at the time. He learned a valuable lesson about what happens when the wrong person says the wrong things at the wrong time, for all the wrong reasons.

"I was working in Honolulu when most hotels were hopelessly overbooked," Brown recalls. "The commitments that hotels in paradise made with customers were done with much speculation with the tour operators who were trying to fill their air charters. It was not unusual to overbook hotels almost 200 percent on some dates, hoping for great 'slippage' (a meetings industry term for the amount of no-show guests or cancellations from a group's commitment), so that we could fill the hotel perfectly at 100 percent, the gold standard of the hotel business."

I can relate to Brown's perspective here. During my formative years in hotels, I learned a tongue-in-cheek phrase from long-timers that was used to glaze over the "open secret" about overbooking: "We're never oversold, we're just under-departed."

Brown chuckles at the memory: "It was a crazy way to do business, to say the least. I was working at a very prominent luxury Waikiki Beach oceanfront hotel. One of my accounts was a large Canadian tour operator. We were heavily overbooked and ours was the deluxe hotel on this particular charter. Unfortunately, we got caught in the overbooking gamble, and it came to pass that we had to *walk* (relocate to another hotel) forty guests from that charter.

"Typically, the day after a group's arrival in Honolulu, there was a breakfast briefing held at our hotel where tour operators sold the optional ground tour programs to their group.

"This particular tour operator was incensed with the news that we had to walk forty of his customers. He demanded that we apologize in front of his group to explain why the folks who had purchased deluxe oceanfront rooms with us would be walked to a very low-grade hotel three blocks inland from the beach, where the description usually says something tricky like 'ocean nearby.' And let me tell you, it was a horrible hotel."

Hotels try to walk a fine line between empty rooms and being overcommitted, walking a few guests. Front desk staffers hate it, because they are the ones passing out the bad news at night to weary travelers who find out they are shut out of the hotel they so carefully selected. But most hotel general managers silently rejoice at a full hotel and don't get too upset with walking a few guests (another "open secret") since it pays a lot of bills. Current net profit margins of a hotel room are over 11 percent.

Brown thought his resort was prepared to receive the blowback: "Normally, our director of agency sales, Charlie, would speak at the tour events. He was a perfectly tanned, silver-haired, handsome Hawaiian man, and he had a very soothing manner. He was a master at the 'aloha spirit,' the perfect representative for this kind of task.

"But oh, no! We had a new director of sales, fresh from the U.S. mainland who apparently wanted to strut his stuff. He informed us that *he* was going to speak to the group. Charlie and I were to flank him in front of the room, facing this rattled charter group.

"The new director should never have opened his mouth," offered Brown.

"He began by introducing industry jargon to our customers, which is a big no-no.

'Sorry folks, we just didn't get the wash' was his opening line. Ouch!

"As you can imagine, these guests did not know what

'wash' was, nor did they care. The more my new director of sales talked, the more angered the group became. He even alluded to the poor condition of the hotel where they were headed. All 223 people in that charter group remained at the briefing to hear this abominable management apology, and how friends who flew with them nonstop from Toronto were being walked to a badly inferior hotel due to our overly aggressive, screwed-up calculations."

These people may have gotten "lei'd" getting off their charter flight at the Honolulu airport. But now they were getting screwed.

Brown has vivid memories of this moment of truth: "These jetlagged guests began shouting obscenities at us, standing up and screaming for all to get their attorneys involved. 'You will pay dearly for this' was among the things we were hearing from the angry customers. Had there been a Hawaiian imu pit close by, I know three hoteliers who would have been roasted right there as the main course.

"All of a sudden, I felt a thump on my chest, and it wasn't a heart attack. I had been pummeled with a powdered donut! It flew in from some unseen person with great aim. To the side of me, our man Charlie ducked just in time as a cream-filled chocolate Bismarck donut sailed past his head. The pastry-missile hit the wall of our ballroom behind Charlie, and I could see the "splat" where the thick chocolate coating was sticking to the wall. I watched it as if in slow motion, inching down the wall, leaving a trail of chocolate icing as it descended to the floor.

"I love donuts, but not as a pocket square on my suit!

"This was an ugly scene and we knew it was time to abandon ship. We slid out of the room and ducked out via a service entrance, running for our lives. It was truly a day where the spirit of aloha was nowhere to be found," Brown admitted, and he carried the lessons from that day with him throughout his career.

He never looked at donuts the same way after that day, either.

Building Your Playbook:

- *Relate this story to your own business. Do you have times where you bend the rules and it backfires with your customers and employees?*
- *What kind of messaging do you manage when it comes to passing along bad news to your customers?*
- *When "fails" start to happen, what can you do the stop them from snowballing?*
- *What are your steps for customer recovery? If you have no set program, now is the time to build one.*

Chapter 53

Calling on your Knights of the Round Table

"I'm not the smartest fellow in the world, but I can sure pick smart colleagues." —Franklin D. Roosevelt

King Arthur of Camelot fame assembled his amazing support team around him and called them his Knights of the Round Table. These brave knights gathered in the castle around a large table that was round rather than rectangular so that everyone who sat around it was seen as trustworthy and equal to each other. Each of them was a confidante of the king, helping to support him and ensure peace in the kingdom. They also shared deeds and strategies among each other.

Inspired by something I had recently seen featuring King Arthur and his knights, I sketched out some ideas of applying the same concept to each of us in our particular life and/or career.

Essentially, I believe that we all need our own Knights of the Round Table in one way or another. We need to have an "inner circle" of people we can draw support from, bounce ideas off of, and share our thoughts, dilemmas, or crises we are facing.

I first introduced this concept to a team from Fort Worth and they really embraced the idea, as have many others since then. It seems to be something that not a lot of people ever give any thought to. I certainly have my own Round Table and I am also on others' Round Tables as we receive and offer help, support, and advice with each other.

Here is how it works:

In terms of professional "knights," I suggest that you write down the names of five-to-ten customers, colleagues, and peers who you feel are part of your personal "inner circle."

We need people around us who can be honest sounding boards for us. Don't just put a bunch of yes-people or kiss-ups around you. Those kinds of people will only tell you what you *want* to hear. You need people who will tell you what you *need* to hear.

Confident, self-assured people and true leaders are brave enough to surround themselves with people who bring value to the table, whether they always agree or not. President Roosevelt employed that tactic while leading our country during World War II. That's healthy. Be on solid ground with your own beliefs and principles. You want supporters, yes. Suck-ups, no.

"I can't win without the amazing support team around me."
—Jordan Spieth

As a professional golfer, Spieth has to hit the actual golf shots but he has coaches, caddies, assistants and family around to support him and lighten his load. Let's face it, no matter our chosen work it gets lonely out there in our world at times. Don't you sometimes feel as if you are taking on the world as a solo warrior? And for those of you who are entrepreneurs or self-employed (or thinking about it), *you really need a Round Table*. Otherwise, you'll be largely operating in a vacuum which is not recommended! I've called on my own knights thinking I was going to go in the direction of "X" and my knights gave me compelling reasons why I should pivot and go in the entirely different direction of "Y."

Call them "sounding boards" or whatever you like but by any name, your knights may give you a perspective you didn't know existed. They might reframe an issue or idea so it looks like something entirely different. They may twist your familiar!

And don't worry, you will have people come and go on your Round Table as you move along in your career or your life. It happens.

How to build your own Round Table

Start with five knights (and by "knights," I mean trusted advisors, without limit to gender, of course). Make a list of those five people whom you consider to be your trusted advisors. You can expand your circle of knights to include as many as you want. But make sure it's a fairly exclusive club. This isn't a Facebook popularity contest in which you think you have to have 150 people on your Round Table who will "like" everything you do or say or else you won't be able to sleep at night.

Ask yourself: Who would I call in a pinch? With whom can I speak forthrightly? Whose opinions do I value? Who do I trust? Who trusts me? Who inspires me?

Now, let's flip the Round Table

I'm going to twist the familiar on you here and add a dynamic dimension to this Round Table idea. I've asked you to identify those people on *your* Round Table. Now, I'll ask you this: "Whose Round table are *you* on?" If I called twenty of your customers or friends and asked them for their five knights, which folks would list you as a member of *their* respective Round Tables?

It's an interesting perspective to ponder, isn't it? Are you 100 percent sure about who would consider you as one of their knights? This exercise goes better if we check our egos at the door. It has forced many people to really give some thought as to who they need to get to know better.

Invest the time and care it takes to be on other peoples' Round Tables as one of their trusted advisors. It will pay off for you personally and professionally. It will increase your referrals and business reach, too. Let your knights know that you have selected them for your Round Table after you explain to them what the concept is, of course. They will most likely be very honored, as you would be, to be one of their knights.

We all face dragons at various points in our lives. Why not have your knights with you to help fend them off and knock them down to size?

Building Your Playbook:

- *Make a list of your knights — give it some solid thought. Think about how and when you will approach them and call upon them.*
- *Commit to calling on your knights when the need arises, and also give back generously to those who consider you a knight of theirs.*
- *If you manage salespeople, have them craft their own Round Tables with the same goals in mind. Knights can be invaluable to salespeople. Note: Don't limit this program just to salespeople, however — **everyone** can use a Round Table.*

Chapter 54

From Ballfields to Business:
Coaching Excellence is Transferable

"Everybody wants to be a success. I've never heard anyone say he or she wants to be a failure. No matter what their definition of success might be—and it's different for everybody—everyone wants to be successful." —Coach Bob Ladouceur

Of course, you don't have to play sports to gain important life lessons. But there is no denying that sports can teach some powerful lessons—both good and bad—and the parallels between sports, business, and life are plentiful. The most important influencers of our lives can often be people such as our head coach, manager, band director, dance team/cheer coach, etc. Their lessons, both inspiring and debilitating, can stick with us forever.

My own sports coaches and business bosses taught me valuable lessons in both the right ways and wrong ways to do things. It's important to have takeaways from both ends of that spectrum. It's how we grow and decide which paths to take in our own journeys and which styles to use. As the legendary UCLA college basketball coach John Wooden once said: "A good coach can change a game; a great coach can change a life."

To help illustrate how excellent coaching (whether in business or sports) can impact the pursuit of quality, the importance of trust and the building of team camaraderie for winning results, I'd like to introduce you to someone who has changed many lives over many years as a high school football coach and teacher. His principles and lessons aptly apply to many aspects of running businesses and ways of operating. And you don't need to know anything (or even care) about football or sports, either. The lessons we'll be talking about here are fully transferable to your own applications in one way or another.

Coach Lad and his leadership legacy

Bob Ladouceur is one of the most humble people I've ever met. Talking to him, you'd never know he even coached one winning game. He's also not some high-flying Wall Street wiz or Fortune 100 C-suite executive. He taught at a high school. But he is a genuine winner by every measure, and real winners don't need to showboat. They let their records, and others, do their talking.

"Coach Lad," as many call him, built quite a football coaching legacy over many years at De La Salle High School in Concord, a city near my home in northern California. In my quest to study more deeply what goes into winning leadership methods, I wanted to see how excellence was achieved and how it was sustained over such a long period. I made it a goal to seek an interview with Coach Lad. My goal was to understand more about his successful methods and practices in hopes of drawing business parallels that people can learn from.

I made my way to the high school one afternoon and introduced myself as he was making his way across the campus after practice. He gave me a firm handshake and a shy smile. After I explained what I do for a living and why I wanted to spend some time talking with him, interviewing him about his methods and insights, he encouraged me right on the spot to stay and walk with him as he did his various duties. He didn't even flinch. "Sure," he said quite kindly. "Do you want to talk now?"

Didn't this man have a million other things to do? I gave him an out for a future appointment, but he made me feel quite at ease to stay. We walked and talked freely around the football field, in the team weight room, and he also escorted me through the locker room and into his office to chat.

It was the first of three such talks I had with Coach Lad. He was very friendly and forthcoming with his insights. He never once looked at his watch or hurried me along. I was respectful of his time, too. He treated me like a friend.

Records don't tell the whole story

In addition to his school duties Ladouceur is a sought-after motivational speaker for business executives and groups wanting to learn his recipe for excellence. What is so special about him is that even with his giant-sized career accomplishments, he values the impact he's had on young peoples' lives more than his coaching records. To put his *football vs. life* orientation into a business context, one could say that he strived for a successful balance sheet in terms of winning (such as we do in business), but he actually cared more about his performers and their development, knowing that the latter will have a healthy effect on the former. Business leaders please take note.

Unlike the all-too-often practice these days by some on LinkedIn to bloviate their mediocre accomplishments and refer to themselves as "a proven winner" there's no need to do anything of the sort with Coach Lad. He retired as a head coach in 2012 with the highest winning percentage in USA high school football history, an amazing 399–25–3 record at De La Salle. In September 2023 ESPN named his 2001 De La Salle Spartans as the greatest high school football team of all time. His teams were also voted to ten national championships and achieved five California state football titles. A dramatic Hollywood film about Coach Lad and the streak, titled *When the Game Stands Tall* (Sony Pictures, 2014) starred actor Jim Caviezel as Ladouceur.

From the weight room to the board room

So you might ask, "OK, that's terrific but it's high school football. What can this coach offer that will be of any help to me or my organization?"

Fair enough. Consider this: We aren't going to be talking football plays here. We'll be examining how proven winning techniques in one application can be used to achieve outstanding results in another. You will discover that Coach Lad's concepts are transferable to a multitude of business applications. I'm betting they will inspire you for your business, too. His outlook on how to excel to achieve better results goes far beyond the goalposts on a football field.

Ladouceur keeps his feet on the ground and his head from swelling when talking about his methods and results: "We were never fighting for wins," he explains in his book *Chasing Perfection*. "We were fighting for a belief in what we stood for, the way we believe life should be lived and people should be treated . . . We were also trying to teach them [the players] accountability."

Preparation, perfect practice, hard work,
and repetition will pay off

During a virtual program where he talked about his formula for success, Coach Lad answered a question about what it takes as a leader/coach to put successful teams out year after year: "Winning was just a by-product of how you approach life, it's an outcome of all the things you do. You don't even have to talk about winning. It comes naturally if you're doing all the other things."

As a business owner, manager, or team leader, take a pause and think: What are those "other things" me and my team should be doing?

Make no mistake. All of this takes work, diligence, and commitment. Coach Lad speaks frankly as to the work ethic it takes to achieve excellence: "It's drilling and redrilling ad nauseam to the point of boredom. There is no way around that. No matter what your system is, there has to be a foundation of technique and fundamentals."

Fundamentals may seem boring, but they are, well, *fundamental* to success. The late, great women's college basketball coach Pat Summitt also felt strongly about work ethic in order to achieve winning results: "By doing things when you are too tired, by pushing yourself farther than you thought you could, you become a competitor. So many people today seem rather likely to give up on the hard things, or not even try them at all."

Applying Coach Lad's ideas to the corporate world:
the "secret sauce"

Amazingly, Coach Lad revealed to me that while coaching,

he only had four team rules each year. They were simple, direct, and serious: "You can't lie, cheat, steal or do substance abuse."

I also asked him for his best advice for businesses that want to achieve sustained success. He offered this: "Be prepared. It's the little things that matter. When you cut corners, it adds up."

To me, that translates to this: *DO sweat the small stuff.*

I immediately recalled a tough budgeting meeting during my hotel days when our hotel general manager told our cut-crazy controller, "You can't cut yourself to greatness." Can you see an application of this for your organization?

I asked Ladouceur if he had an overall goal for any particular season or game. He replied:

"Our goal is to put ourselves in a position where success is possible. We don't think we will win every game, but we want to put ourselves in a position to win."

Aha! To me, that idea seemed like a "secret sauce." You can't ensure that your people will always win and you can't ensure that they won't flub up occasionally. You also can't promise them moonlight and magnolias every day, either. But what you *can do* is set people up for success and put them in a position to be successful. Essentially, it's about having the right people in the right places, doing the right things. How does that square with your organization?

"The most important words that have helped me in life, when things have gone right or when things have gone wrong, are 'accept responsibility.'" —Billie Jean King

While Coach Lad held himself and his coaching staff accountable for their actions and efforts, his players also drank deeply from the cup of accountability, and maybe even more so. After all, they had to execute the plans and make the actual plays on the field. Given the school's national football prominence, they felt that they had very high standards to uphold.

In business, it's the same thing. Everyone should own a piece of the accountability pie, from top executives/owners to middle management and frontline staff. Everyone should uphold the brand promises and customer commitments.

During our talks, Coach Lad also shared with me his core values, staying constant, year in and year out:

Hard work
Discipline
Technique
Learning how to get along with each other

Those don't just sound like high school football core values, do they? How would they sound if you adopted them for your organization or business team?

I also asked him which traits among those he taught to his players would be most applicable to people in the business world as a starting point: "What we try to instill in our kids is responsibility, commitment, and accountability. I'd start there," he told me.

Those three attributes sounded like a great place to start in a program for a new resort client of mine. The sales and services team was having some fits and starts gelling together. At times, they pulled in different directions.

Three-by-five commitment cards
—it's all about trusting one another

I had heard about the De La Salle trust and accountability program involving three-by-five cards. Coach Lad elaborated on his tradition for me. It works like this:

The night before a game, the team meets at a player's home for a pasta feed. Afterward, the team (and *only* the team, no parents) goes into a large room or the garage together. Each player gets a three-by-five card and writes down a goal that he wants to accomplish for the game and is pledging to do for the good of the team. In turn, each player stands up and reads his commitment card to teammates and coaches. They hold each other accountable for the results. It is a very profound moment for all.

And the results are the stuff of record books.

If high schoolers can do such a thing,
how about adults in business settings?

For the resort group, I set it up thinking that if high school athletes could do this, so could adult business professionals. That's what I told them. I was wrong. The initiative had very limited success.

Only a couple of the people lived up to their commitments made to each other. Many were uneasy about even putting a commitment down in writing. There was almost no accountability in the group, including the management team. I doubt that any of them had ever been asked to do such a thing. There was clearly a lot of strength and conditioning work for me to do with this client.

When I returned home, I visited with Coach Lad again

and I explained to him what had happened. I was frustrated by the exercise. Maybe I had done it wrong. Maybe the method was incorrectly applied. He listened, and then he offered this: "No, Gary, that's not it. I'd say it didn't work because they don't know each other that well yet."

With the coach's answer, it all came into focus for me.

While Coach Lad's players got to know each other through months of practice and being in the classrooms together, the resort sales and management group were virtual strangers. They didn't have high trust in each other quite yet. They didn't feel invested in each other enough to make meaningful, binding commitments. They weren't comfortable as a group yet. Were they afraid they'd get reprimanded if they didn't meet their commitments? Clearly, what I was attempting to do was uncharted water for them.

Reworking the plan for a better result

I went back to the drawing board and reworked the exercise. I gave it another try on my next training installment for that company six months later. I presented it in a different manner. It worked much better given the six additional months of interaction the team had with one another.

Everyone learned from this episode, including me. The company's managing director gained a measure of self-realization, too. I relayed to him that I had gone back to chat with Coach Lad about our first tepid attempt with this exercise, and I shared what the coach had surmised was the reason it hadn't worked.

The experienced hospitality executive looked me in the eye, shook his head in an apologetic manner, and remarked, "As a resort group, we should be embarrassed. And you were right, Gary. If a bunch of high school kids can do this, so should we."

Touchdown!

Building Your Playbook:

- *Using Coach Lad's criteria for building a strong team, rate your own team in the areas he listed. How does your team stack up?*
- *Do you have team rules? What are they? Are they working? Are they respected and followed?*
- *What are you doing to create an atmosphere of accountability on your team?*
- *How do you sustain long-term success like Coach Lad discussed? Do you practice, focus on fundamentals, rinse and repeat?*
- *How about trying the three-by-five card commitment exercise? Is your team ready for such a thing?*

Chapter 55

Coaches Can also Teach us What NOT to Do

"Looking back, I've learned the most from the bad coaches, really, how not to act, how not to coach, how not to treat people. So I always say, no matter what situations you're faced with, how bad it is, you can always walk away and learn. You can always rise above it." —Jennie Finch

Finch was an Olympic gold and silver medal-winning softball pitcher and All-American at the University of Arizona and *Time* magazine's "most famous softball player in history." Her career offered many moments to glean lessons from her coaches. Her take on this illustrates how we can often learn more from the bad than the good.

Think of this: Do you pay more attention to your driving speed in your car after you get stopped for an expensive ticket, or when you simply pass a speed limit sign that you see on the side of the road? Yup, I thought so.

While growing up, I generally enjoyed playing sports. I learned some good lessons from most of my baseball and football coaches. But I never had the opportunity to play for a coach on the level of Bob Ladouceur or Pat Summit. The most impactful "wrong way" lessons occurred during my senior year in high school playing varsity football. I'll share a couple of them here as unfortunate examples of how *not* to lead.

As you read these episodes, think about similarities that translate to your business and how you would do things differently as the coach or team leader.

Some rules don't apply to everyone equally

Our head coach had given us team rules during our pre-season workouts. We were expected to abide by them or else face expulsion from the team. They were the standard high school fare like no smoking, no drinking, keep your grades up, no suspensions, that kind of stuff.

One of our talented players, who I recall our head coach believed had college football potential, was caught drinking during our preseason "hell week" practices. Instead of backing up his own rules and making the tough call about this player, our coach called all of us varsity players to the gym. He explained that this player had been caught drinking and had thus broken a team rule. But he was leaving it up to a vote of us teenage players to decide whether our classmate was to miss the season or play on the team for his senior year. Many of us were confused by this; did we have team rules or not?

Now, years later, I can think of several leadership flaws exposed by our coaching staff during this episode; specifically, a lack of a leadership "spine" comes to mind, plus rules for some but not others, and favoritism, too.

As it turned out, we had a fairly forgiving team of fellow players. Either that or the guys who liked to drink a bit figured they would have a "get out of jail free" card to use in the event they were busted during the season, too.

The little paper ballots were collected in a box and the coach read off the results, like when the TV show *Survivor* reveals who goes home. A majority of our players voted to keep this classmate on the team, but not all. As it turned out, there were consequences for this episode.

Our coaches lost respect from a number of the players

that day in the gym. No one ever divulged how they voted, but something changed from that point forward as far as our team chemistry. We didn't know it at the time, but the team seemed fractured. We seniors had won the league championship together as sophomores but in this, our final season, we limped our way to four wins and five losses—not the big year that we had envisioned.

"That episode told me that our coaches' rules were totally meaningless," recalls Dave Harvey, a friend of mine and a fellow senior on the team. "They passed them out for us to follow and a few weeks later, they're asking us seventeen-year-olds to decide for them whether or not to enforce their own rules. That's upside-down."

As it turned out, the coach didn't do the reprieved player any real favors, either. College football coaches didn't come knocking on his door with scholarship offers and sadly his drinking problems worsened during the school year—another lesson to be learned. The player whose season our coach had rigged to be "saved" kept repeating his habits. He needed help, not a favor.

In trying to keep this one player happy (and maybe selfishly wanting that athlete on the team because he was thought to be a strong asset to our defense), our head coach lost respect from some of the other team members because he eschewed his leadership responsibility of enforcing his own rules. Despite our coach's large physical stature, to some he looked smaller and weaker after that vote in the gym.

Let 'em suffer?

Many years ago, a reporter asked head football coach John McKay of the Tampa Bay Buccaneers this question after another ugly loss by his team during their abysmal inaugural season: "Coach, what do you think of your team's execution?" He calmly answered: "I'm in favor of it."

Although my high school football coach didn't physically execute anybody, he concocted a twisted kind of lesson by letting some of our players suffer miserably through a horrible experience, even when reinforcements were standing by, more than ready and willing to jump in. This is a story of what NOT to do.

As that season unfolded, our hopes for a conference championship faded quickly. By the time of a mid-season, three-game losing skid, our coach apparently gave up on what was my graduating class's senior season. He was starting to sit the seniors and play more juniors so as to give them experience for the following season. The coaching term for this is "playing for next year." Of course, this didn't sit well at all with us seniors, who had waited three years to play our final season of football together and enjoy our senior experience. With a league title two years prior, we had talent on the squad.

We seniors decided to hold a seniors-only meeting in the weight room before practice to talk things over. Feelings were running strong; frustration had bubbled over. The previous week, we had been dominated by our cross-town rivals 34-7. That really stung. Worse, many of us hadn't played a down, standing on the sidelines in a pouring rain. Double sting.

The game was largely decided by halftime, yet our coach

left the overmatched juniors in the game. At one point, we had just one senior playing among the twenty-two positions on the field. We seniors bristled on the sidelines as the rain drenched us. We weren't getting a last shot at our rivals. We weren't getting a shot to come out and maybe get some of our team pride back with a score or two.

At our meeting, we aired our frustrations with each other and then called the coaching staff in to hear what we had to say. As mentioned, our head coach cut a dominating figure—a large-framed, ex-collegiate lineman who stood about 6'5," which intimidated many of the guys. For some reason that I don't recall, my teammates asked me to speak for them. Oh sure, let me get my head chopped off!

I was fairly nervous, but I marshaled enough courage to ask him this question (as it's been more than a few years, I may not have all the exact words in order, but the essence is here): "Coach, on Friday we were getting wiped out by halftime. We'd like to know why you stuck with the juniors and kept them in the game in the second half. We're seniors and we practiced hard all week, fired up to have one last shot at our rivals. Why did you keep the juniors on the field for the blowout? Didn't we deserve the chance to see what we could do? After all, our last season here is running out of games."

His answer was incredulous, and a big fat lead balloon to our ears: "Well, the players out on the field got themselves into that hole, and I wanted them to have to suffer through what they created."

We were stunned. No one said a word. I was only in high school but that sounded like the worst leadership cop-out decision that I had ever heard. Harvey recalls the scene, too: "Where were the other coaches on this? They didn't say a word." Did the juniors really learn any lessons by "suffering?" There was never any evidence of such a thing. It worked to further fracture our team, that's for sure.

The following week or so, we seniors figured the assistant coaches must have somehow talked some sense into our head coach because we saw some increased playing time during the second half of the season. We played with enough intensity to win three out of our last four games. We got a measure of satisfaction by winning our very last game, too, which meant a lot to us as we closed out our football playing careers. But make no mistake—we were playing for each other, not the coach. He was already playing for next year.

Building Your Playbook

- *Can you cite examples in your life when coaches or leaders either inspired you by their good decisions or disappointed/angered you by their bad decisions?*
- *Have you ever had to show "tough love" to a team member when they screwed up or broke a rule, even though it would put a strain on the operation in some way?*
- *Can you think of any of your (or others') decisions that adversely affected team dynamics, and what you learned from that?*
- *How would you fill in this sentence: Integrity on my team (or in my organization) is _____?*
- *How important is integrity and respect in your organization? How is it manifested?*

Chapter 56

The Best Coaches Keep Things Simple

"Self-praise is for losers. Be a winner. Stand for something. Always have class, and be humble." —John Madden

During our friendly albeit competitive backgammon matches over frequent lunches, my friend John Vella, a former Oakland Raiders offensive lineman and All-American football player at the University of Southern California, will often share insights with me from his days in the game. We have a lot of laughs over the shenanigans of his former teammates and his stories of epic games and "inside stuff" about preparation, focus and coaching.

The nuggets he's shared with me about his beloved coach, the late John Madden, intrigued me enough to include them here for you. They offer solid lessons for business leaders and managers to model and make their own. I think you will find that they translate quite nicely to leading and directing business units and organizations.

In addition to being a professional athlete, Vella owned and operated his own set of retail stores after his NFL playing days. Thus, he not only knows the approach to being successful in large, established-brand organizations such as the Raiders and USC, but he also faced the challenges of being a small business owner and building his own brand from the ground up.

One particular afternoon, I asked Vella to take me back to the time when the Raiders were preparing for their Super Bowl XI against the Minnesota Vikings. Did the team do anything significantly different from its normal business-as-usual routines employed during the regular season? I was thinking about businesses that have to crank it up for their own type of annual event or campaign. Does that call for a whole new playbook and a new set of procedures?

Not according to John Madden. "Coach wanted to keep the routine before the Super Bowl as normal as possible," Vella recalled. "He gave us five or six days off the first week after the AFL [American Football Conference] championship. He didn't want to over-prepare us. He didn't re-do our playbook just because it was the Super Bowl. We stayed true to who we were. We went with what made us successful." The approach worked brilliantly, as the Raiders prevailed convincingly 32-14 over the Vikings, capping a stellar 16-1 overall record that season.

As his big lineman's hands moved his backgammon pieces deftly around the board during one of our lunch matches, I asked Vella about Madden's overall approach to coaching, to uncover any savvy business applications. After all, Madden was an NFL Hall of Fame coach. He compiled an impressive 112-39-7 record during his career, winning an impressive three out of every four games he coached.

Breaking it down in little bits can improve focus

"He had us focus on what we were supposed to do—our jobs—and center on worrying about ourselves and not what the other guy was doing or not doing," Vella mused. "'Do your own job,' he'd say. He constantly drummed it into us to think about the next play. I remember him saying 'the next play, the next play. Don't think about the next quarter or the next game down the road, or the fact that we are playing the Steelers in two weeks—just the next play.'"

Thus, Madden's success was breaking things down in plainspoken little bits. I shudder when I think of how many aspiring managers and team leaders think they have to complicate the uncomplicated, or put on airs that they are something they aren't just to impress others. They manage via a bunch of convoluted approaches and sophisticated mumbo jumbo when handling internal issues, giving directions, writing emails, and talking to customers. They look to impress others with their faux sophistication, which is usually not their forte.

Madden seemed to fly in the face of all that. "He didn't put on airs," recalls Vella. "He coached to make things uncomplicated, basic, and understandable." Madden's business approach to football was similar to other successful coaches and leaders. He treated his players like adults and didn't over-manage them. In his world, team success was rooted in *fundamentals*, which is an idea that should never become obsolete, especially in business. You've read about Bob Ladouceur saying that very same thing in another chapter. For people tasked to lead others, *performance and results* ultimately matter, not flowery language, excuses, or confusing procedures.

Smart leaders have to know when to loosen the reins too. Amid all of the grueling work, Madden also allowed his players (many of whom were free spirits) to blow off some steam when they needed to. Thus, the Raiders were fairly loose and confident going into that Super Bowl. Conversely, the Vikings were coached by the stricter, more buttoned-up head coach Bud Grant, and they came into the game more tensed up. It showed in their play during the lopsided game.

Sometimes, teams of people can be too uptight, honed

to too fine an edge. Madden knew his players and where he could push or back off when needed. Smart leaders know their people.

Team rules: the K.I.S.S. method works best

Madden kept it simple in terms of team rules, too, specifically the Raider dress code. He was more concerned with his players' football work and focus, not so much in their attire on road trips. While many NFL coaches stipulated coats, ties, suits, and the like, Madden was revolutionary. As Vella tells it, "He said, 'Look guys, we don't have any coat and tie rules here, but just make sure your Levi's are clean, OK?'"

The relaxed dress code was just one example of how Madden, as Vella puts it, "picked his battles." That's a key trait for a leader to have, to be able to read their audience and decide what is really important and what is superfluous. While Madden eased off the dress code, he was demanding in his expectations for total focus, hard work, and full effort on the field. Business owners and leaders can use this, too. Focus on the important things that really matter and be more flexible on the small stuff that is often just *stuff*.

Vella chuckles when he explains Madden's three simple, overarching team rules in lieu of a lengthy list: "Show up on time, pay attention, and play hard. Do that and we'll all get along just fine." His motto about rules in general was equally straightforward: "The fewer rules a coach has, the fewer rules there are for players to break."

Business leaders have to have a good dose of authenticity and humility, too. Some even have to work at appearing imperfect and fallible (even human?). John Madden set his tone through his self-effacing manner: "I never professed to be perfect. When I do something wrong or something stupid, I laugh at myself."

Whether in sports or in business, getting people to focus starts with Job One

Vella stressed that focus was extremely important to Madden and the Raider coaches. Instead of getting caught up in things they couldn't control, the players were coached to focus on their Job One — right in front of their noses. "We were coached to focus on our three feet of turf around us, the job at hand. We had one job to do, and for me, I was always looking for that edge to do mine better. My Job One was protecting our quarterback (Hall of Famer Kenny Stabler) for five seconds so he could make a play."

Though keeping pressure away for five seconds doesn't sound like a long time, in the violent world of professional football it is easier said than done. But having that specific Job One goal helped dial Vella and his teammates in with a crystal clear understanding of what was expected of them.

Similarly, here are three steps I use in a direct approach to Job One that have proven to be successful when working with my management training groups:

Make sure everyone on the team knows and understands what their Job One is.

Dial in your focus on your immediate job right in front of you; do first things first.

Understand how your role contributes to the overall goal/production/bigger picture.

To summarize, there are all kinds of coaches with all kinds of approaches. Some are more successful than others. You have to find out what works best for you so that you and your teams can be successful. Your leadership style will (and should) likely evolve over the years as you engage with new bosses, new teams, new responsibilities, and additional experiences coming your way.

John Madden's coaching method for success was employing the K.I.S.S. method. Maybe you roll a bit differently. But you can't argue with the man's legacy. Those Madden Raiders were the third winningest NFL team in the 1970s and also hoisted a Super Bowl trophy.

Like the man said: **"Show up on time, pay attention, and play hard. And we'll get along just fine."**

Building Your Playbook

- *What is your management style? Do you break things down in small bits to help with understanding and comprehension for your team?*
- *If you are a team member, same question about your manager or team leader.*
- *What are your (or the organization's) team rules? Are they simple to follow? Are they actually followed? Is your organization too heavily ladened with rules?*
- *What would be your first five things you would do on your team or within your business if you adopted the K.I.S.S. method? Would you eliminate redundancies? Streamline processes? Communicate easier? Cut some red tape?*

Chapter 57

The Roads of History Lead us Back to Today

*"As America decides how to move forward,
as we do we must not forget there is still much
more we can learn from the past." —Brett Baier*

People have asked me if I have an all-time favorite coaching or speaking gig, a most memorable assignment I've treasured over the years. While I truly cherish all of my opportunities to work with people and help them develop and grow, those times when I've had the honor to draw upon one of my lifelong passions—history (specifically, the Civil War), and parlay it with modern-day business coaching, are especially dear to me.

My love for our nation's history led me to twist my own familiar and develop a part of my enterprise I call "Battlefields to Business." Combining history with my core business as a speaker/coach seemed like such a natural to me. I drew inspiration from George Santayana, who famously coined this phase:

"Those who fail to learn the lessons of history are doomed to repeat it."

The Civil War bug bit me early, when my dad bought me The American Heritage Golden Book of the Civil War when I was in second or third grade. I was hooked. I still know it by heart. I also treasured watching Civil War movies and shows on TV back in the day, though blissfully unaware at my tender age that most of them were historically inaccurate.

Fast-forward to eighth grade, when my parents took my brothers and me on a family road trip from our home in Michigan for Easter vacation to Gettysburg, Valley Forge, Atlantic City, and Washington, D.C. My dad loved working some history into trips. Years before he had stopped for a visit to Gettysburg with my mom as his new bride on their way to the Poconos for their honeymoon. Yup, my dad was always a true romantic.

Such a place as Gettysburg, I had never seen. Books and movies were great, but nothing beat the realism of being there. We traversed the various auto stops around the vast national park in our family's Vista Cruiser station wagon, getting out at many of the key sites to walk the fields, read the markers, climb on the rocks, and inspect the cannons with my brothers. I was like a kid in a candy store, absolutely smitten with the place. It was astonishing and awe-inspiring to me to think that my own shoes were walking on the same fields where 172,000 Union and Confederate soldiers fought it out during their bloody struggle in July 1863. That same feeling still comes over me to this day. Since that first trip as an eighth grader, I've been fortunate to return to Gettysburg many times. With each visit I make it a point to explore parts of the battlefield that I have not yet experienced, which leads me to new discoveries each time.

An experiential business program springs forth from a hobby

A few years ago, I was about to take my studies and enthusiasm for the topic to a new level. I was speaking at a meetings industry conference in Richmond, Virginia. I mentioned a historical reference in my remarks to help make a point. Virginia is a state teeming with rich history, so audiences there are very likely to pick up on such a thing.

At the coffee break, I was approached by an audience member, Victoria Matthews, a sales representative from Fredericksburg, Virginia. She had tuned in to my historical reference, asking me if I ever thought of combining my business knowledge with history, and offering training seminars that encompassed both. I lit up like a Christmas tree.

"That's exactly what I've been dreaming of doing," I enthusiastically responded. "It would be terrific to do programs on the actual historical sites and battlefields. How could we explore doing such a thing in your Fredericksburg area?"

Matthews went on to explain her destination, a history-rich region that boasts four major Civil War battles: Fredericksburg, Chancellorsville, The Wilderness, and Spotsylvania. She loved the idea of combining lessons from history with business lessons for today, a model that offers real experiential learning when done on actual historic sites. The spark that led to my "Battlefields to Business" programs had been lit at that coffee break!

Working with Matthews and her wonderful local resources in Fredericksburg, we've done some very experiential programs for groups. I refer to such programs as "the ultimate adult field trip," because we take teams of executives and employees out to explore the historic sites (programs are available in any location where history took place, not just battlefields) and combine that with post-tour debriefs and group workshops that tie back the lessons of history to today's business challenges.

We incorporate fresh air and exercise in walking around

the sites, team-building, camaraderie, problem-solving, designing presentations, etc. It's a very immersive experience for groups and executives that want to twist the familiar with their learning initiatives. One might ask, "How does an event from all those years ago relate to today's business dilemmas and challenges?" It's a fair question. Some of the historical aspects that I incorporate to help today's business organizations include:

Preparation/design of a plan
The importance of effective and clear communication
Accountability of leaders and their (business) units
Allocation and effective use of resources
Dealing with "shift happens"
Taking advantage of situations that present themselves on the spot
Managing/leading through change
Sustaining success
Cutting one's losses
Succession-planning for sudden management turnover
The qualities of successful leadership

My most challenging training mission so far

What happens when a customer throws you what appears to be a very complicated, tough assignment—in effect they twist your familiar in an extreme way. Does it excite you, scare you or challenge you?

I love such a challenge, it gets my creative juices flowing. One such group was an organization that booked my Battlefields to Business program in the beautiful historic town of Fredericksburg, Virginia, once the scene of a violent battle in the cold winter of December 1862. Today, the town is wonderfully friendly and quaint. Even with modern-day advances such as fast-food restaurants, hotels, and big-box stores like any other city, the downtown area that runs on both banks of the Rappahannock River seems like a walk back in time. It is a lovely city and I always enjoy going back there.

This particular client group presented an altogether unique challenge to me—they were non-sighted people. Virginia's Business Opportunities for the Blind represented non-sighted and nearly non-sighted business owners and professionals from around the state of Virginia, gathering for their annual educational conference.

My first thought: What was their motivation for booking an outside "field trip" to a battlefield where so much of the experience is in seeing the battleground, the cannons, the markers, and trying to visualize how the battle unfolded? I asked the meeting planner that very question. She admitted that it surprised her, too, but that the planning committee had a very vocal and persuasive member who was passionate about American history. She laid out the challenge to me: *Can you do this for us?*

Game on.

As I viewed it, my initial challenge was this: How do I make an event like this, and the lessons to be learned from it, come alive for people who cannot see? The light bulb went on in my head that if they couldn't "see" the battle, then maybe I could work it so that these people could "feel" the battle.

Working with Victoria Matthews again, she put me in touch with the wonderful team at the Fredericksburg National Military Park. I explained the group to them and requested various battlefield relics and replicas to be made available to us for a "feel and tell" type of program. I asked for cannon balls, a rifle, a bayonet, bullets, and a soldier's field pack. When the meeting planner heard my plan, she was enthusiastically on board.

Feeling is believing

The program rolled out flawlessly, thanks to teamwork. We assembled the group in the visitor orientation room at the Fredericksburg battlefield site, where the film was played so the group could at least listen to the narration and pick up the audio story of the events. Their sighted partners and family members watched the film alongside them.

The descriptive and patient licensed guide brought out the cache of battlefield pieces and artifacts I had requested, which were passed around the room among the group of fifty or so people. I was a bit anxious to see how the group members would respond to feeling and touching the Civil War materials and relics. I needn't have worried. My goal was to have as much of the battle come alive for them as possible. The participants found the most surprising thing about the pieces was their sheer weight.

We then guided the participants and their sighted guides and spouses onto the battlefield area known as Marye's Heights, the Confederacy's line of defense during the battle. We led the group to an original house that was present at the battle, situated in the center of the defenders' works. Bullet holes from the battle are still located in the wood siding. The park ranger encouraged the group to put their fingers in the bullet holes. There was a real "buzz" among the participants with questions and comments flying about, which the planner in charge of the group later told me clinched it for her that this program was a home run. It was one of my proudest career moments.

The success of seeing a plan come to light:
It's all in the preparation and small details

We next led them to a preserved section of the original stone wall, which played a very important part in the battle. The Southern army used it to repel the onslaught of the Northern troops. We encouraged the participants to take a knee to see how it might have felt to brace against the wall while firing a musket. There was much discussion and electricity going on among the participants as they inspected the stone wall with their hands. I never felt prouder of an original vision of an assignment playing out so successfully. I've never forgotten that feeling.

One of the things I kept silently reminding myself over and over again as the tour evolved was what NOT to say. It is so natural in a setting like that for a person with sight to say something like "As you can see . . ." I'm not trying to be glib or disrespectful here, but things like that are easy to say to people without even thinking. I was deathly afraid of letting something like that slip out and offend someone. Thankfully, it didn't happen.

We finished the program with a debriefing workshop back at the hotel, where I helped them apply the lessons of the tour and the elements of the battle to their current business and management challenges. People remarked how much fun the learning experience was, despite the serious subject matter. The feedback was tremendous.

But the people in the group weren't the only ones who learned something that day.

Want to learn something? Walk in someone else's shoes

Experiencing things from another person's perspective is a good thing to do. And trying to think what would appeal to someone without sight is not as easy as it sounds. At the time of this program, my own brother-in-law was in the throes of going blind, so I had a lot of newfound empathy about losing one's sight.

I took pause at many points along the battlefield tour myself, thinking how easy it was for those of us with sight to take for granted being able to see the beautiful trees, hills, and landscapes. As I said earlier, I had to work hard to remember not to say something so natural to me, such as, "Folks, take a look at those trees about a mile down the road . . ."

What trees? What does a tree even look like? What does a mile look like? What does a road look like? In addition to being one of my most memorable and fulfilling training events I've ever done, it was also a very sobering day for me.

I admired these folks for wanting to get outside of their comfort zones, to twist their familiar (and mine too!); to go on an outdoor adventure to learn new things; to ask questions and apply the lessons from a battle in 1862 in order to help move their businesses forward.

Indeed, the roads of history can lead us back to today.

Building Your Playbook

- *What has been your toughest, most challenging assignment of your career?*
- *What made it so, and how did it turn out?*
- *What kind of difficult or unique assignments does your company or team perform? How do they turn out?*
- *What resources would you need in order to pull off a tough, unusual assignment that you or your team has been given?*
- *Have you thought about turning one of your passions or interests into a business opportunity?*

Chapter 58

Selling Styles: Consultancy vs. Commodity

"My greatest strength as a consultant is to be ignorant and ask a few questions." —Peter Drucker

Every salesperson at some point begins to develop their personal style. Sometimes it just happens, other times it's a struggle to find it. Some never really get comfortable in any style and leave the ranks of sales. That's OK, it's not for everybody.

Great salespeople have their core selling style, yet also have the ability to "morph" their style, chameleon-like, to fit a particular customer's buying style. It's NOT to be called a phony, as some unknowing people have commented over the years. It's more about being flexible in styles so that the salesperson and the customer can relate to each other better.

Customers want to buy from people they know, like, and trust; people they can believe in. The term "different strokes for different folks" applies to sales as much as it does management, coaching, teaching, music, sports, you name it. It's not a cookie-cutter world, and salespeople shouldn't be cookie-cutter either. Sales author Jeffrey Gitomer weighs in with this take:

"Great salespeople are relationship builders who provide value and help their customers win."

You may not be able to close a sale in the first five minutes, but you sure can lose it

Through my own selling experiences, research, and work with scores of salespeople and buyers from all kinds of industries, I've found that given the choice between a consultative-style sales approach and a commodity-based sales approach, most customers prefer to buy from the former. I know I do.

Building a rapport, especially in the initial stage, is substantially more successful than pitching your product's features and statistics. People often decide in the first few minutes whether they want to stay with you or hit the road. Be solid in your opening step or you may not get to the second step.

I prefer being consultative in my own sales approach. I learned early on that even while you may be selling a commodity, selling it via a consultative approach will endear you to more customers and also set you up for more repeat sales, too. That is golden. Conversely, many customers can't stand pushy, canned salespeople. People want to buy—they just don't want to be sold to.

So what actually goes into being a true, solid, consultative salesperson? It can be a subjective conversation, to be sure. To help you here in an effective, concise manner, I've developed twelve *Personal Traits of Consultative Selling*, drawn over my own sales career and my coaching/consulting projects.

Please keep in mind that most everything in selling and buying has an element of "nuance" to it. I would never dream of presenting you with an inflexible set of rules meant to be followed in absolutely the same exact way in every interaction. That's not the real world, is it? It's much more nuanced than that, so please factor that into your takeaways from this chapter.

The Consultancy Traits:
stop selling and start helping people buy

Before diving in, please take note: these traits are not magic beans. They are blended common sense and proven tactics. They aren't the one-size-fits-all variety, either. The challenge is to put them to use at the best moments, in the right ways, with the appropriate customers. No solution applies to everyone in every circumstance. Your ability to apply different brush strokes and nuances to these traits will separate you as a true professional from the commodity order-takers, the slick talkers, and the pedestrian salespeople so full of themselves that they often don't see just how off-putting they can be to people. Don't be one of those folks.

Time out! What if your job title isn't in sales—why bother to read this? Because you sell, believe me. In our own way, just about every day, we all "sell" to other people in ways we don't even think of as "selling." We sell ideas to one another, we sell alternatives when we want someone to do something different or change their mind; we sell and negotiate just to compromise on the color of the drapes or which school we want to go to, or who gets to pick the restaurant that evening. When someone "buys" your idea you are selling! These traits will work for you, too.

No matter your sales experience, this section will help make you better - with practice and artful application, of course. Consider this your consultative sales "strength and conditioning" playbook:

Stop just selling "stuff:" Be more solution-driven rather than product-driven. Help people buy by offering solutions to their dilemmas, needs, wants, and pain points. Be service-oriented vs. transactional. Remember, people don't buy features (what something is or has), they buy the benefits (what something does).

Be a great listener: Listen 90 percent, talk 10 percent of the time in the initial conversation. Ask your questions, and then *zip it*. People like to talk about themselves so lead with your questions, not facts. Don't feature-vomit a bunch of factoids on your prospects. We learn by listening, not by talking.

Dial in to customers' WIIFM (what's in it for me): It usually revolves around the Four P's—*Pain, Panic, Pleasure and Purpose*. It helps to look at the entire buying process through the buyers' eyes, not yours. What are they going through, what are they thinking? Are my points delivering a WIIFM or putting them to sleep?

Work to be a believable expert and a trusted advisor: Customers may be silently asking themselves, "Why should I put my faith, trust, and business in your hands?" There is no one single way to do this, but if you *do the right things and do things right*, and if you are smart, honest, and truthful, you will likely engender the buyers' trust. That is paramount because so much flows from that. People will even pay more for goods and services from people they trust and believe in. They will refer others. Trust-building never goes out of style.

Ask great questions: You will be much more successful in sales if you learn to ask compelling, revealing questions in an "interview style" that actually mean something to the prospect. No one wants to feel they are just being checked off a form like a telemarketer. Use both open (to expound) and closed (to confirm) questions properly.

Try these questions: Why did they reach out to you? What are they looking to gain, accomplish, or fix? What are their pain points? What are their hot buttons (likes) and cold buttons (dislikes)? What are their deciding factors or buying criteria? Who makes the decision? What is the process? Are they under any time deadlines?

Find out who your competition is: Try to get it to an apples-to-apples comparison during your presentation process where you can point out the "gaps" and how your organization can fill those to the advantage of the customer. Why is the customer considering other alternatives?

Be a consummate, engaged consultant: Great listener, honest, trustworthy, authentic, transparent, timely, and detail oriented. These are consistently the top attributes I get when surveying customers in my buyer panel programs when I ask about the traits they most want in their salespeople. These attributes don't really change all that much between different industries, regions, or economic conditions.

Customize your approach vs. one-size-fits-all: Make your customers feel special, like you're in it just for them. People don't like to be treated like the rest of the crowd. I've never met two clients exactly the same anyway; they all want to feel special. Find creative ways to customize your approach to each buyer.

Be easy to do business with: Buying can be a hassle. Buyers want to do business with those who make it easy doing business together. They don't want to jump through hoops or fight through layers of the org chart just to get answers. You'll want buyers to see you as part of their team, in their corner, clearing out as much of the clutter for them as you can.

Enthusiasm is contagious: If you aren't excited about your product/service/organization, then who is? You'd be surprised at how many customers complain about a lack of enthusiasm in their salespeople.

Be a great storyteller: Have some great stories ready to go with the points you are making to help drive home the point or make it memorable or funny, etc. Sixty-three percent of people remember stories, while just 5 percent remember statistics/facts. Stories are emotional and that's the bigger driver in sales over logic and numbers. Yes, numbers do matter, but how *much* do they matter? That's for you to find out by asking. Generally speaking, *people buy with emotion and justify it with logic.* Studies generally agree that 80-95 percent of buying decisions are led with the emotional side. As sales guru Zig Ziglar put it: "Logic makes people think and emotion makes people act."

Own the follow-up: This is a key salesperson's responsibility, and if you want to be thought of as consultative, you'll own the follow-up and not take the lazy way out by asking your customer to "let me know if you have any questions." To me, that's the worst way to end an email, too. It's severely overused, mundane, and unnecessary. It makes your writing bland—and who wants to be bland?

Customers have a lot going on and they can't (or shouldn't) be expected to remember follow-up steps or circle-back dates. If you want the sale, you have to manage it and you have to own the follow-up. You are actually helping them stay organized. It's a courtesy and it's also smart business. Pick up the phone, send the email. Manage the process, or you will be left to having the process manage you.

"You don't sell what you're trying to sell—you sell what your customers want to buy."—Mario Alioto

With this phrase, one of my longtime business friends offers the credo of being a consultative salesperson. Mario had a long run working for the San Francisco Giants, ultimately reaching the position of Executive Vice President of Business Operations. He played a major role in the Giants organization, especially during the incredible span of three World Series championships in five years. His marketing ideas and creativity are well-recognized and admired within the professional sports world.

Mario also lives by another solid gold belief when it comes to understanding how customers respond to a consultative approach vs. being treated like commodities. It's a great way to put a bow on this chapter:

"You have to know who your best customers are, and then take great care of them."

Building Your Playbook:

- *What are your personal consultative sales attributes? Do they match any of those discussed above?*
- *How are they working for you? Any that you would like to develop/improve upon?*
- *Do you or your organization have a culture/expectation of consultative selling, or more of a commodity selling approach?*
- *What are your top three sales attributes and how do you make them work for you?*
- *What can you work into your own sales (or team) methods to develop more of a consultative approach to selling?*

Chapter 59

The Art of Communication:
Are We Still in This Together?

"The single biggest problem in communication is the illusion that it has taken place." —George Bernard Shaw

A re you as frustrated hearing about "poor communication" as I am? I can't think of a coaching client or organization I've worked with that didn't have the area of *achieving better communication* at or near the top of its list of concerns.

Adding to that, we heard a constant dose of the battle cry "We're in this together" in many different industries while the Covid-19 pandemic was raging. Considering that so much of our ongoing communication between buyers and sellers still needs serious work, the question is: *are we still truly in this together?*

Let's "business up" for better communication with each other

There is no denying that communication of one type or another permeates every corner of our lives and businesses. We absolutely need effective communication—just imagine life without it. Whether we are talking, listening, reading, writing, or signing, it is like the air we need to breathe, an absolute essential to doing good (or any) business together.

With waves of new people entering the business ranks all the time, modes and styles of communication are changing, but is it all necessarily for the better? The barometer of success for effective communication is not in how cute or fancy or brief we make it. Instead, it must stand the litmus test of whether it is clear and understood by both parties.

We know that while some communication can be wonderfully clear and easily understood, at other times it can be fraught with errors and confusion. That's why we have to keep working at it.

So let's work smarter. Let's do something I call "business up." It refers to kicking up our games a few notches and doing things better. We can all stand to clean up our communication toolboxes in some way or another. And we don't need advanced degrees to do it, either. It's a two-way street with customers and their supplier-partners. Both senders and recipients share the responsibility for successful communication.

Be accountable and own the issue

I've employed a classic phrase to help remind me that I need to do my part first and make sure my own communication house is in order: "If it is to be, it's up to me." That focuses me on doing everything within my power to do the right things: listen fully, write plainly, respond quickly, and speak to be understood.

One of the most frustrating things about achieving sparkling clear communication is that even when we do all those things correctly, the other party can still ignore us, not listen, misinterpret our messaging, miss important details, etc. It's maddening!

Still, I suggest we strive to help the other parties be successful. By helping someone communicate with you better, you get the win, too. I once offered to a client that if he responded to my emails sooner—he apparently had a rabbit hole in his inbox where things went to die—I would be able to get my part completed quicker and we could get our combined project finished—to the benefit of both of us. He saw great advantages in that and kicked his responses into higher gear.

Your communication moments of truth can make or break the mission

As we go about trying to do business with each other, there are hundreds of *moments of truth* involved in the process. And along those paths most of those moments tie back to the need for effective communication with others. It's mission critical. How do you and your business colleagues stack up?

Here are a few key questions to help avoid the classic communication pratfalls, or at least keep them to a dull roar:

Do we give each other our full attention when communicating? Are we active listeners or just passive listeners? Let's pay better attention to each other.

*Do you clearly express yourself in order to be understood when speaking and writing? As the sender, your messaging may seem crystal clear to you, but do the receivers see and hear it the same way? Remember: people don't process and comprehend information at the same levels. Write and speak **plainly**.*

Do we often interrupt the other party, finishing their sentences for them?

Do we avoid jumping to conclusions or making assumptions when someone is communicating with us? Don't let your personal notions cloud what the other person is sending to you. Hear them out.

Do we assume that the other party will totally understand our exact meaning behind our emojis and "lol" responses? A lawsuit involving a thumbs-up emoji in response to an offer made on a text was ruled by a judge to be a legal acceptance and therefore constituted a contract. Be careful that being cutesy doesn't turn into an expensive "oopsy."

Where does someone start to improve their communication program? It's easier than you think. In fact, it can be embarrassingly simple. Just pick up the phone. Return calls, answer emails, respond to appointment requests and voice messages. Write understandable and clear emails, RFPs, and contracts. Say what you mean and mean what you say. Don't ignore people (unless it's spam or telemarketers). This isn't rocket science.

The "No Update-Update"

If my conference and workshop audiences are any gauge, communication courtesies need a lot of work. Many salespeople and customers alike vent about the lack of response from other parties after trying to reach them. It's usually more salespeople than customers having this issue, as they try to close business or get some kind of response on their proposals. But customers share their own horror stories, too.

The term "ghosting" applies here. People from all parts of the country in different industries are being ignored by one another.

Thus, many years ago I came up with a term based on those stories, and I started imploring my audiences to employ the "No Update-Update." I am always met with a lot of enthusiasm and applause for this idea.

Simply defined, it's the courtesy of getting back to someone, even if there is no tangible update on the decision, RFP, negotiations, etc. The idea is to at least acknowledge their attempts to reach you. Let the other party know that although there is no real update, you hear them and haven't forgotten about them. That in itself is an update. Give them a time frame for when they can loop back. This thoughtful step lets the other party know that even though there is no progress to report yet, you are alive and well.

Give them your best guess as to when they should loop back or when you will be contacting them. It's not a hard thing to do, really. It's thoughtful and polite. At least they know you are paying a bit of attention and courtesy to them.

It's the Golden Rule. And in the current state of communication, we could use a good dose of it.

Building Your Playbook:

- *Have you ever been frustrated by a lack of response from someone you were trying to reach? How did that make you feel? What did you do about it?*
- *What can you do to improve your response rate, and that of your team?*
- *Many customers suggest to salespeople that they mix their media when trying to reach them over several attempts, such as phone, email, video, handwritten note, etc. Don't always do the same thing with the same message. What methods would you use to get a response, and how would you apply them?*

Chapter 60

Learning From a Child:
How Truly Simple Things Can Be

"Sometimes a change of perspective is all
it takes to see the light." — Dan Brown

Sometimes, the best lessons come from the simplest sources. One of the best lessons I ever received in communications came about quite by accident in one of those little moments that happen in life that resonate for years.

The initiator of this lesson was my younger son Michael, when he was about five years old.

I was working in my office late one afternoon when he approached me and asked me if he could go outside and play ball with some of his friends. My wife and I encouraged outside play for our boys as much as possible, so my answer was going to be yes. But I asked him a question first, just to check if he had left his room in a mess.

"What shape is your room in, Michael?"

He knocked me out of my chair with his simple answer: "Um, square?"

His voice tone and face signaled to me that maybe he thought I was giving him a pop quiz on knowing his shapes, perhaps a parent's qualifying question in order to be able to go outside and play.

I looked at him, taking his answer in. It was brilliant. And practical. I thought I'd have some fun with this. "Is that really the shape of your room?"

"Yes, dad," he said again, "My room is in the shape of a square."

I burst out in a wide smile, gave him a loving hug and said, "You're right, Michael, that's perfect. That is exactly what shape your room is. Go and have some fun outside with your friends."

I sat there at my desk for a moment, reflecting about what a lesson that was for me in communication and different perspectives between me and my young son. I saw in this a powerful lesson on communication: one question, two different perspectives, and two possible answers.

The following points, while intended for everyone, are especially applicable for those people who lead teams and organizations and frequently send emails, memos, and directives to their teams:

> *Never assume what we are sending is what the other party is receiving (and vice versa).*
> *Never assume that our perspectives and the other parties' perspectives are aligned with each other.*
> *Keep in mind that not everyone will comprehend the same words the very same way.*
> *Remember that people can look at the same question or set of words in entirely different ways.*

Every day, communication with others is often fraught with misfires, assumptions, and imperfections. This topic comes up with participants in 99.9% of my workshops. It's an issue that has been around for a long time and continues to be a top concern of organizations everywhere.

Interpretation and comprehension between people can differ greatly, such as figurative vs. literal, subjective vs.

objective, generational references, regional dialects, phraseology, you name it. Is it any wonder that communication (or lack of) gets blamed for a lot of things? Keep this in mind: your idea of what is right is not everybody's idea of what is right.

That idea leads me to one of the best tips I can recommend in order for you to be an epic communicator, whether sending or receiving: it's really about different strokes for different folks. By keeping that in mind you will communicate better in all types of applications – verbal, written, online, etc.

And here's the fun part. You never know when a truly impactful lesson will come your way, totally out of the blue, from the most unexpected sources. As my episode here illustrates, for me it was as the beautiful song by Aurora suggests, "through the eyes of a child."

Building Your Playbook

- *Can you think of a time when you made an assumption in questioning or listening? What happened?*
- *Can you recall examples of when people took away different things from the same memo, email, or comments in a meeting? Could it have been written/spoken any differently to clear up the confusion?*
- *What steps can you take to improve yours and your team's questioning and active listening skills in order to help avoid communication pratfalls?*

Chapter 61

Sales Boothmanship
—It Takes More than Just Showing Up

"There is no such thing as an attention span. There is only the quality of what you are viewing. This whole idea of an attention span is a misnomer. People have an infinite attention span if you are entertaining them." —Jerry Seinfeld

D o you remember your first tradeshow booth experience? I sure do remember mine. I was one of six seniors representing Michigan State's School of Hospitality Business in our school's booth at the National Restaurant Association show in Chicago many years ago. It was "lights, camera, action" for us wide-eyed college students, getting our first taste of a national gathering of hospitality business companies from all over the country. It was exciting, dazzling, and a lot to take in. The entire experience convinced me I had made the right decision to get into such a robust industry.

We got to our booth with lots of enthusiasm to "work it" and represent our school. Great, there we were, proudly wearing our name badges. *But how were we supposed to do this?* No one had coached us on anything. We figured it out using common sense and observing others in our neighboring booths. Essentially we shook hands, smiled, talked up our program, and made sure not to do anything to embarrass our school or faculty. Things were less complicated in those days.

Many years later I still chuckle at that experience,

considering all of the conventions and events I've participated in as a salesperson in the booth or a customer in the aisles. "Boothmanship," as it's called, is truly an art form if done correctly. Tragically, it's seldom taught in many sales training programs or orientations to sales. When I cover the topic in workshops, I get a lot of the "Wow, I never knew there was so much to it" kind of comments.

The booth, the whole booth, and nothing but the booth

According to NAFA Fleet Management Association, "Boothmanship is the art of combining booth design and booth etiquette to attract, connect and win over attendees." So at its most basic level, the art of boothmanship comes down to grabbing prospects' attention so that they enter your booth space, feel welcome, and remain entertained and engaged on some level so as to keep them talking to you and not talking to your competitors across the aisle. It's about engagement and entertainment, as Seinfeld suggests.

Many salespeople think the overall carnival atmosphere of the show is enough to carry the day and the rest will take care of itself. But that is far from the truth. You can't just show up and begin handing out pens and expect the customers to flock to your booth to load you up with leads.

Salespeople should carry plenty of business cards, too, which are not out of fashion by any means. Cards represent you and your brand. They help people remember you better, and vice versa. Write notes on them to capture details of your conversation in the booth for follow-up. Trade shows can get crazy-busy and if there is a lot of traffic in your booth, trying to remember all the people you met and what you talked about is a tall order.

I cringe when I hear a salesperson say, "I forgot my business cards." Ouch. You are a professional. Don't be a schlub. Go to such events prepared!

Put your best efforts into this to get yours and your company's ROI from working the booth. After all, it's not a cheap endeavor given your expenses of air travel, hotel, registration, booth shipping, giveaways, time involved, entertaining customers, and a myriad of other components that go into attending a trade show/event.

Are you adding to the noise or standing out from the crowd?

There are ways to increase your effectiveness in your booth, and also things to avoid doing so you don't become lost in the shuffle or turn away your prospects. Some of my twelve "dos and don'ts" that follow here may sound embarrassingly simple or basic. Don't be fooled, they are on this list because they still frequently happen:

Buyers: give the registered attendee list an advance screening (if available) to pre-pick your places and people to see so that you don't run out of time. Prioritize your walking route and then see others after your prime "hit list"' is complete. Salespeople: peruse the list and earmark those prospects/customers that you want to make a point of seeing. Set up an appointment to meet at the show if possible.

Don't set your booth up like a mine field that is hard to maneuver around. Cutesy may catch the eye, but it has to be practical to accommodate traffic, too. Recently, a vendor put a Christmas tree right in the middle of a booth, making it impossible and clumsy to move around. When she went on a break, her boothmates moved the tree to the outside corner.

If you have games, videos, live demos, etc., practice using them before the doors open. Check for glitches; otherwise you look unprepared for "show time."

Name badge 101 please! The proper place for your badge is upper right chest/lapel area. If you are wearing yours on a lanyard around your neck, have the badge at the proper strategic height. People shouldn't have to bend down to your waist to read your name. And dear heaven, make sure your badge is turned print-side out so people can read it. Duh. It's comically tragic to see name badges being worn backwards. Come on, don't be sloppy, your personal brand is at stake.

What will you say as a greeting? What kind of questions will you ask? Open questions do a good job of getting the other person to open up. Active listening works like a charm. Remember, we learn more from listening than we do from talking. Don't feature-vomit in your booth and take up all of the buyer's time with your data dump! Buyers at the show want to be inspired, not lectured.

You are very much "on stage" as a salesperson in a booth. Smile, have fun, and keep good eye contact. Project that you are enjoying the experience, unless you are auditioning to be a guard at Buckingham Palace in your next job. Too many salespeople wear the "my ankles hurt and my back is killing me" look on their faces. It's not a welcome sign for customers to want to engage in conversation with you.

Break up the reunion! Exhibitors like to visit each other in their booths. That's great, but that's not why you are there. So have your hugs and chats, but when customers walk in your booth, disperse the reunion and excuse yourself so you can fly over to the customer. They came into your booth for a reason, and it's your job to find out why.

No eating! However, breath mints are strongly suggested.

No standing in the booth checking your mobile phone. If you have to put out a fire back at work, ask a teammate to cover for you and do it outside of your booth or walk a few feet away. Standing in your booth staring at your phone tells a customer, "Don't come in here and bother me, I'm busy." According to *Trade Show Advisor*, over 80 percent of what show attendees remember is directly relevant to booth staff performance and actions.

Show some care and interest in prospects visiting your booth! A colleague and I were looking for information on planning a sales retreat for a corporate client. Two of the salespeople were huddled around a desk in their chairs while one of them was sitting on top of the desk. Classy look. They were having a fun time looking at photos on one of their phones. They finally noticed us looking at a brochure and one of them said, "Let us know if you have any questions," then went back to looking at the phone in their huddle. No greeting. No questions. No interest. No engagement. No thanks. My colleague and I almost apologized for being a bother to them.

Follow up on your hard work and don't let the conversation fly-bys and moments with prospects get lost in the blur. Put your collection of business cards to good use for that. If you've taken notes as I suggested earlier, it will go much easier (and better) when you write your follow-up notes. Think handwritten cards, too, as they will definitely stand out as twisting the familiar. Most salespeople don't bother with them because it's too much work. Stand out from the noise, remember?

Own the follow-up on a timely basis. Experienced salespeople do NOT count on customers to remember everyone they met at the event and everything they talked about, let alone follow up with salespeople. If you are in sales, YOU own the follow-up, and make it timely, not weeks or months later. I often get boilerplate sales follow-up emails six months after an event. Those companies have wasted their time, money, and effort. Forget it.

> *"Some people have no idea what they are doing, and a lot of them are really good at it."* —George Carlin

Carlin must have attended a trade show or two. Rise above your competitors and take advantage of live prospects walking around. They're right in front of you and much easier to talk to than chasing them down on emails, phone calls, and texts.

Engage the spirit of this book and find ways to stand out from the rest of the competitive noise at the show so that you can increase your chances for more leads and better engagement. And buyers/customers – do your part to be good partners in this arena, too. Be forthright with salespeople and don't lead them along if you have no intention of doing business with them. Business Courtesy 101 includes responding to salespeople who follow up with you on a timely basis after the event. No ghosting!

With the professionalism, courtesy and savvy we've discussed here, salespeople and customers alike can achieve outstanding results from their experiences. Everybody is on stage, one way or another, so bring your A game and let's have fun with this. You'll see better ROI for the time, money, and energy you expend when attending tradeshows and events.

And who knows? Maybe you'll hone your skills to such a high level that you'll be able to keep Jerry Seinfeld's attention, should he ever visit your booth. After all, when you twist the familiar, extraordinary things can happen!

Building Your Playbook:

- *Do you (or your organization) have tradeshow booth sales strategies in place? How do they work? If not, can you draw some up?*
- *What are you trying to accomplish in your booth? Are you there to inform, inspire, generate leads, close sales, entertain, or increase brand awareness? Maybe it's all of those. Your mission should drive your booth design and sales tactics during the show.*
- *Does your booth appeal to buyers? How do you know? When planning a reboot, you might want to ask some customers for their suggestions and feedback on booth design. Also, get professional input on the latest booth trends from those that do it for a living.*
- *Seek training for your salespeople. Don't just throw them to the lions in the booth. The business of booth selling is a fiercely competitive, serious business. Some industries have more "fun style" trade shows, while others are more serious, drawing companies that come to write multi-million-dollar agreements. Either way, business is at the core. Plan accordingly.*

About My Back Cover Photo

We all have our favorite places. One of mine is Pebble Beach, California. I know it sounds cliché, but it's a slice of heaven to me and my family, a very special and beautiful place that often calls us to visit there.

The weathered wooden bench in my photo is on the rustic boardwalk running parallel to the sea, overlooking North Moss Beach, commonly referred to as "Spanish Bay Beach." We often walk down the winding footpath from the Inn at Spanish Bay, past the first green of its golf course, making our way to "our bench," as our family refers to it. We've sat there countless times over the years, watching the surf crash against the craggy rocks, sometimes downing a sandwich or a snack. It was my dad's favorite place to sit and ponder about things as the Pacific Ocean rolled its breaker waves inexorably in his direction.

Besides the awesome, unfettered view of God's handiwork, the bench has an added charm for us. A small, weathered plaque was built into it, and it has always meant something very special to us in its profound simplicity. I hope you find inspiration in it, too. The plaque reads:

REST – MUSE
COUNT BLESSINGS

A Special Thanks

I am indebted to everyone who helped bring this book to life. First, a big thank you to each of the people within these pages who offered me their unique episodes and input for the purpose of helping others learn from their stories. My early editors, Peggy Spear and Janine DeFao Hayward, deserve salutes for taking my original manuscript and rambling notes and helping to trim, edit, and make them better. My final editor, Lily O'Brien, provided careful eyes and a deft touch to my final draft, and her experienced professionalism shines throughout. It's said that authors should never edit their own books and it's the truth.

My heartfelt thanks goes to the team at ALIVE Books, including Eric Johnson, his wonderful and savvy wife, Peggy, and their exceptionally creative Art Director/Designer, Alex Johnson. I walked into Eric's office in Alamo, California, a few years ago, inspired by his article on book publishing in his *ALIVE Magazine*. I told him I was writing a book, explained it briefly, and he was willing to be patient and take a chance on me. Thanks, Eric, for your guidance, suggestions, support, and the faith in me to cull my 350,000-word leviathan into a single work.

And I must thank most of all my beautiful, loving, and supportive wife Marie, whose gentle prods of, "How's your booking coming along?" in the early stages turned to the more direct approach of, "So when is your book going to be finished?" as time marched on. Without her encouragement and checking on me every so often during my marathon writing sessions until 2:00 a.m. or later on many nights, I'd probably still be struggling with my quest.

And certainly not the least of all, a big thanks to you, my readers. I sincerely wish you the best of luck on your journey. I will be pleased if my ideas, stories, and coaching tips presented in these pages help you create new successes, find answers to your dilemmas, and provide some form of motivation for you to conquer your mountains. Please write to me and let me know how things turn out. Who knows, if I publish another book, your story may be in there!

Gary Hernbroth
Danville, California
April 2024

Gary is available for customized speaking and coaching appearances, such as keynotes and educational sessions, training workshops, executive retreats, facilitation, consulting projects, and one-on-one coaching. He can be reached at:

Website: trainingforwinners.com
Facebook: facebook.com/trainingforwinners.com
LinkedIn: linkedin.com/in/garyhernbroth/
LinkedIn: linkedin.com/company/training-for-winners
X (Twitter): @Gary_Hernbroth
Email: gary@trainingforwinners.com

The Man in the Arena

"It is not the critic who counts; not the man who points out how the strong man stumbles, or where the doer of deeds could have done them better. The credit belongs to the man who is actually in the arena, whose face is marred by dust and sweat and blood; who strives valiantly; who errs, who comes short again and again, because there is no effort without error and shortcoming; but who does actually strive to do the deeds; who knows great enthusiasms, the great devotions; who spends himself in a worthy cause; who at the best knows in the end the triumph of high achievement, and who at the worst, if he fails, at least fails while daring greatly, so that his place shall never be with those cold and timid souls who neither know victory nor defeat."

———

(Theodore Roosevelt, 1910)

Disclaimer

The information contained in this book is for general information purposes only. The content is provided by Gary Hernbroth and while he endeavors to keep the information up to date and correct, he makes no representations or warranties of any kind, express or implied, about the completeness, accuracy, reliability, suitability, or availability with respect to the book or the information, products, services, or related graphics contained in the book for any purpose. No intent of legal advice is being made by the author. Any reliance placed on such information is therefore strictly at the reader's own risk.

About the Author

Gary Hernbroth is an award-winning professional speaker, business coach, and author. Recognized as one of the leading voices in the hospitality and meetings industry, he was honored by Connect Meetings as one of the "Top 15 over 50 Professionals in the Events Industry", and by Smart Meetings as a "Best of the Stage - Industry Expert" award winner. Gary's customers appreciatively refer to him as their strength and conditioning coach, as he has inspired hundreds of audiences and organizations from a diverse array of industries since 1995.

Gary achieved his first byline as a writer in sixth grade for his school paper, and won his first writing award from *The Detroit News* as a senior journalism student in high school. Gary earned his bachelor's degree from Michigan State University's School of Hospitality Business, helping him to launch an 18-year career in luxury hotels before forming his Training for Winners business. Born in Texas, he grew up in Michigan and currently lives in Northern California. Gary enjoys   playing golf with family and friends, travel, supporting his favorite sports teams, and kicking back to classic rock/pop music.

ABOOKS

ALIVE Book Publishing and ALIVE Publishing Group
are imprints of Advanced Publishing LLC,
3200 A Danville Blvd., Suite 204, Alamo, California 94507

Telephone: 925.837.7303
alivebookpublishing.com

www.ingramcontent.com/pod-product-compliance
Lightning Source LLC
Chambersburg PA
CBHW020814270326
41928CB00006B/371